DATE DUE

MAY 1 1 2006 RECI			
MAY 08 2006			
MAY 0 2 2008			
RECEIVED MAY 0 6 2008			

IRISH POETRY AND THE CONSTRUCTION OF MODERN IDENTITY

IRISH POETRY

and the
Construction of
Modern Identity

Ireland Between Fantasy and History

STAN SMITH
Nottingham Trent University

IRISH ACADEMIC PRESS
DUBLIN • PORTLAND, OR

First published in 2005 by
IRISH ACADEMIC PRESS
44 Northumberland Road, Dublin 4, Ireland

and in the United States of America by
IRISH ACADEMIC PRESS
c/o ISBS, Suite 300
920 NE 58th Avenue
Portland, Oregon 97213-3786

Website: www.iap.ie

British Library Cataloguing in Publication Data

An entry can be found on request

ISBN 0-7165-3329 -4 (cloth)
ISBN 0-7165-3330-8 (paper)

Library of Congress Cataloging-in-Publication Data

An entry can be found on request

Printed in Ireland by Betaprint Ltd

For Hilda Warburton (*née* Flannery)
and for
Keir, Rhianna and Iona Mackenzie

Contents

Preface

The present volume requires some explanation. My original intention was to collect most, if not all, of my writings over the last quarter century, published and unpublished, in the field of twentieth century Irish literature. However, when I came to put this material together, I was aware of repetitions and other features which in my opinion required a more serious editing. The more I engaged in this, the more it seemed to me that the original material should be rewritten to bring out more clearly the developing argument these writings have been conducting, over twenty-five years, about an unprecedented century of Irish literary creation, and of far-reaching political and cultural change. This argument concerns the role of Irish Modernist writing in constructing the model of a specifically Irish modernity. Re-engagement with this material led to the writing of much new work, as well as the reconfiguration, rather than simply the rehearsal, of old themes.

In the 1970s, initially on the suggestion of Augustus Young and of Michael Smith, the editor of the Dublin-based little magazine *The Lace Curtain*, I wrote several essays on those first Irish Modernist poets to break free from a 1930s Ireland dominated equally by the rhetoric of Yeats and the politics of de Valera and 'Ourselves Alone' – Brian Coffey, Thomas MacGreevy and Denis Devlin. These essays were regarded at the time as ground-breaking, and it has been suggested frequently over the last few years that I should make this material available in collected form. The present project, however, required something different, and to that end I have here updated and shortened the Devlin essay, which first appeared in *Irish University Review*, and have shortened and revised the work on Coffey and MacGreevy to integrate it with extended accounts of Padraic Fallon and Austin Clarke in a new reading of this generation. The opening chapter, 'Historians and Magicians', reconsiders ideas first raised in a plenary lecture at the 1979 IASAIL conference, published in *Literature and the Changing Ireland* (Gerrards Cross: Colin Smythe, 1982), edited by Peter Connolly. A postscript to my study, *The Origins of Modernism: Eliot, Pound, Yeats, and the Rhetorics of Renewal* (Hemel Hempstead: Harvester Wheatsheaf, 1994), revisited briefly and provisionally the discussion of Beckett undertaken there, only to conclude: 'But that is another story.' The present book is an attempt to supply part of that story, drawing out the specifically Irish implications of the account of Modernism charted in that book. In reconsidering 'What was I saying', it agrees with Vladimir that 'we could go on from there'. Of course, as Estragon observes, 'You can start from anything'. What I have started from, in writing of Joyce and Yeats in the first two chapters, is a rethinking of some aspects of the IASAIL paper and of a previously unpublished keynote lecture, 'New Tales in Old Tubs: Modern Critical Theory and Irish Modernism', delivered at the Royal Irish Academy, Dublin, in 1990.

Of the more recent work in this volume, the second chapter on Heaney is reprinted with some changes from the collection edited by Neil Corcoran, *The Chosen Ground* (Bridgend: Seren Books, 1992), but here finds its proper place as part of a developing argument. The last three chapters, on Mahon, Muldoon and Carson, were successive contributions to the biennial Research Symposium on Northern Irish Poetry at the University of Ulster (Coleraine) organised by Elmer Kennedy-Andrews, and a version of the first has appeared in the collection, *The Poetry of Derek Mahon* (2002), which he edited for the Ulster Editions and Monographs series published by Colin Smythe. I am grateful for the opportunity the Symposium provided to think seriously about these poets, and in particular about Ciaran Carson, whose work I had not considered at any length before, but who became, for me, a major find. Other essays incorporate material from a variety of sources, but constitute substantially new accounts of the poets considered. In addition to the sources cited above, preliminary versions or draft sections of material here have appeared in the following journals: *The Lace Curtain, Irish University Review, Bullán: An Irish Studies Journal, Irish Studies Review, Modern Language Review, Yeats Annual*, and in the collections *Poetry in Contemporary Irish Literature* (Gerrards Cross: Colin Smythe, 1995), edited by Michael Kenneally, and *Locations of Literary Modernism* (Cambridge: Cambridge University Press, 2000), edited by Alex Davis and Lee M. Jenkins, and I would like to express my thanks to these editors and publishers for the opportunity to explore aspects of the argument developed here. As always, I am indebted beyond measure to Jennifer Birkett, for her wise observations and advice, but, most importantly, for being there.

There is, inevitably, a range of registers in the present volume. I was struck, nevertheless, in reassessing it for publication, by the consistency it displays, and its complex interdependence. It was because I saw in ostensibly diverse material the same kind of cohesion which I had sought to achieve in previous books, which I had envisaged from the start as unitary projects, that I decided my argument would best be served by a complete reconfiguration of the whole work. I have not reprinted anything simply for the sake of completeness. Essays on Devlin and on Brian Coffey's *Death of Hektor*, for example, can be found in Coffey's *Advent VI: Denis Devlin Special Issue* (1976) and *Etudes Irlandaises* (December 1983) respectively, but did not contribute significantly to the argument developed here. I think the centre holds.

I
Historians and Magicians: Ireland Between Fantasy and History

Mythological Presents

For Estragon in Samuel Beckett's *Waiting for Godot* (1952; 1954)[1], responding to Vladimir's importunate demands to recall what happened yesterday, history is simply 'Another of your nightmares'. The echo of Stephen Dedalus's famous remark in *Ulysses* calls up, too, another aphoristic saying, that it is better to be a people without history, living in an existential present which has neither guilt nor recrimination as its heritage. We do not need a history that sits like a burden on the shoulders of the living, Estragon suggests: 'You can start from anything.' For Vladimir, however, finding somewhere to start from means returning to unfinished business:

> V.:   What was I saying, we could go on from there.
> E.:   What were you saying when?
> V.:   At the very beginning.
> E.:   The beginning of WHAT?
> V.:   This evening ... I was saying ... I was saying ...

But Estragon cuts him short: 'I'm not a historian.'

This antithesis offers a parable for two contrary impulses in Irish history and literature. For Vladimir the past tells us who we have been, without which we cannot know who we are and will be. But for Estragon the past is suppositional, a figment invented to keep others happy ('I suppose we blathered') which, once invented, takes on a spurious narrative certainty: 'Blathering about nothing in particular. That's been going on now for half a century.' It is, rather, for Estragon, the games we invent in the present which give us meaning, identity, purpose:

> E.:   We always find something, eh Didi, to give us the impression we exist?
> V.:   *(impatiently)* Yes, yes we're magicians. But let us persevere in what we have resolved, before we forget.

Vladimir's irritated sarcasm focuses an opposition here not only between two personalities but also between two modes of historical exegesis. These modes can be seen to have dominated the Irish literary and political imagination, at the time of Beckett's writing in 1952, for the half-century of blathering since the emergence of a modern movement for national independence. Both interpretations, however, have a common factor, *discourse*, as Vladimir indicates later, when a fallen Pozzo calls for help. Symptomatically, Vladimir's own gospel of action and commitment remains simply words, the fiction of doing something, not its actuality:

> Let us not waste time in idle discourse! Let us do something, while we have the chance! It is not every day that we are needed ... To all mankind they were addressed, those cries for help still ringing in our ears! But at this place, at this moment of time, all mankind is us, whether we like it or not ...

What's at issue here is an old ambiguity in the word 'history' itself, obscured in English by the evolution of two words and concepts from the same root, but one preserved in the French 'histoire', the Italian 'storia'. For 'history' is both events and the narrative in which we inscribe them, simultaneously the discourses of action and of language. The whole problematic of the play derives from the fact that we cannot separate out, except for brief moments, 'history' as event from 'story' as interpretation. Beckett is here exploring the roots of the *ideological* – that rich, elusive, opaque, mystifying medium in which we misperceive and misrepresent to ourselves the significance and texture of our being-in-the-world. It is something indicated already, in the opening song of Act II, with its receding, never completed narrative of the dog's death in the kitchen, and of all the other dogs which came running to write his epitaph. The endless recursion of the song repeatedly embeds within itself its own repetition, and therefore like history never reaches any conclusion, a multiple embedding which, like Zeno's paradox, always puts an uncrossable and infinite distance between start and finish, narrative and event. A similar process occurs towards the end of the play when Vladimir, watching over a sleeping Estragon, envisages a similar regression in space: 'At me too someone is looking, of me too someone is saying, he is sleeping, he knows nothing, let him sleep on. I can't go on. What have I said?'

The infinite recession of interpretations, of 'sayings' in which the self and its acts all disappear, arouses a kind of ontological anxiety about the narratives in which one will be recalled. Vladimir too knows that history is a kind of nightmare, between the present of 'saying' and the past of what has been 'said', both of which shape the future of what is yet to be uttered:

> Tomorrow, when I wake, or think I do, what shall I say of today? That with Estragon my friend, at this place, until the fall of night, I waited for Godot? That Pozzo passed, with his carrier, and that he spoke to us? Probably. But in all that, what truth will there be?

This question lies at the centre of Irish history in the last century, kept alive by that stone at the heart of all, the unfinished business of 'the North'. What stories do we tell about the events that may have happened, and how do we test their veracity? What consequences will those stories have for the future? Is there any reliable 'history' to be found, or are all the versions we have of the past fairy stories told by ideological magicians, fantasy fare on which the heart grows brutal?

The end of *Molloy* (1951; 1954) takes this procedure further, separating, by a deliberate change of tense and person, and the negative mode, these two dimensions of 'history'. In the retelling of experience, or in its simultaneous telling and acting, we are at once 'historians' and 'magicians', spinning our ideological rationales out of the very stuff of language and event. Significantly, Beckett does not simply dissociate the past tense of the written from the living present of the writer. In the run-up to the book's final sentence he relates this to a larger process of acculturation, that learning of a language in which the child is appropriated to history, made a party to its terms, learning to reproduce in its own life the experiential paradigms of its forebears:

> I have spoken of a voice telling me things. I was getting to know it better now, to understand what it wanted. It did not use the words that Moran had been taught when he was little and that he in his turn had taught to his little one ... But in the end I understood this language. I understood it, I understand it, all wrong perhaps. That is not what matters. It told me to write the report. Does that mean I am freer now than I was? I do not know. I shall learn. Then I went back into the house and wrote. It is midnight. The rain is beating on the windows. It was not midnight. It was not raining.[2]

Writing the report turns the present tense of events and voice into the past tense of print. But the story is apparently present, and the 'real' events apparently past; and the relation between them is one of direct contradiction. 'I speak in the present tense,' says Molloy at the beginning of the book, 'it is so easy to speak in the present tense, when speaking of the past. It is the mythological present, don't mind it.'[3] Such reassurance leaves the reader at sea in a fabular confusion of times. History as events is here turned into a magical story, to be taken with a pinch of salt.

The Hearing of History

It is perhaps one of the most repeated motifs in modern Irish literature, signalled in the opening sentence of *A Portrait of the Artist as a Young Man* by a cunning textual duplicity. For this most sophisticated of avant-garde novels, with all its elaborate aesthetics, chooses to introduce itself, and gives away the secret of all narrative, with that most primitive and fundamental of formulae: 'Once upon a time and a very good time it was ...'[4] Joyce indicates here the doubleness of any literary text. At the end of *Molloy*, the text tells us not to believe it just as it solicits our credence. So, here, Joyce warns us that this is a *story*, at the moment that he announces the opening of Stephen Dedalus's *history*. We can, as naive realists, hear these words simply as the *content* of this history (this is Simon Dedalus, dramatically caught in the act of telling his son a tale). At the same time, as subtle formalists, or as even more naive readers, we can hear these words as the formulaic opening of the whole story we are about to read (for how else do all good stories begin but 'Once upon a time ...'?).

The formula, that is, is both form and content, signifier and signified. The close of *Portrait* points towards a time beyond the bounds of Stephen's present life while simultaneously indicating a real world beyond the book's frontiers, speaking of 'the *spell* of arms and voices' and the tall ships' '*tale* of distant nations'. But the ending also points back to the beginning of the book, in a circular movement which makes it precisely the *product* of the future time only imputed, not yet realized, in those closing paragraphs. The story exists, that is, in Beckett's 'mythological present'. (The same temporal paradox lies behind Stephen's inversions of the parent/child relation, here and in *Ulysses*.) The opening of *Portrait* similarly initiates a structuring analogy between the articulation of characters in a story and a society's articulation of its subjects. We are witnesses, in these paragraphs, to the simultaneous genesis of child and text, 'young man' and 'portrait'. Stephen is constructed as a *subject*, a conscious ego, by learning to recognize his place in a story: the story his father tells him about himself, the story through which 'his' family, 'his' church and 'his' nation donate him a role and an identity. The text here enacts, in appropriate nursery-tale terms, what Jacques Lacan has identifed as the 'mirror phase' in the construction of the human subject.[5] The child learns who it is by seeing itself as an object of the other's gaze, an image in its parents' eyes which it then learns to identify with the 'me' in the mirror. Just as, in the story his father tells him, the moocow coming down the road is grammatical subject, and the 'nicens little boy named baby tuckoo' initially only the object of the sentence, so in Stephen's life the father precedes and names the son, assigns him his place in an already constituted tale. Stephen's role is simply to confirm this role. Recognizing himself in the mirror of the tale, and thereby learning that trick by which, happily ever after, he remains that person he has recognized himself to be: 'His father told him that story; his father looked at him through a glass ... He was baby tuckoo.' Identity is then simply a matter of acknowledging the properties and appurtenances, and in particular the self-uttering discourses, that go with the role ('He sang that song. That was his song').

It is significant, then, that the narrative moves on, from impromptu nursery-tale, through rhyme and the child's familiar landscape, to the larger history implied in the names of Michael Davitt and Parnell. In acquiring a language the child is simultaneously acquired by it. History is a mode of discourse in which we simultaneously discover and lose ourselves. For it is at the very moment that we acknowledge, 'yes, I am baby tuckoo', that we enter into that closed ideological universe where we will forever remain that which we have indisputably established ourselves to be. This is what Stephen puzzles over when he speaks of the soul's birth, 'a slow and dark birth, more mysterious than the birth of the body' (p.231). Nationality, religion, language, may be for *Stephen* the nets which the self has to evade; but *Joyce* presents us with an image of Stephen forever trammelled in the language which has constituted him. He may reject allegiance in a language not his own ('Non serviam'); but those words are at the same time a sign of the potency they strive to renounce. The very possibility of rebellion has been instilled in Stephen's soul by the tales his culture tells him, so that in revolt he can only cast himself as a Luciferian rebel angel. He may refuse the linguistic nationalism of Davin; he may, forced by the verbal puzzlings of the old English dean, come to feel that the English language is, first and foremost, the agency of an alien oppression. But that language is inscribed in his own soul: it would be more accurate to say, *his soul is inscribed in that language*:

> The language in which we are speaking is his before it is mine. How different are the words *home, Christ, ale, master,* on his lips and on mine! I cannot speak or write these words without unrest of spirit. His language, so familiar and so foreign, will always be for me an acquired speech. I have not made or accepted its words. My voice holds them at bay. My soul frets in the shadow of his language. (p.215)

Stephen's mistake (not shared by Joyce, as the pun on 'familiar' indicates) is to assume that language is ever anything else. English is Stephen's *family* tongue: the whole book demonstrates how, in passing through the changing idioms of infancy, school, church, politics, art, the 'young man' is also being recruited. The 'unrest of spirit', the 'fretting' of the soul, is not that of an Irishman in the shadow of English; it is that of all individuals in the shadow of the language which has made them what they are. Always, as in the parent/child relation, there is an oedipal struggle against, as well as attraction to, the language which tells one what to think, an obscure intuition that one is *being thought*, that one is a *vehicle* for meaning, rather than its instigator. Language is not just form and not just content in *Portrait*. It is the real hero of the book. Language utters Stephen in the very moment that Stephen struggles to master and transcend language. No man 'makes' or 'accepts' its words: they make and accept him.

Bewildered by the politics of his first grown-up Christmas dinner, discourses into which he has not yet been initiated, the young Stephen senses obscurely that this is something to do with the unreliable nature of language.

The episode opens with his awareness that the same word can mean quite different things, that signifiers enter into promiscuous relations with the realm of the signified, wondering 'Why did Mr Barrett in Clongowes call his pandybat a turkey?' The mystery of the sign resides in its arbitrary relation to the object. 'Turkey' is here a single signifier with two distinct signifieds – what *Ulysses* jokily calls 'homonymity'. But that later and equally famous episode in *Portrait* referred to above offers two signifiers with one signified: 'funnel' and 'tundish'. In each case, it is the social context, embodied in the institutional power of a patriarch – father, schoolmaster, Dean – which establishes meaning and usage.

Stephen is initiated into the unreliability of ideological signifiers from his earliest moments. Such shifting and shifty allegiances are held in place by an authority which derives from beyond the linguistic: 'Dante has two brushes in her press. The brush with the maroon back was for Michael Davitt and the brush with the green velvet back was for Parnell' (p.7). Neither name is explained, and for the young Stephen they are empty and self-sufficient formulae, not pointing at an object in the external world but expressing a subjective fixation of his Aunt's. The brushes are self-referential magical fetishes, tangible signifiers of signifieds which themselves have cut adrift from their referents – the real historical men – to become icons of Dante's feelings. That 'for' implies not only 'dedicated to', but 'stands in for' – replaces. Dante's allegiance is absolute, a fanaticism. At the Christmas dinner, however, it has been replaced by an equally absolute but contradictory obsession. The signifier 'Parnell' is now charged with hatred. In each case, the word is an index of subjective interpretations. But each time, Dante has not changed, in her own self-perception. She is always absolutely in the right, knows exactly what she means.

What Stephen learns throughout *Portrait* is the power of discourse to conscript us under its sign, to make us render 'false homage to a symbol behind which are massed twenty centuries of authority and veneration' (p.277). Stephen penetrates this opaque, language-beguiled world at the point at which he learns to separate out signifier from signified and both from referent, abolishing centuries of antagonism with a cool, childlike analysis of language's betrayals. Aunt Dante doesn't like Stephen to play with Eileen because Eileen is a Protestant,

> and when she was young she knew children that used to play with protestants and the protestants used to make fun of the litany of the Blessed Virgin. *Tower of Ivory*, they used to say, *House of Gold*! How could a woman be a tower of ivory or a house of gold?
>   ... Eileen had long white hands. One evening when playing tig she had put her hands over his eyes: long and white and thin and cold and soft. That was ivory; a cold white thing. That was the meaning of *Tower of Ivory*. (p.40)

6

Ideology yokes signifier and signified by violence together. Stephen's escape lies in forcing open a gap between them *in the name of the referent*. For him, such ideological conflicts can be resolved to simple confusions of metaphor and metonymy. One awakes from the nightmare by recognising that it is a compendium of tales told by idiots. Already, here, lie the seeds of Earwicker's universal dream, in a night as long as history.

Throughout the Christmas squabble (pp.30–44), which focuses so many Irish contradictions, history is lived as a discord of discourses: election addresses and pulpit sermons, oaths and prayers, 'The language of the Holy Ghost', 'and very bad language if you ask me', 'the language he heard against God and religion and priests in his own home', 'the language with which the priests and the priests' pawns broke Parnell's heart', and so on. The correlation of language and power is recurrent throughout the book. Stephen feels himself the specific target of the hellfire sermon's rhetoric ('Every word of it was for him' [p.131]), registering consciously a process that has been happening unconsciously throughout the formation of his identity – what Louis Althusser calls the 'interpellation'[6] or *calling* of the subject to be that being history has assigned to him ('God could call him now...'). This moves on at once to a larger recognition, the acceptance of his place in the narrative history, along with all the others who had been called, named and judged:

> The English lesson began with the hearing of the history. Royal persons, favourites, intriguers, bishops, passed like mute phantoms behind their veil of names. All had died: all had been judged. What did it profit a man to gain the whole world if he lost his soul? At last he had understood... and when he spoke to answer a question of his master he heard his own voice full of the quietude of humility and contrition. (p.143)

The 'hearing of the history' is a significant phrase, describing a process which is never complete but has repeatedly to be ratified by its counterpart, the subject's self-estranging hearing of his own voice, as if another's, joining in the liturgy. And such a contracting-in leaves the soul, finally, not its own, but a 'mute' creature, appropriated to some exterior discourse.

Althusser's account of the process of the originally theological concept of interpellation is apposite both to the religious context here, and to Stephen's larger dilemma:

> As St Paul admirably put it, it is in the 'Logos', meaning in ideology, that we 'live, move and have our being'. It follows that for you and for me, the category of the subject is a primary obviousness: ... it is clear that you and I are subjects (free, ethical, etc...). Like all obviousnesses, including those that make a word 'name a thing' or 'have a meaning' (therefore including the obviousness of the 'transparency' of language), the 'obviousness' that you and I are subjects – and that that

does not cause any problems – is an ideological effect, the elementary ideological effect. It is indeed a peculiarity of ideology that it imposes… obviousnesses as obviousnesses, which we cannot fail *to recognize* and before which we have the inevitable and natural reaction of crying out (aloud or in the 'still, small voice of conscience'): 'That's obvious! That's right! That's true!'[7]

If such a cry is that which Stephen utters, Althusser also has a description of the wider rituals which incorporate even the prenatal child into a particular history: 'Before its birth, the child is… always-already a subject, appointed as a subject in and by the specific familial ideological configuration in which it is "expected" once it has been conceived', and by 'all the rituals of rearing and then education in the family'.[8]

There are two complementary extremes to language in *Portrait*, each of which is a snare that may threaten the integrity of the constituted subject. One is the cry, brutal, inarticulate, falling below the human. The other is the *inscription*, as a crudely physical presence. Speech at its most spontaneous and inarticulate, disjunctive, interruptive, the exclamatory moment in which Estragon lives, is one threat: 'From the foul laneways he heard bursts of hoarse riot and wrangling and the drawling of drunken singers' (p.113). But there is also *script* at its most brutal, incised by clumsy and brutish labour in the desk tops at Belvedere or in the anatomy theatre (Vladimir's residual, oppressive past, telling us nothing is ever new): 'The letters cut in the stained wood of the desk stared upon him, mocking his bodily weakness and futile enthusiasms' (p.103). At times, the two extremes meet in hostile conspiracy, as when he hears 'a cry which was but the echo of an obscene scrawl which he had read on the oozing wall of a urinal' (p.113). In between, is the prison-house of articulate discourse, where his father endlessly spins an imaginary, self-aggrandizing present out of imaginatively embroidered memories, retold tales of 'heroism':

> Stephen walked on at his father's side, listening to stories he had heard before, hearing again the names of the scattered and dead revellers who had been the companions of his father's youth. And a faint sickness sighed in his heart. (p.103)

Even revolt, such as Stephen's at Clongowes, is second-hand in such a world, an already-written story, only made real for the new subject when it is taken up into the printed schedule: 'A thing like that had been done before by somebody in history, by some great person whose head was in the books of history' (p.60). The transition here from 'history' to 'the books of history' is so subtle as to be barely noticeable, but it reinstates the dialectic process by which event and narration mutually constitute each other. The same dialectic is ironically refigured in the unexpected shift at the end of *Portrait* from the cool translucent narrative to the fragmentary, disjunctive items of

Stephen's diary. The crude fragmentariness of Stephen's written text reproduces as script the lyric fragmentariness of speech, chant and song in the opening pages. The openness of the *voice* has been sealed off into the closure of *writing*. At the moment the subject writes of escape, the book closes and imprisons him in the text. As a model of the way in which the subject relates to the hearing of history, it is a complex and subtle parable.

Plastic M'Intosh

The paradigm that links *Portrait* to *Ulysses* is that of the escapologist. And it links the birdman Dedalus to that quintessential wandering seme, Leopold Bloom, né Virag, a.k.a. Henry Flower, erroneously L. Boom, sometime Ulysses, by turns No Man and Everyman, with only his body as the constant referent of a protean identity. Bloom speaks of the hermeneutic crisis in language which itself circulates the signifiers in periphrastic bombast: 'the difficulties of interpretation since the significance of any event followed its occurrence as variably as the acoustic report followed the electrical discharge'.[9] *Ulysses* is preoccupied with the power of discourse to create signifieds which exist only in discourse:

> – And tell us, Hynes said, do you know that fellow in the, fellow was over there in the...
> He looked around.
> – Macintosh. Yes, I saw him, Mr Bloom said. Where is he now?
> – M'Intosh, Hynes said, scribbling, I don't know who he is. Is that his name? (p.104)

Bloom's (dubious and unintended) authority, as with the word 'Throwaway', inserts new signifiers into a world that takes them literally, endows them with a *soi-disant* referent. The word 'sign' in Bloom's exclamation itself takes on a sneaky duplicity: 'Where has he disappeared to? Not a sign. Well, of all the. Has anybody here seen? Kay ee double ell. Become invisible' (p.104).

The fabulous disappearing Kelly from the Isle of Man becomes No Man, as the noun itself becomes invisible in the curtailment of Bloom's speech ('well of all the'), evaporating like the man in the brown mac. If Bloom is a referent with several signifiers, constituted as several signifieds in different discourses, the spurious name 'M'Intosh' is a single signified that does not match up with the mystery man it seems to indicate.

Molly Bloom likewise invents signifieds for uncomprehended signifiers: 'Unusual polysyllables of foreign origin she interpreted phonetically or by false analogy or both' (p.647), turning even the word 'metempsychosis' into 'met him pike hoses', making 'alias' into a 'medacious [sic] person mentioned in sacred Scripture' (p.647). At the heart of script is someone else, an 'alias' – like the fictive Henry Flower, the misattributed M'Intosh, the ghost of Paddy Dignam. Metempsychosis by periphrasis and misperception is in the very nature of textuality. This is a world of floating signifiers as wayward as the ubiquitous but erratic sandwichboard men advertising HELY'S store. The protean plasticity of the signifier flashes briefly from the folds of this plastic 'M'Intosh'.

Stephen has already grasped the emptiness of the signifier, which names 'things that were not: what Caesar would have lived to do had he believed the soothsayer: what might have been: possibilities of the possible as possible: things not known: what name Achilles bore when he lived among the women' (p.182). Yet in *Portrait* he had assumed the hermeneutic burden of trying to reconstruct a real history, to impute behind the play of signifiers a set of referents who actually did this and that and the other, in a past which once existed as substantially as the city in which he now moves:

> The crises and victories and secessions in Roman history were handed on to him in the trite words *in tanto discrimine* and he had tried to peer into the social life of the city of cities through the words *implere ollam denariorum*. (*Portrait*, pp.203–4)

As prodigal with his cash as with his words, however, Stephen in *Ulysses* also knows that money and language flow like water over the palm and off the tongue, knows that rights and property and debts alike are in the end nothing but 'In words of words for words, palabras' (p.188), as, in his reflection on the idea of adultery, his careful reiteration of the phrase 'what he calls' loosens the tight grip of possession: 'a man who holds so tightly to what he calls his rights over what he calls his debts will hold tightly also to what he calls his rights over her whom he calls his wife' (p.194). Language may function like a knife in the hand, murdering to dissect: 'Unsheathe your dagger definitions. Horseness is the whatness of allhorse' (p.174); but it is also, appropriately for such a novel, a Trojan horse, carrying mayhem within it.

Ulysses steers a mid course between the wandering rocks of discourse, charting a mid career between Scylla and Charybdis, the vertiginous whirlpool of the signifier and the hard rock of the signified. The home Bloom seeks is that final referent in which meaning can be anchored in the whatness of all-horse. This is the nub of the textual aporia that figures throughout the book. All exchanges involve translation, which always entails both loss and addition of meaning. Texts exist only in being communicated, and in that communication we are constantly mistaken and taken amiss, just as Stephen is unaware of what the Queen's Hotel means for Bloom (the place where his father killed himself), just as, in Bloom's recollection, Molly metempsychoses 'metempsychosis' into 'met him pike hoses'. Language, as its very condition, involves misprision: it is the very site of the other, the site of the Fall. As such, it is intimately entwined with the body. For Bloom and Stephen to meet in the library or newspaper office would be to place their meeting under the sign of the sign. Significantly, it is in the realm of the material body, the untranscendable referent, that their encounter is prepared and realised: cemetery, hospital and brothel.

The Moving Finger Writes

Joyce's novels are full of hands, in a kind of running joke (a 'let your fingers do the walking' joke). In the passages I have already cited, for example, there are Eileen's cool white hands, the young Stephen's hand hot from the pandybat, the father's hand that detaches the parson's nose, or Dante's holding the hairbrushes. There is, too, the adolescent hand that has carved the word 'foetus' in a desk top, writes *fin de siècle* poems, or unsheathes dagger definitions. This is a hand that 'holds so tightly to what he calls his rights'. Stephen, to indicate the funnel / tundish to the old dean, has to make his point, at one point, by pointing. The hand, one might say, is fingered throughout the text. It is the bodiliness of the sign, the pointing finger, that preoccupies *Portrait*. The index finger *indicates*. The history of signs is also a history of material bodies, of fingers that point.

Ulysses likewise refuses to unhand us, reminding us that, just as human subjects are not disembodied voices but material bodies, with limbs and organs, so texts are material things, written by hands which hold pens. In the classroom, Stephen is lost in reveries about Aristotle and the potentialities of the actual, while the class is reading 'Lycidas' from its textbooks:

> Talbot repeated:
> – Through the dear might of Him that walked the waves,
>   Through the dear might ...
> – Turn over, Stephen said quietly. I don't see anything.
> – What, Sir? Talbot asked simply, bending forward.
> His hand turned the page over. (p.23)

Language, we know, can speak of things that are not, like the language Achilles spoke among the women, or Christ walking on the water. But books, to be read, need hands to hold them. Reading is a physical act. Texts are material things. Collected works are usually heavy volumes.

The same point is emphasised in the reader's first encounter with Bloom, a little later. Bloom has collected the breakfast kidneys from the butcher. In the process he has found himself reading the (Zionist) newspaper in which

11

they are wrapped, which, if only to complicate the relations between sign and referent, contains pictures of 'blurred cropping cattle, the page rustling' (p.52). That last play on words seems totally irresistible: images are cropped, but not by cattle, cattle are rustled, but not by pages. The text is full here of hands, Bloom's own, holding the newspaper-wrapped package, the pork-butcher's, cutting the meat, the recollected hands of breeders in the market, poking the rumps of cattle, the 'thick wrist' and 'Sodachapped hands' of the woman in the shop, in Bloom's memory/fantasy whacking a carpet on the line. But this is only the half of it. Ingestion has its consequences, for texts as for meat, and the end products of the two kinds of consumption are brilliantly merged in a twentieth-century tale of a tub, that lavatorial episode in which Joyce explores the back passages of writing.

When Bloom reads the tabloid weekly, *Titbits*, at stool, it is difficult to distinguish the acts of textual ingestion and physical excretion: 'Quietly he read, restraining himself, the first column and, yielding but resisting, began the second. Midway, his last resistance yielding, he allowed his bowels to ease themselves quietly as he read, reading still patiently that slight constipation of yesterday quite gone' (p.61). Bloom has been reading a prize story, which has given him the idea of writing one himself. However, the text's way with words is rather more abrupt: 'He tore away half the prize story sharply and wiped himself with it' (p.62).

The history of the body is reproduced in the history of texts, just as the hospital where bodies are born and the cemetery where they are interred are reproduced in the novel by newspaper offices, where discourses come hot off the press, and library, where the sign is laid to rest, awaiting the last judgment and resurrection, as Stephen obscurely records: 'Coffined thoughts around me, in mummycases, embalmed in spice of words. Thoth, god of libraries' (p.182). As Swift remarked in 'The Battle of the Books': 'it is with libraries as with other cemeteries'.[10]

In *Ulysses*, the Stephen who at the end of *Portrait* had departed euphorically to pursue the tales of distant nations finds himself lured back into his own claustrophobic Irish narrative, cabined, cribbed, confined like Hamlet, bounded in a nutshell, afflicted by bad dreams. Locked in the classroom, still transmitting a double inheritance to others, he has himself become the teller of history in an hour when, for him, history is a nightmare from which he wants to wake up. A nightmare, not because, in some archly aesthetic way, he is contemptuous of the world's demands, but because, as in a nightmare, one is lived, as if without volition, by the story which constitutes one's consciousness. It's for this reason that apocalyptic wishes lurk just below the surface of Stephen's (as of Bloom's) mind. History is again a double field: 'Fabled by the daughters of memory. And yet it was in some way if not as memory fabled it'. On the one hand, history is the deadly reality of a 'corpsestrewn plain', and, on the other, a 'phrase the world had remembered' (p. 21).

For Stephen, it's this doubleness which makes the nightmare, as it is for the schoolboys he is teaching: 'for them too history was a tale like any other too often heard, their land a pawnshop' (p.22). Infinite possibility is fossilized into finished event, in the text of the history-book, and the text of the past:

> Had Pyrrhus not fallen to a beldam's hand in Argus or Julius Caesar not been knifed to death? They are not to be thought away. Time has branded them and fettered they are lodged in the room of the infinite possibilities they have ousted. But can those have been possible seeing that they never were? Or was that only possible which came to pass? Weave, weaver of the wind.
> – Tell us a story, sir.
> – Oh, do, sir. A ghoststory... (p.22)

The oral story seems, to the class, an escape into a spontaneous, open future, from the 'fettered' discourse of the history book. The movement in this sequence between history and story now contains a larger contradiction, between necessity and freedom, determinism and possibility: the story-teller magician deals with the realm of speech, where each next word is as yet unuttered and therefore unpredictable. That escape lies in the fantasy of a 'ghoststory' complicates matters. 'Lycidas' itself, since it imagines the posthumous life of a dead man, is a kind of ghost story. But in that sense, all historical records endow their subjects with a posthumous existence, are textual ghosts of the events they purport to report.

In the classroom, Stephen's memories are of the prison-house of *print* which is also a kind of graveyard, recalling, for example, 'the studious silence of the library of St Genevieve where he had read, sheltered from the sin of Paris', his brain 'impaled' like those around him (p.23). And it is a characteristic rhythm of the book, in which the script of libraries, newspaper files, schoolbooks, sandwich-men, documents, tracts, bills, accounts, alphabets, letters, all *conscript* (literally) the future but at the same time incarcerate the past. That process is signalled by the slavish dependence of teacher and pupils on the brute fact of the book from which the poem 'Lycidas' is being recited: the spoken (but pre-ordained) words are interrupted by the pause required manually to turn the page. Speech and print are reunited by a brief, mute action. The final collocation of a weary tyranny and the 'mummery' of script is contained in the sums, 'writ[ten] out all again' which Stephen has to correct.

The gamut of language which runs from cry to hieroglyph is the primary matrix of *Ulysses*. The book, like the city it transcribes, is an interpenetrating flux of discourses, none of them privileged. And these discourses are not coterminous with individual subjects, but cut across them, so that, for example, Gerty MacDowell's identity is the nexus where the discourses of True Romance and Mariolatry converge. The same words and phrases are repeated by different individuals; Bloom has a knowledge of matters too arcane to be typical of his particular consciousness. At the moment where we move from Gerty's to Bloom's consciousness, it is difficult to decide precisely where one ends and the other begins. Physically separate, they interpenetrate in discourse. Joyce in *Ulysses* does not set out to depict a world of autonomous subjects. Rather he reveals the extent to which our common experience is constructed out of language, so that, in a sense, we do not utter it: it utters us. Equally, he is not simply engaged in a series of parodies of linguistic forms. Rather the text spells out the multiplicity of ideological forms through which history is articulated.

Blank Pages

There is a rather touching moment at the end of *Ulysses* where Stephen and Leopold negotiate the very Derridean question: 'How was a glyphic comparison of the phonic symbols of both languages made in substantiation of the oral comparison?' (p.648). This they do by writing parallel Irish and Hebrew letters on 'the penultimate blank page of a book of inferior literary style entitled *Sweets of Sin*', a mildly salacious text, of the kind read with one hand, which reminds us of the bodiliness that underlies all textuality, just as the periphrastic idiom reminds us of the great gulf between signifiers and signifieds. The Irish and Hebrew melodies they then respectively sing depend on the vulnerable vocal cords of each, and upon the limits of their power to recall the words, 'in consequence of defective mnemotechnic', which is compensated for by 'a periphrastic version of the general text'. In other words, they make them up.

Stephen writes his name in Irish and Roman characters. Bloom sings a Hebrew hymn and Stephen hears 'in a profound ancient male unfamiliar melody the accumulation of the past'. This past is not a tradition that exists in splendid independence of its human subjects, as Bloom's forgetting and paraphrase remind. Rather, it is a past taken over, *translated*, in every transmission. Encountering the ghost of Joyce at the end of 'Station Island', in the volume of that name, Seamus Heaney puts into the mouth of a dead man words which turn in the mouth itself into an incongruously material image of *writing*:

> his voice eddying with the vowels of all rivers
> came back to me, though he did not speak yet,
> a voice like a prosecutor's or a singer's,
>
> cunning, narcotic, mimic, definite
> as a steel nib's downstroke, quick and clean.[11]

This translation, or taking over, of speech into writing prevents us from translating the simile into metaphor and thence into an ideologically charged and spurious literalness. That pen sticks in the maw. Deconstructing the conventional image of the bourgeois subject as disembodied voice, the poem simultaneously reminds us of its own textuality.[12] It homes in on writing as a physical act, something effected by that hand which also grasps the ash plant, grips that of the younger writer, and which Joyce once joked no-one would ever want to kiss who knew what other things it had done besides writing *Ulysses*. As soon as the writer opens his mouth he puts his pen in it, so to speak.

The Dedalus/Bloom exchange does not evoke the inheritance of a Coole Park or a Municipal Gallery, Yeats's celebrated repositories of Irish history and culture, of fixed properties nailed down once and for all in their place. Rather it is a negotiation, on the basis of inadequate means, between the volatile, shifting, transitory human subjects who translate that inheritance, take it over (in the sense both of appropriating and carrying forward) and who in so doing forget, misremember, confound, compound, collocate and collate discourses which can never be restored to some imaginary pristine authenticity. Yet this does not mean that we are all necessarily solitary misleaders and misreaders of discourse. On the contrary, once the noise of communication is seen to enter into its very meaning, a provisional, unsure, cautious, but legitimate exchange becomes possible, as Stephen's and Bloom's mutual reflection merge in a 'common study'.

Joyce's portrait of 'a good man', however, is not without its shadows and complications. The fissure between history and story accounts for the most remarkable absence in *Ulysses*, ostensibly simply a matter of dates. By pitching the events of *Ulysses* in a mythological present ten years before its writing began and eighteen years before its publication in 1922, Joyce omits the central historic events which determine its whole significance. This is a day like any other, and it is lived by its actors as if it will go on forever. But the writer and every reader know what none of these characters can: the fact of world war and postwar revolutions, of insurrection and fratricidal struggle, of Europe as a battlefield between 1914 and 1918, of imperial collapse and the revolutions it precipitated between 1917 and 1922, of Dublin at Easter 1916, of those dragon-ridden days in Ireland between 1919 and 1922, where rebellion turned into the civil war ongoing as the book appeared. In this context, the apocalyptic fantasies of Stephen and Bloom, the violence of the Citizen and the rumpus with the British soldiers, all take on a new and ominous significance, one denied to the people imprisoned in the text. Written out as stories, they are forever refused knowledge of that real world which brutally negates their (in retrospect) prelapsarian innocence. *Ulysses* is, finally, a presentation of the world before the Fall. The last words of the book embed the fabled Dublin of 1904 in the context of the historic Trieste, Zurich, Paris of 1914–21 where it was written, as another casualty of that long record which reaches back through Tarentum, Asculum, Carthage to Troy itself. When we consider that it was Ulysses/Odysseus himself who designed the Wooden Horse that betrayed Troy, we have to ask again how innocent is Leopold Bloom, as the average man, of the guilt of history? Do the sadomasochistic, *Uebermensch* fantasies, the daydreams of revenge and the 'horse-play' of the brothel (all unfulfilled 'stories') not have something to do with the real *nightmare* of history? Is innocence not, perhaps, history's Trojan horse? The violence of that real future, of fifty years and more of blathering yet to come, if we look closely, is everywhere predicted, spoken in advance and not heard, in the body of the text. And it is in that world of historical event, those blank pages still to be written on, and not in the mythological present, that, finally, the negotiations of fantasy and history have to be played out.

NOTES

1. Samuel Beckett, *Waiting for Godot* (New York: Grove Press, 1954); original French version, *En Attendant Godot* (Paris: Editions de Minuit, 1952).
2. Samuel Beckett, *Molloy* (Paris: Olympia Press, 1954; original French version, Paris: Editions de Minuit, 1951); in *The Beckett Trilogy* (London: Picador, 1979), p. 162.
3. Ibid, p. 26.
4. James Joyce, *A Portrait of the Artist as a Young Man* (New York: W.B. Huebsch, 1916); this edn. (Stockholm: Zephyr Books, 1945), p. 7. Hereafter, page references are indicated in the text.
5. Jacques Lacan, 'The Mirror-phase as formative of the Function of the I' (1949), trans. Jean Roussel, in *New Left Review*, 51, Sept.–Oct. (1968). See also the essays included in Lacan, *The Four Fundamental Concepts of Psychoanalysis*, ed. Jacques-Alain Miller (London: The Hogarth Press, 1977).
6. Louis Althusser, 'Ideology and Ideological State Apparatuses', in *Lenin and Philosophy and Other Essays*, trans. Ben Brewster (London: New Left Books, 1971), p. 160.
7. Ibid., p. 161.
8. Ibid., p. 165.
9. James Joyce, *Ulysses*; this edn. (London: The Bodley Head, 1937), p. 637. Hereafter, page references are indicated in the text.
10. Jonathan Swift, 'The Battle of the Books' (1704); this edn., *A Tale of a Tub and Other Satires*, introd. Lewis Melville (London: J. M. Dent, 1909), p.148.
11. Seamus Heaney, *Station Island* (London: Faber and Faber, 1984).
12. W. H. Auden works a similar variation on the difference between voice (speaking) and hands (doing / undoing) in 'September 1, 1939', which admits its liberal ineffectualness in proclaiming 'All I have is a voice / To undo the folded lie'. On this see my *W. H. Auden* (Oxford: Blackwell, 1985), pp. 27–30.

II

Making it Up:
W. B. Yeats

Analysing the Tub

Jonathan Swift's 'Author's Preface' to *A Tale of A Tub* offers a significant metaphor for the dilemma of the critic attempting to read the narratives of Irish history, so permeated by fable and confabulation, by way of explaining his title:

> [S]eamen have a custom, when they meet a whale, to fling him out an empty tub by way of amusement, to divert him from laying violent hands upon the ship. This parable was immediately mythologised; the whale was interpreted to be Hobbes' *Leviathan*, which tosses and plays with all schemes of religion and government, whereof a great many are hollow, and dry, and empty, and noisy, and wooden, and given to rotation: this is the leviathan, whence the terrible wits of our age are said to borrow their weapons. The ship in danger is easily understood to be its old antitype, the commonwealth. But how to analyse the tub, was a matter of difficulty; when, after long inquiry and debate, the literal meaning was preserved; and it was decreed that, in order to prevent these leviathans from tossing and sporting with the commonwealth, which of itself is too apt to fluctuate, they should be diverted from that game by *a Tale of a Tub*.[1]

What Swift means by this little allegory is worth considering. It may be that the empty receptacle of the text keeps the cultural exegete, or partisan appropriator and fabulator of narratives, from laying violent hands on the commonwealth or 'interpretive community' itself. But in what way, and to what end? Stanley Fish, a critic of a different kettle, who might well enquire, 'Is there a tale in this tub?', has premised that there is no original meaning which can be established for a text, but only a series of interpretations which in the end derive their authority from the contemporary institutions which sustain and authorise them, and the persuasive or even coercive rhetoric of the critic (or cultural context) in enforcing his, her, its authority. Swift however has seen it all before, ironically considering it 'fit to lay hold on that great and honourable privilege of being the last writer; I claim an absolute authority in right, as the freshest modern, which gives me a despotic power over all authors before me' (p. 85).

Swift's textual tub is not empty. It overflows with tales. The central difficulty is how to endow any of these tales with authoritative status. The authority of the text clearly cannot derive from the author. We don't need Roland Barthes to tell us, since we already have Swift's word for it, that 'It is another pattern of this answerer's fair dealing to give us hints that the author is dead' (pp. 19–20). Nor can authority derive from the reader alone, either, for, in Swift's words, 'for the greater part the reflector is entirely mistaken, and forces interpretations which never once entered into the writer's head' (p. 17). Trapped in the hermeneutic circle, it appears that we cannot appeal beyond it for the validation of our interpretations.

Swift himself had identified the central deconstructive problem: what constraints do we place upon interpretation? How far can you go? It is the issue raised in the *Tale*'s central parable about Christian exegesis, in which three sons, Peter, Martin and Jack compete for control over the interpretation of an ultimately unknowable original. But if Peter's elaborately decorated coat travesties that original, Jack's attempts to strip all away will only end in tears, denuding and impoverishing it. The text here is an aporia, radically unstable, endlessly re-readable. But it is definitely not a nullity. As Swift knew well, and satirised in *Gulliver's Travels*, much blood had been shed, in the long, fractious history of a Christianity beset by heresy and schism, over questions of interpretation as trivial, almost, as which end to crack open an egg. In Ireland, as Yeats fretted in 'The Man and the Echo', and as many other Irish poets have subsequently reiterated, the relation between event and interpretation has been a particularly bloody one, written, often, on the bodies as well as the minds of its subjects.

Taking It Over

Seamus Heaney's poem 'The Disappearing Island', in *The Haw Lantern*, offers an interesting gloss on Swift's allegory. It speaks of mariners who 'presumed to found [them]selves for good' on an island which then 'broke beneath [them] like a wave'.[2] For it was in fact the back of a basking whale, that 'seemed to hold firm/Only when we embraced it *in extremis*'. The text is not an empty tub into which the story-tellers pour their tales. Rather, it is very like a whale, and in this it partakes of the character of the rest of the material world. It is subject to misinterpretation, can be mistaken for an island of solid meaning until it plunges to unplumbable depths, taking its Captain Ahab pursuer with it. The whaling motif, as I discuss in a later chapter, is picked up by Ciaran Carson's 'Auditque Vocatus Apollo', a poem specifically about the way the god of poetry is summoned to make sense of inchoate experience.[3] The text, that is, is not only a disembodied chain of signification. It is also a material body, subject to all the physical constraints of the material. That realm of social and political practice, *hors texte*, that endangered species, the Third that tends to get left out, left over, in any discussion of the Saussurean Trinity, the referent, is precisely where these fabulations find their (provisional) grounding, on what may not be, after all, solid earth, but simply the whale's back. This is the real Derridean 'supplement' – that unknowable and shifting ground which is experienced only through the mediation of our various semiotics, but which rolls and slides remorselessly under signifier and signified alike, a leviathan of discourse, beating its enormous tail/tale.

It is not difficult to see 'The Disappearing Island' as a poem about the hermeneutics of Irish history. There are good historical and political reasons why contemporary critical theory, with its extreme distrust of the sign as a guide to the real, its preoccupation with the endless deferral of meaning, should have a particular, positive application to Irish culture. Heaney suggests them here and in a poem in the same volume such as 'Parable Island'. The latter is itself a parable about the nature of story-telling – in particular, about those mythologisings of history in which national cultures are constructed. Parable Island is a place where everyone thinks in parables, a world of 'shifting names' homing in on an illusory 'point where all the names converge' beneath a mythical mountain, where 'the ore of truth' may be mined – one day. In fact, parable is always-already retrospectively at work on the island, so that no 'original idea' can ever be genuinely grasped. Irish history, Heaney suggests, has been a struggle of referentless parables, of discourses which often engage with each other, but in the process brutally override any actual events in the material world. At times, that referent has avenged itself in a murderous return of the repressed, irrupting into what had seemed like a purely cerebral play of signifiers, a rough beast slouching to be born, Furies climbing the stairs, a terrible beauty bursting into discourse.

In 'A Tale of Two Islands: Reflections on the Irish Literary Revival',[4] whose title recalls its Swiftian as well as Shavian antecedents, Heaney contrasted Yeats's attempt to forge 'a coherent Irish tradition' with the position of Joyce, 'content to inherit the shattered one which history bequeathed him'. The hermeneutic crisis at the centre of modern theoretical debate is, however, not only centrally relevant to the two strands of Irish Modernism Yeats and Joyce respectively represent. It was in some senses identified in advance by both of them. When Heaney in the lecture *Among Schoolchildren* speaks of Joyce as 'deconstructing the prescriptive myth of Irishness which was burgeoning in his youth and which survives in various... forms to this day',[5] he identifies a recurrent moment in his own writing as well as Joyce's. But it is also something we can find throughout Yeats's poetry.

Yeats is always trying to have his way with history. Yet that history remains as unaccommodating as its repeated 'figure' (both literal body and literary trope), Maud Gonne, remained in his life. Throughout Yeats's master-narratives another history speaks, and it is the strength of his poetry that it everywhere utters this alternative history, even as it tries to marginalise and transform it. Indeed, the *meaning* of his texts is often just this contention between conflicting interpretations, a struggle for hegemony within the poem itself. Yeats's poems, that is, deconstruct themselves as we read, their masterful narratives inscribing in image and trope a plurality of voices which say, slyly or shyly, vehemently or with reserve, 'So *you* say, Willy...'.

It is a paradox, or a logical inconsistency, or simply the *hubris*, of contemporary critical theory in its post-structuralist, deconstructive and postmodernist modes, that though it mounts an intense assault upon metaphysics, it enshrines, in the conviction of its own otherness, that most ancient of metaphysical notions – the idea of a *beyond*, of an *origin* somewhere else. But critical theory is not an oracular message from spirit instructors, come to give us 'metaphors for poetry'. It is constructed here and now, in the academy or in the streets, by situated, particular subjects who bring with them the whole baggage of their historical and cultural imbrication. To adopt the title of one of Heaney's poems in *The Haw Lantern*, we all start from the frontier of writing. There is nowhere else to start from. Deconstruction is an effective strategy for subverting sovereign meanings, refuting irrefutable authoritative readings. But it is in itself no more than a strategy. It is not, and by its own terms of reference cannot be, an alternative system. Heaney's 'frontier of writing' is not a beyond, but the immanent horizon of any text – a limit imposed from within the text upon the play of interpretations. This limit derives from the fact that the text is the product not of a transcendent subject, but of a language which is a material thing, impersonal and collective and charged in every syllable with historical meanings. The powerful discourses of gender and of class are inescapable horizons of any text, because they are ineluctable elements of that discursive unconscious from which the text derives, what Heaney calls 'the unconscious of the English language'. Hence the fecundity of feminism as a mode of reading *against the grain* of a text, without in any way simply importing perspectives extraneous to it. A reading of 'Michael Robartes and the Dancer', for example, which starts by contrasting the wordy and self-contradictory rhetoric of male seduction with the sharp rhetorical questions of the woman, works on what is there in the words even as it overturns the patriarchal self-satisfaction in which the text basks. Likewise, we cannot now read the historical and mythic paradigms embodied in 'Leda and the Swan' without inverting its missionary positions, acknowledging the full force of that moment of female revenge on the patriarch, 'Agamemnon dead', which comes at the very climax of poem and rape alike.

Heaney's account of translation in an interview in *Salmagundi* is apposite here.[6] Heaney speaks of 'the notion of translation as taking it over... in two senses – in the slightly imperial sense and in the original etymological sense of carrying a thing across' – across, that is the frontier of writing, but in the process also appropriating it, making it one's own. Heaney speaks of seeing the 'oblique applicability' of the Ugolino episode in *The Divine Comedy* to the Northern Irish situation: 'So one foraged unfairly into the Italian and ripped it untimely from its place.' The echo of *Macbeth* is singularly appropriate in this account of child-devouring patriarchs. With *Suibhne* too, he says, he 'wanted to pull it out of the Irish', with all the resonant *double entendre* of that phrase. What Heaney says of translation is true of all interpretation, which in one sense is always a taking over, an appropriation and translation into one's own – another Heaney keyword – preoccupations. From Joyce's and Yeats's making it new with Homer, through Louis MacNeice's repossession of Greek tragedy, Derek Mahon's revisitings of French poetry, to Heaney's and Ciaran Carson's versions of *Suibhne*, *Beowulf* or Dante, and Paul Muldoon's reinventions in turn of MacNeice, Auden et al. in '7, Middagh Street' or of the Pantisocratic Wordsworth, Coleridge and Southey in *Madoc*, such taking over and over-taking has been a central element in Irish literary discourse. Characteristically, Beckett trumps them all in translating himself in reverse, from French into English, and then into German. As the parodic Morris Zapp reminds us in David Lodge's novel *Small World*, in that most authoritative of modern discourses, the lapel badge, 'Every decoding is another encoding'.[7]

The most principled formulation of such a position is perhaps Walter Benjamin's idea of the discursive 'constellation' – in which, he says, the critic 'grasps the constellation which his own era has formed with a definite earlier one'.[8] This is not the same as a subjective and capricious expropriation of the past, because what link the two moments in a single constellation are the shared historical discourses that underlie both. As Heaney goes on to say, 'a writer is not different from a reader, in that the common ragbag of orthodoxies and assumptions is what a poet has to work with as well'. The literary text, as Heaney taught us to see in his first collection of essays, *Preoccupations*, is always *pre-occupied* by the traces of its referents, of its historical a priori. It is, indeed, very like a whale.

Fabular Darks

Contrasting Joyce and Yeats, Richard Ellmann remarks, before going on to discuss their respective views of history:

> Yeats has no barrier about subjects, but in responding to unexalted occasions he guards a verbal formality. Even at his wildest, he maintains the poise, the authority of language. It is just this poise and authority which Joyce seems always to be disturbing, as if he were mounting a revolution against that worst of tyrannies, the lexical kind.[9]

In Yeats's poetry the ego appears to arrive fully formed on the stage of history. He may, in 'A Dialogue of Self and Soul', speak of 'that toil of growing up; / The ignominy of boyhood; the distress / Of boyhood changing into man', but the starting-point of his poetry is always the already-constituted subject, 'The finished man among his enemies'.[10] Childhood hardly exists for the poet as a stage in his own being. He can look at children from the outside, 'A sixty year old smiling public man', and even, in imaginative sympathy, respond to the recovery of another's childhood as story, 'a tale that she / Told of a harsh reproof, or trivial event / That changed some childish day to tragedy – / Told...'[11] The sequence 'tale... Told... Told' here, foregrounded by enjambment, tells it all. That this actual person is spoken of, only periphrastically, as 'a Ledaean body', indicates that the mythologising principle has already infiltrated even the world of social and material relations. Maud Gonne is no longer a person but a signifying practice, appropriated to a fabular tradition, her subjectivity expunged in the very process of apparently evoking it.

For Yeats, the child, like Maud Gonne here, is almost always an external object, taken up into the fluent medium of the poet's own subjectivity, as in 'A Prayer for my Daughter',[12] where the poet walks and prays, evoking a possible future for his offspring out of his own magical imagination. 'A Prayer for my Son' indicates why he shies away from acknowledging infancy as a state through which he himself has passed. The child, like God, 'can fashion everything / From nothing every day, and teach the morning stars to sing'; but its essential vulnerability, as object and dependant of others, undermines this naive solipsism, even when the child is Christ:

> You have lacked articulate speech
> To tell your simplest want, and known,
> Wailing upon a woman's knee,
> All of that worst ignominy
> Of flesh and bone.[13]

Lack of articulate speech places one at risk among one's enemies, exposes one to 'ignominy'. When, occasionally, Yeats does advert to his own childhood, as in the first section of 'The Tower', it is mediated through a literary filter – here, the Wordsworthian mode and shrewd use of the disowning negative:

> Never had I more
> Excited, passionate, fantastical
> Imagination...
> No, not in boyhood when with rod and fly,
> Or the humbler worm, I climbed Ben Bulben's back.[14]

The autonomy of the subject, its freedom from history, lies in its power of 'articulate speech', a power which, spinning a cocoon of imaginary selfhood out of the 'fantastical / Imagination', insulates the self against the world.

Of the fantastic in literature, Tzvetan Todorov argues that it 'can subsist only within fiction; poetry cannot be fantastic', because, unlike fiction, poetry does not have a referent in the external world against which the deviations of fantasy can be measured.[15] This works as a definition of lyric and symbolist poetry; but it hardly bears up against a poetry such as Yeats's which again and again takes as its theme and locus the major events of a familiar, verifiable history. What Yeats in fact does is to appropriate the realm of history to poetry precisely by converting it into story, transforming it into that literary mode which Todorov calls the 'fantastic'.

According to Todorov, the fantastic has, at its centre, a deliberate 'transgression' of what the text had previously imputed to be reality:

> The reader and hero ... must decide if a certain event or phenomenon belongs to reality or imagination, that is, must determine whether or not it is real. It is therefore the category of the real which has furnished a basis for our definition of the fantastic ... By the hesitation it engenders, the fantastic questions precisely the existence of an irreducible opposition between real and unreal ... If a certain apparition is only the fruit of an overexcited imagination, then everything around it is real.

'Easter 1916'[16] is a poem centrally concerned with the process by which an everyday world undergoes this 'transgression' by a force it cannot interpret. Unequivocally posited on 'real' events, it takes the *real*, the discourse of history, and encloses it within the text, not as some external referent of the words, but as an *interior perspective* of the poem, against which the *transgressions* of the imagination, of magic, have to be set. The more we examine the text, the more this interiorization of 'history' becomes apparent.

Like *A Portrait of the Artist*, 'Easter 1916' signals its literariness. It opens, for example, on a close: 'I have met them at close of day.' This closure seals out the discourse that preceded the poem as the ending opens anew on that discourse: 'A terrible beauty is born.' Throughout the poem there is an insistence on its status as a linguistic artefact. Language, as recurring motif, calls attention to the fact that the poem itself is made up only of those events which we call words. From the start, the variety of forms language takes in the world of history offer alternative versions of the function this poem might be fulfilling, and the functions it is resisting: 'polite meaningless words', 'a mocking tale or a gibe', political 'argument' that makes the voice grow shrill, even the 'call' of hens to moor-cock, and the mother's 'naming' of her child, England's 'keeping faith', 'For all that is done and said', and so on. Only halfway through the poem does it declare itself for what it is, at precisely the moment that the most intractable aspect of the real, the loutishness of history's 'casual comedy', is transformed into the purity of 'song', and reality itself is retrospectively reduced to the unreality of 'dream' ('This other man I had dreamed / A drunken vainglorious lout... / Yet I number him in the song'). But it is only at the end that this transubstantiation is completed, and it is signalled, noticeably, by a shift from the open, fluid spontaneities of speech and action to the finality of *script*, in that elegiac listing with which the poem concludes ('I write it out in a verse...').

The 'transgression' in this poem is a purely verbal event: the assertive repetition of those words, 'changed, changed utterly: / A terrible beauty is born'. We, of course, locked in our guilty historicity, know exactly what is meant. That which is not spoken, the absent centre of the poem, we can supply, from our knowledge of a history in which we are all involved. Yet it's a remarkable operation, when we think about it. As in 'All Souls' Night', the poet / magician is conjuring with our connivance. There too, nothing is actually summoned up except words, names, stories, yet we are left feeling that we have participated in some mysterious séance, that the fantastic has invaded the realm of the quotidian.

Todorov speaks of the process by which, in fantastic literature, the reader becomes a character in the text. The text, he says,

> must oblige the reader to consider the world of the characters as a world of living persons and to hesitate between a natural and a supernatural explanation of the events described... [T]his hesitation may also be experienced by a character; thus the reader's role is so to speak entrusted to a character, and at the same time the hesitation is represented, it becomes one of the themes of the work.[17]

Yeats achieves this identification by moving from the opening 'I' of the poet to the implicating 'we' of the final section ('We know their dream'). Both poet and reader alike are faced with the problem of interpretation: is this 'transgression' an imaginary or an actual event? But the reader, unlike the 'hero', has a further problem; required to ask: are we reading a history of events external to the poem, does the text have a referent? Or are we reading a story, something which exists in its own right, without reference to anything external even when it is appropriating that externality to its own interior discourse?

Yeats allows for this doubleness by the sequence of unanswered questions around which the text is constructed, questions which bring the 'I' of poem and of reader into an uneasy identity before the incomprehensible order of things. Each of these questions in turn is closely bound up with the motif of language, either directly ('What voice more sweet than hers?') or because it is at once answered by a changing of the subject, away from deeds to the words into which we have to displace them ('O when may it suffice? / That is heaven's part, our part / To murmur name upon name'; 'What is it but nightfall? ... Was it needless death after all? ... / For England may keep faith / For all that is done and said'). The final strategic withdrawal from the historical question to the unequivocal affirmations of story is also that transit from speech to script: 'And what if excess of love / Bewildered them till they died? / I write it out in a verse...' The date which concludes the poem, unlike the title, pointedly refers to the time of that writing out, and not to the time of the events described.

Wherever story touches history in Yeats's poetry, the rhetorical question is not far away. And this is not simply a matter of Yeats's liberal uncertainties. Rather it is the very function of poetry to articulate this hesitation, this stuttering in language, within which its meanings are located, parentheses which willingly suspend not belief but disbelief, bracketing a textual reality with hints and rumours of a real world where questions have to be answered. In this world, fantasy is not just a literary mode but a political reality on which the heart feeds and grows brutal, a world where images are not contemplative but efficacious ('And yet they too break hearts'), and 'fanatics invent... / Fantasy or incident / Not worth thinking of' ('Quarrel in Old Age') that disturb the living stream.

Yeats asks this question, about the relation of fantasy to history, in 'The Statues',[18] again without providing an answer: 'When Pearse summoned Cuchulain to his side / What stalked through the Post Office?' The poem's meaning lies precisely in this unanswerableness. Did Cuchulain, a 'real' supernatural force, stalk through the Post Office? Did Pearse merely 'summon' something out of his own dark, and was it a phantasm, an imaginary thing? *What* did stalk? Nothing, perhaps. But the sentence is posed in such a way that, though it affirms nothing, the interrogative pronoun, in taking a verb, presupposes that *something* did the stalking. The historian would ask a different question. 'Did anything stalk?' or, even more sceptically, 'What on earth did Pearse think he was up to?' Yeats's sentence describes a pseudo-event, like all the events of literature.

The question functions in exactly the same way in, for example, 'The Second Coming': 'And what rough beast...', where the concreteness of the verb 'slouches' disguises the fact that this is a fantasy evoked by words ('The Second Coming! / Hardly are those words out...').[19] 'A Stick of Incense',[20] likewise, juxtaposes two questions which imply a supernatural transgression of the natural, with a subversive and yet strangely innocent statement of secular scepticism which is *not* an answer to the questions but merely a counterposing assertion. The answer lies in the silence between the couplets: the *meaning* of the poem is the juxtaposition of these incompatibles. Again, those famous and harrowing lines in 'The Man and the Echo' where Yeats agonizes over his political responsibility, lines apparently raw with uncertainty and remorse, asking 'What have I done?' actually perform the same, *literary* function: 'Did that play of mine send out / Certain men the English shot?'[21]

The question seems to point backwards, towards an anterior, historical world, in which art has its effect directly, as propaganda and provocation. But in fact the lines constitute only themselves. Whether *Cathleen ni Houlihan* provoked men to die for Ireland is beside the point. Now and in time to be, *in this poem,* the conjunction has occurred. In the *story* of this particular poem, a play may have sent men out to die. This throws a critical light back upon that earlier statement:

> All that I have said and done
> Now that I am old and ill,
> Turns into a question till
> I lie awake night after night
> And never get the answers right.

The formulaic couplings here indicate the fabular nature of this questioning, which becomes more explicit in that last aggressive interrogation of the oracle:

> ...O Rocky Voice
> Shall we in that great night rejoice?
> What do we know but that we face
> One another in this place?

'That' and 'this' have no real location outside the text. 'That great night' is simply the 'fabulous formless dark' which encloses 'this place', the circumscribed text. Art itself becomes the echo which gives us back our own words, strangely transformed, turning the historic conditional / subjunctive, 'Sleepless would lie down and die', into a fictional imperative, in the mythological present: 'Lie down and die'.

It is for this reason that, having raised the problem, Yeats can drop it, with a cunning changing of the subject which masquerades as an aesthetic muffing of his lines: 'But hush, for I have lost the theme, / Its joy or might seem but a dream.' We are then distracted away from the text by a cry which seems to come from beyond but which is really only its final invention, distracting the poem into closure: 'A stricken rabbit is crying out, / And its cry distracts my thought.' For the (historical) men sent out to die *in this poem,* Yeats cares as little as for the legendary Oisin in 'The Circus Animals' Desertion': 'But what cared I that set him on to ride?' They are simply 'themes / ...That might adorn old songs'.[22]

Having warned us that history is only a set of themes, metaphors for his poetry, Yeats's stories leave us with a sense of the fatuousness of historical action. Like Beckett, but with confidence and joy, he shouts: 'Nothing to be done; everything to be written out.' And this itself is an ideological strategy, a way of coming to terms with the paralysis of an Ireland that, having almost destroyed itself in inconclusive civil war, seemed to have nowhere anymore to go. An urgent and imperative history is thus transformed into an image out of *Spiritus Mundi*, a theme in the Great Memory. In the last sentences Yeats wrote for *A Vision* in February 1925, he confessed this with his usual gnomic insistence:

> I can recognise that the limit itself has become a new dimension, that this ever hidden thing which makes us fold our hands has begun to press down upon multitudes. Having bruised their hands upon that limit, men, for the first time since the seventeenth century, see the world as an object of contemplation, not as something to be remade...[23]

Language becomes the lonely tower in which the subject confronts history, a world yet to be remade. In the words added in 1934–36, in even more pressing times, this is spelt out with greater candour: 'How far can I accept socialistic or communistic prophecies?', he asks, and, without answering, replies, climbing to his 'proper dark' out of history, into the 'fabulous dark' of story – 'Then I draw myself up into the symbol and it seems as if I should know all if I could but banish such memories and find everything in the symbol.' Yet the mythological present of the symbol can in the end offer no solace for the victim of history's memories, as he ruefully concedes: 'But nothing comes.'[24]

The Irish Construction Industry

Yeats's essential role in the construction of an Irish national identity, both in his agitations, propaganda and writings in the decades before independence, and in a handful of poems in the vein of 'Easter, 1916', did not end with his death. He has continued, as a discursive practice, to play a similar part ever since, as the site of a contention as to what constitutes an 'essential' Irish identity. Having opted for Arthur Griffith's 'constitutionalist' Free State, he came to despise the parochial, exclusivist Ireland which emerged in the 1920s and 1930s. At the same time, because of his Anglo-Irish Protestant background, he was reviled as little more than a crypto-Brit by the 'Catholic Celtic' Nationalist irreconcilables of de Valera's IRA, and his life was threatened during the Civil War. None of this contradictory history seems to be known to Carmel Jordan, whose *A Terrible Beauty: The Easter Rebellion and Yeats's 'Great Tapestry'*[25] appropriates Yeats to an exclusivist construction of Irishness, a 1990s NORAID version in which he is the unequivocal champion of the kind of fantasy fare on which the heart had grown brutal for over a century. By contrast R. F. Foster's *W. B. Yeats. A Life: The Apprentice Mage, 1865-1914*,[26] coming from a Protestant Anglo-Irish background similar to Yeats's, in demonstrating the precise negotiations and complexities of Yeats's alleged 'Ascendancy' origins, depicts Yeats as a kind of performance artist who was always simply playing at being himself, a prestidigitator and trickster for whom no subject position was final. It would be convenient to argue that Yeats's true position lies somewhere between these two representations. But it would be closer to the truth to say that Yeats's mercurial shape-shiftings resist such easy accommodations. Simultaneously and impossibly both wave and particle, Yeats's texts coast between the Scylla of absolutist allegiance and the whirlpool of a postmodern relativism in which all absolutes drown.

Yeats, Carmel Jordan says, accurately enough, was 'not interested in a fac-tual linear view of Irish history, but in an epiphanic one where the image is predominant' (p.71). For her, however, this makes him an unreconstructed worshipper at the shrine of physical force nationalism, celebrating with her 'The terrible and splendid things ... that have made up the history of Ireland – violence, bloodshed and death, and the splendid poetry and song that has grown out of that blood' (p. 37) – and often more in the blood than the poetry, as in her digression on Bobby Sands, for, 'Although his poems were not great, the passions that lay behind them were, and ... he endorsed his poetry with his blood' (p. 33), which is to endow the manual act of writing with a partic-ularly gory physicality. When it comes to strands of Irish nationalism other than the spilt religiosity of Padraic Pearse, Jordan is at a loss. Michael Davitt goes unacknowledged. Parnell appears once, in a quotation from Pearse. Most significantly, of the three passing references in her study to the socialist James Connolly, two confuse him with the Abbey actor named in 'Three Songs to the One Burden'. In the same vein, Jordan ignores the complexity of Yeats's Anglo-Irish background, and slides over his contempt for Paudeen's Ireland, blaming it all on the British, for 'one must realize that life for the Irish was so barren under British rule' that it led to 'a burning hatred' and a 'notion of beauty inextricably tied up with their concept of nationality' (pp. 54-5), which meant that 'the Rising, in a sense, was their aesthetic masterpiece' (p. 61). In Jordan's 'external', diasporic reading, all Yeats's Irish contraries have merged into a homogeneous Catholic Celtic myth peddled in the souvenir shops. In this dark fabulation, 'Ireland has always been 'a Druid land' (p.55). The perpetually reiterated 'unbroken continuity' (p. 27) of Ireland, the 'unbroken continuity and permanence of the Gaelic tradition' (p. 15), 'the unbroken continuity of the Irish imagination' (p. 38), the 'unbroken continu-ity of the Gaelic tradition' (p. 38), all guarantee that Pearse in 1915 'was not preaching some "new" radical gospel of blood sacrifice' but reiterating 'a belief that pervades Irish history and literature – a belief that is deeply embedded in the racial imagination' (p. 65).

Jordan's Ireland is a land of (plaster) saints, its beautiful lofty things pre-served in the tourist brochures for visiting Americans seeking their roots, like the cute folkloric anecdotes about the 'sod of death' or the Stone of Destiny, deployed to explain the central image of 'Easter 1916'. Her account of the Rising is simple hagiography, expounding the 'sheer poetry' of The O'Rahilly writing his epitaph in his blood, or offering a 'brief description of the heroic struggle of the Irish people during the centuries of English rule' (p. 55). Its heroes always 'eagerly took up [the] call' and 'gave new life to Ireland's ancient symbols and icons by passionately endorsing those symbols with their blood' (p.25). Performativity is all, in a dramaturgy of insurrection which surely would have satisfied Yeats's thirst for a nation as 'some great theatre' where a people might realise itself. Joseph Plunkett's set-piece death-scene is 'a perfect reflection of the Irish poetic tradition he so passionately embraced' (p. 30). Carmel's text, indeed, is full of passionate intensity, comparing Pearse approvingly to the Japanese fascist Mishima in his belief that 'bloodshed is a cleansing and a sanctifying thing, and the nation which regards it as the final horror has lost its manhood' (pp. 67–8). Enthralled by this decadent mélange of Swinburnian and Sacred Heart sadomasochism, Jordan sometimes gets quite carried away – by, for example, 'the highly erotic imagery' of a hero's blooming wounds in one poem (p. 30), the wife who 'voluptuously immerses herself' in her martyred husband's blood in another (p. 40), or the 'highly erotic' picture of Cuchulain's bleeding body, 'his soft skin ... furrowed with sword cuts', in a third (p. 68). It is, however, a startling revelation of what it is like to live these murderous innocences from within, and an indication of just what Yeats had to dissociate his poetry from in espousing the cause of national independence. At the same time, as I shall suggest later, Yeats's poetry shares enough of the assumptions of the tradition of blood sacrifice to make such an appropriation unsettling, destabilising the balance and moderation which generations of interpreters have sought to restore to his contentious and intemperate texts.

By contrast, the Yeats who emerges from Roy Foster's biography *The Apprentice Mage* is a juggler of roles who can never be pinned down in any single subject position, all performance. A maker on the make, it is primarily himself that he is remaking, in a world with no serious allegiances or commitments. Foster demonstrates the links between Yeats's 'continuing reworking of his poems' and 'his own heroic self-construction' as 'an impresario of his own image' (p. xxv), deploying a mage's 'alchemical capacity' (p. xxvi) to transmute the events of a crowded life not only into art but also into a fabricated personal history, 'always with an eye to how people would see things afterwards' (p. xxxi).

Though Foster insists that his biography is about facts (what Yeats did), not interpretation, the book's artistry and artfulness constantly belie the modesty of the claim. If Foster detects both retrospective rewriting and deliberative forward planning in Yeats's self-fashioning, the biographer himself practises the same kind of hindsight as foresight, exemplified at times in the very act of diagnosing it: 'Thus early, he was preternaturally conscious of the need to impose a shape on his life, and able to anticipate the way it would look in retrospect' (p. 45). Yeats inherited his retrospective pattern-making, Foster suggests, from his father John Butler Yeats, the shared middle name itself an instance of the family mythmaking that led Yeats in consecutive versions of a poem unblushingly to revise an ancestor from Jacobite to Williamite loyalist without in any way compromising his claim to being peculiarly Irish. Despite Yeats's disingenuous claim that 'I have never advertised myself in my life' (p. 377), Foster depicts a figure who 'early on showed his gift for enhancing life' (p. 14), even down to 'the question of self presentation in frontispiece portraits' (p. 373). Yeats's remarkable ability to enter collaboratively into the fantasies of others transformed not only his own life but the lives of all those around him, and of Ireland itself, into a phantasmagoria. His 'great talent for managing publicity' (p. 280), Foster says, lay at the epicentre of an 'informal freemasonry' and 'reviewing mafia' (p. 108) constantly engaged in self-promotion, assiduous networking, literary and political hustling, 'high-hatting' (p. 475), and (a recurrent concept) mutual 'log-rolling'. Foster writes with admiring irony, for example, of the 'carefully choreographed' row with M. K. Magee (p. 201) and 'the controversy so successfully orchestrated' (p. 212) over the Abbey Theatre.

For Foster, such 'hard-headed marketing' (p. 69) seems to have been a characteristic of the largely Protestant literary Irish of his day, as indicated by illuminating comparisons with Shaw ('two young *déclassé* Irish Protestant bohemians, on the make in literary London' (p. 64)), with Wilde ('another middle-class Irish Protestant who had remade himself' (p. 81)), and, *inter alios*, with Katherine Tynan's 'country "salon" and the determined self-promotion of her circle' (p. 73). The impulse of a spiritually hyphenated literati to forge a multicultural Irishness, which Foster sees as close to the heart of Yeats's project, is something not far removed, perhaps, from Foster's own agenda. 'The cultural roots of Irishness [...] strike a problematic note' for the Yeats family, as 'from the 1860s on, a sense of cultural and social marginalization and insecurity haunted the Irish Protestant universe' (p. 5). In this version of Yeats, every event and anecdote can become the metonymy of a larger acculturation, in which a 'family history brings together all the emblems signifying the decline of an Ascendancy elite' (p. 9), whether it is Yeats's honeymoon diphtheria, the speculative Oedipal dimension to his slow reading and bad spelling, or his father's response to the Phoenix Park murders: 'Symbolically, during the trial of the Invincibles, he sat in court and made sketches' (p. 31). For Yeats, Maud Gonne, we are told, 'represented tragic passion' (p. 88), and the idea of *representation* is indeed at the heart of Foster's narrative. By the early 1860s, Yeats was already 'representing himself as a mage' (p. 100) and had 'become a news item' (p. 135). His lover Florence Farr, who 'helped define the New Woman', even saw her own love-making as 'a stage performance' (p. 137).

What the biographer's relentless pursuit of this collective fictioneering denies to his subject, however, is any claim ever to be importantly earnest. In 1912 Yeats wrote that 'I am becoming mythical even to myself' (p. 453). For

Foster, he never stops putting on a show, whether in his 'epical construction' (p. 462) of Parnell, or his invention of 'the emblematic meaning of Synge's death' (p. 400). At times, he seems to be doing what he accused the largely Catholic Young Ireland movement of: 'substituting a traditional casuistry for a country' (p. 419). Even the 'discovery of his own voice', assisted though not instigated by Ezra Pound, involved a species of ventriloquism as, at Stone Cottage, dictating letters to Pound, Yeats took on the latter's 'didactic staccato' (p. 505). Similarly, at a séance, he behaved 'like a gross exaggeration of the Idea of a Poet as laid up in heaven', and came to speak in the magisterial tones of his spirit guide Leo Africanus (p. 487).

Yeats's Mittens

Foster at times seems to regard Irish nationalism as simply a rather successful form of political theatre. In his *Memoirs* Yeats confessed that at times he felt as if his political machinations were magicking Fenianism into being: 'I formed a grandiose plan without considering the men I had to work with, exactly as if I were writing something in a story' (pp. 226–7). For Foster, if 'the Irish identity [...] was forged in revolution' (p. xxviii), Yeats was in on the forgery. For all his Burkean organicism that thought the state a tree, nationhood for him, as for Stephen Dedalus, was a fabrication that had to be hammered into an artificial unity from a 'complex tangle of historical allegiances as well as personal relationships' (p. xxviii). If its liberal Irish Protestant *parti pris* ensures that Foster's will not be the definitive biography, its grasp of 'the uneasy collusions of Irish life' and the 'need to keep up ecumenical appearances' (p. 338) in the construction of a nationalist movement is a powerful corrective to the simplistic sectarian versions of Yeats peddled in the thoroughfares.

Yeats wrote in his *Autobiography* that 'the idea of a nation' could be sustained only when there is 'a model of it in the mind of the people'. Though that model might be called, 'in a mood of simple feeling', 'Cathleen ni Houlihan' or the 'Shan van Voght', it is not a straightforward, unitary icon but 'a complex mass of images, something like an architect's model'.[27] As he had observed just before this, 'All civilisation is held together by the suggestions of an invisible hypnotist – by artificially created illusions'.[28] The poet, then, is a kind of Svengali, maintaining the hypnotic trance in which a nation comes to be that which it fantasises, coming to accept as reality, in the words of 'The Municipal Gallery Revisited', 'An Ireland the poets have imagined, terrible and gay'.[29] In 'Magic', in 1901, Yeats wrote of poetry and music having 'arisen … out of the sounds the enchanters made to help their imagination to enchant, to charm, to bind with a spell themselves and the passers-by', creating 'the seeming transitory mind made out of many minds' which could rediscover 'the genius of the family, the genius of the tribe'.[30] The nation that poets imagine is not an hypostatised object, an entity, but a process, an ongoing performance, ultimately, a theatrical self-representation. In the theatre, he wrote in 1899 in 'The Irish Literary Theatre', in a phrase he attributed to Victor Hugo, 'the mob became a people'.[31] Deploying the same phrase in April 1934, in writing of how 'the mob reigned' in contemporary Ireland, preventing it from finding any authentic, unifying symbol of itself, Yeats spoke of a nation as itself 'some great theatre', where a people, simultaneously actors and spectators, could watch 'the sacred drama of its own history'. True self-knowledge for a nation would not be an abstract, formulaic thing, for 'Such knowledge thins the blood. To know it in the concrete we must know it near at hand.'[32] That emphasis on blood knowledge is central.

If, at times, Yeats sees nations as constructs, built from the top down by political and literary elites, who may, like his own fantasised Anglo-Irish, not even belong to the majority tradition they substitute for, at other times he can claim as one of Protestant Ireland's greatest achievements the political theory of Edmund Burke, who 'proved the state a tree' – an organic, natural growth, not an artefact at all. This central aporia in Yeats's thinking about nationality derives from a familiar conflict between Enlightenment and Romanticist models of nation-building. Marjorie Howes' *Yeats's Nations: Gender: Class, and Irishness* reconfigures these contradiction in a series of incisive readings which situate Yeats's thoughts, early and late, about 'race', 'nationality' and 'kindred' within the mutating discourses of 'femininity' and 'sexuality', and the changing significations and locations of women within Irish society in his lifetime. Howes rightly argues that 'the changing ways Yeats imagined Irishness' all have 'specific configurations of gender and class' as their warp and woof, no matter how diverse the plaids they weave. Instead of 'the question of nationalism', which, she says, 'tends to produce reductive analyses... attacking or defending Yeats's politics', she addresses 'the question of nationality', which 'emphasizes the particular structures of his various conceptions of Irishness, their relation to social, political and cultural discourses, and their changes and continuities over time'.[33]

Yeats's early adaptation of the Renan/Arnold concept of a 'feminised' Celticism takes on, in this perspective, a new and unexpectedly radical complexion. *The Countess Cathleen*, obfuscating the actual relations of Irish landlord and tenant beneath the evasive iconography of female martyrdom, is seen by Howes as an attempt to forge a sympathetic bonding of peasantry and Ascendancy against an emerging Catholic middle class which frequently attracted Yeats's contempt in sexualised terms (the 'eunuchs' who jeered Synge off the Dublin stage, outraged by mention of a woman's shift). All that 'theatre business', where Yeats believed that a 'mob' might be transformed into a 'people', finding 'one mind for an hour or so',[34] likewise shares in the dubious erotics of representation, linking the occult preoccupations of the *Anima Mundi* with issues that Howe locates in the bedroom of the Big House.

There, she demonstrates, sexuality miscegenated with a specifically Anglo-Irish idea of 'kindred' to take on dynastic obligations, pointing towards Yeats's later preoccupation with eugenics and the 'rule of kindred', and the 'race philosophy' adumbrated in such late works as *Purgatory*.

A passing remark of Yeats's in *Letters to the New Island* sets up, however, an altogether odder problematic of nationality. Yeats observed there, as early as September 1888, that

> To the greater poets everything they see has its relation to the national life... But to this universalism, this seeing of unity everywhere, you can only attain through what is near you, your nation, or... your village... One can only reach out into the universe with a gloved hand – that glove is one's nation, the only thing one knows even a little of.[35]

Never one for consistency, Yeats wrote elsewhere, in 'A Coat', that 'there's more enterprise / In walking naked',[36] and he can sometimes be seen, in his later years, unpicking the stitching of the national garment, with the impatience of one who has lost the thread. The metonymy of the glove, in its peculiarity, is itself distinctly postmodern. On the one hand (so to speak), one's nation is clearly superficial, no more than a thin layer of fabric interposed between a pre-existent self and the pre-existent universe, an emptiness waiting to be filled by a warm and capable, living hand. On the other – left-handedly – it is 'the only thing one knows even a little of', the truly pre-existent mediator between two blank potentialities.

But gloves actually blunt the sensitivity and efficiency of the hands they keep from existential frostbite. What would happen if Yeats's nations lost their mittens? Yeats himself gave something of a clue in his broadcast on 'Modern Poetry' in 1936, speaking of that terror in which all profound philosophy is founded: 'An abyss opens under our feet; inherited convictions, the pre-suppositions of our thoughts ... drop into the abyss. Whether we will or no we must ask the ancient questions: Is there reality anywhere?'[37] In the sonnet 'Meru',[38] Yeats revels in this invigorating vertigo. Civilisation, the poem concedes, may be 'hooped together, brought / Under a rule' by 'manifold illusion', but this is the mere 'semblance of peace'. Despite its terror, human thought cannot desist from 'ravening' down the centuries, like those barbarians who overthrow the longest-lived empires, 'raging and uprooting' illusion, until it enters again into 'the desolation of reality'. It is with the ancient questions spoken of in 'Modern Poetry' that a 'postmodern' enquiry into Yeats's sense of Irishness must start, acknowledging the 'manifold illusion' of a constructed and capricious nationality, for which so many in this last century have died, but which may be gone before the dawn comes round.

Set-ups and put-downs

Addressing central questions of national identity and identification, Yeats's poem 'Blood and the Moon' (1928)[39] deploys the image of the moon as part of a potent trinity of traditional tropes, together with his Norman tower at Thoor Ballylee and the 'odour of blood' linked to it in the title. Yeats's metonymies are ferociously totalising, sweeping all before them in the insistence on their emblematic, synecdochic character. Yeats allows no equivocation: this is a 'powerful emblem' which he has masterfully 'set up'. But the astonishing confidence of this entirely subjective construction – he is making it up – is qualified by the admission that it is 'in mockery', a defiance of traditional constructions which is ferociously antagonistic and antithetical. The mockery is that of the Swift invoked later whose Anglo-Irish contradictions found utterance as '*Saeva Indignatio*'. There is no delicate stalking of significance here, but a thunderous, overweaning voice, which asserts itself and its emblems precisely by denunciation. The tower itself, with a ruined roof, duplicates the poet's sense of his own, Ireland's, and the age's defective character:

> In mockery I have set
> A powerful emblem up,
> And sing it rhyme upon rhyme
> In mockery of a time
> Half dead at the top.

The self-regarding analogy is with Amphion, the music of whose lyre raised the walls of Thebes without the need for physical labour as, Yeats would like to have believed, his writing helped forge the Irish nation state from inchoate raw materials. This is the obverse of that self-important questioning in 'The Man and the Echo' about responsibility for the violence of the independence struggle and the civil war that followed it. Thebes, of course, was a city notoriously torn by fratricidal civil war, something which adds resonance to Yeats's use of the figure of Oedipus in the later poems. Here, tower, self and nation are all alike constructed not only in material stone but in ideology, the 'bloody, arrogant power' of the race 'Uttering, mastering it' creating a 'powerful emblem' which magically holds together edifice and state. That the tower is 'Half dead at the top' converts it into a metonymy which expresses, on the one hand, the condition of the subject, Yeats himself, and, on the other, of the state to which he is subject. Yeats is visualising here the traditional cartographic image of Ireland as the Poor Old Woman whose head is the six-county Ulster statelet, with Lough Neagh as the eye: hence 'Half dead at the top' because, as yet, incompletely rebuilt.

Nationhood is not an act of natural construction. It is essentially a work of artifice, for the nation has to be ideologically 'uttered' to be validated. Yeats imagined that his own 'Easter 1916' was the originary 'uttering', the bloody christening anthem of the Irish state. The poem is indeed still widely sold in reverential mock-scroll form in tourist shops throughout present-day Ireland, alongside the rebels' declaration of statehood. He consolidates his bid for a totalising iconography in language of a decidedly statist nature. This uttering is at one and the same time a declaration of independence and oath of allegiance: 'I declare this tower is my symbol; I declare / This winding, gyring, spiring treadmill of a stair is my ancestral stair.'

But it is also an act of appropriation, claiming to self, tower and state a retrospective metonymic lineage of great Anglo-Irish figures all of whom would have been astonished to find themselves in such company: Goldsmith, Swift, Berkeley and Burke, the latter indeed a sworn opponent of the idea of Irish independence. But it is Burke, who 'proved the State a tree', who is here explicitly invoked as the founding, ratifying father of Yeats's idea of Irish nationhood, rejecting the 'mathematical equality' of British democracy for the 'unconquerable labyrinth' of an oligarchic Ireland. Further ratification for Yeats's act of ideological invention is provided by Berkeleyan idealism. By divine appointment, Berkeley 'proved all things a dream' (all the better to raise city walls with music, then) – even 'this pragmatical, preposterous pig of a world, its farrow that so solid seem'. But if such a farrow will 'vanish on an instant if the mind but change its theme', this is not the effortless act by which Amphion sang Thebes into existence. Traditionally the old sow that devours her farrow, Ireland can find authentic nationhood only in the kind of ethnic cleansing that cleared out most of Yeats's own Anglo-Irish Ascendancy compeers from the ancestral sty.

To cope with this bitter and anfractuous reality, Yeats deploys another metonymic sleight of hand, invoking Swift's 'Saeva Indignatio' to provide 'The strength that gives our blood and state magnanimity of its own desire'. With remarkable cool, he inserts a surreptitious first person plural into a poem which has, till this point, been composed of a dissociated 'I' and a series of abstract third persons. He does not, however, start with a 'we', which would be to presume upon a collective subjectivity yet to be constituted. Rather he prepares the way by using the possessive adjective 'our' to qualify a supposedly objective 'blood and state' (Yeats's title has here mutated into a recollection of Shirley's 'The glories of our blood and state'[40]). This then takes on impersonal subjectivity in the 'magnanimity of its own desire'. Such savage indignation consumes all that it does not embrace with 'intellectual fire'. Out of that burning a collective 'we' may then be plucked. In the past seven centuries of this tower, Yeats proposes, generations of soldiers, assassins, executioners have shed blood out of 'abstract hatred' or 'blind fear'. But what is original, and originary, now, is the significance of this new blood-letting. It is a meaningful, a totalising act, not simply one of a potentially endless series of meaningless atrocities. There is 'Odour of blood on the ancestral stair'; and only after that claim to an 'ancestral' lineage has been staked can Yeats speak of a 'we, that have shed none', who now '*must* gather there' (my emphasis), compelled by national fervour to that same blood sacrifice out of which all nations are constituted, to 'clamour in frenzy for the moon'.

The splendour of Yeats's emblems enables him to slide over the actual violence and uncertainty of this national setting forth. The totalising metonymic compulsion, first uttered in the aggrandising emblems of tower, moon and blood (violence, but also lineage), is finally embodied in a sequence of free-floating pronouns, forging a 'we' out of disparate 'I's, 'he's and 'they's, to such an extent that the poem's final question, a pertinent enquiry as to whether nation-building is worth the candle, seems merely rhetorical, easily dispersed by a return to the grand emblems of tradition:

> Is every modern nation like the tower,
> Half dead at the top? No matter what I said,
> For wisdom is the property of the dead,
> A something incompatible with life; and power,
> Like everything that has the stain of blood,
> A property of the living; but no stain
> Can come upon the visage of the moon
> When it has looked in glory from a cloud.

The image of a moon bursting in glory from the clouds is straight from that Shelley invoked early in the poem. But it does not resolve the anguishing about the price paid for nationhood of the previous section (which included the extirpation of Yeats's own Anglo-Irish Protestant minority). The 'stain of blood' here begins to recognise that blood has been shed in the process, but, in a kind of conceptual anacoluthon, the image displaces itself to become instead the figure of lineage, affiliation, ancestry, the 'blood relation' that binds a people together by the 'rule of kindred'. What the poem envisages in its subliming of innumerable 'I's into a collective 'we' is that goal prescribed in the *Autobiography*,[41] to create 'an Irish literature which, though made by many minds, would seem the work of a single mind'. 'Blood and state', it would appear, are the same thing, and they find the completion of their trinity in power. Power, Yeats insists, is a property of the living. The living alone possess, and can shed, blood. But if 'property' can mean a quality or attribute, it also alludes to real estate. For Yeats, always, 'state' and 'estate' are closely linked, as in the poem 'Ancestral Houses' in 'Meditations in Time of Civil War'. It is in the exercise of power by 'some powerful man', by architects and artists serving him who are themselves 'Bitter and violent men', that poem proclaimed, as the Civil War drew to an inglorious close, that a nation discovers its authentic images of 'The sweetness that all longed for night and day, / The gentleness none there had ever known'.[42] If a state is a people linked by blood,

blood shed as well as blood inherited, it is also a tract of land, and a tract of words, owned by someone.

Yeats spoke in 'In Memory of Major Robert Gregory' of how John Synge 'dying chose the living world for text'.[43] Close to death himself in 'The Municipal Gallery Revisited' in 1937, revisiting the 'images of thirty years' preserved in the gallery, Yeats found himself compelled to admit that the pictures record not 'The dead Ireland of my youth, but an Ireland /The poets have imagined, terrible and gay'. Artist and poet as historians have been converted into magicians in this display of masterful images. The poem remains ambiguous as to whether it sees this, finally, as imposture or essential truth, a falsification of the real history of its times, or, on the contrary, a redemptive transfiguration of the 'living world' into an 'imagined' text, 'that tale, / As though some ballad-singer had sung it all'. The refractory, contentious historical personages Yeats knew are now written up, written into a shared textuality, becoming images in 'the common tongue', in that 'book of the people' spoken of in 'Coole Park and Ballylee, 1931',[44] where all conflicts and divisions are resolved into a unitary national myth. It may be that future generations can trace 'Ireland's history in [the] lineaments' portrayed in the Municipal Gallery. But the arbitrary bricolage of the art collection, its images juxtaposed without reconciliation, is the *only* place where all are reconciled. So, too, the Swiftian battle of the books may be silenced on the library shelves. In the real world, however, its thunder continues to deafen. It is easier to make up a story than to make up a quarrel. The dual meaning of 'making it up' catches a central dilemma for the historian, as for the magician story-teller, for to make up stories may be to exacerbate rather than abate that quarrel. The Thebes whose walls Amphion sang effortlessly into being famously suffered civil war over several generations, because of a primal curse of internecine division sown with the dragon's teeth. In the myth of Thebes' origins, the outsider Cadmus (who brought the alphabet and therefore writing with him) founded Thebes by fomenting strife among the indigenous children of the dragon, then allying himself with the survivors of the struggle – a powerful if possibly unintended analogy for Ascendancy hegemony in pre-independence Ireland. Yeats's national metonymies all strive towards the condition of music, synthesising conflict, orchestrating discord, creating a unitary, all-encompassing emblem out of disparate materials. But the national self-image then constructed, so different from the squalid conflicts and accommodations of the post-independence decades, as this subtext suggests, comes at a price.

NOTES

1. Jonathan Swift, *A Tale of A Tub* (1704); this edn, introd. Lewis Melville (London: J. M. Dent, 1909), pp.33–4. Hereafter page references are indicated in the text.
2. Seamus Heaney, *The Haw Lantern* (London: Faber and Faber, 1987).

3. See below, Chapter 12.
4. Seamus Heaney, 'A Tale of Two Islands: Reflections on the Irish Literary Revival', in P. J. Drudy (ed.) *Irish Studies I* (Cambridge: Cambridge University Press, 1980), pp. 1–20.
5. Seamus Heaney, *Among Schoolchildren* (Belfast: John Malone Memorial Committee, 1983).
6. Seamus Heaney, 'Interview' with Rand Brandes, *Salmagundi* (Fall, 1988), pp. 4–21.
7. David Lodge, *Small World* (London: Penguin Books, 1985), p. 251.
8. Walter Benjamin, 'Theses on the Philosophy of History', in Hannah Arendt (ed.) *Illuminations* (London: Fontana, 1973), p.265.
9. Richard Ellmann, *Eminent Domain* (New York: Oxford University Press, 1967), p.55.
10. W. B. Yeats, *The Winding Stair* (New York: Macmillan, 1929).
11. W. B. Yeats, *The Tower* (London: Macmillan, 1928).
12. W. B. Yeats, *Michael Robartes and the Dancer* (Dundrum: Cuala Press, 1921).
13. Yeats, *The Tower*.
14. Ibid.
15. Tzvetan Todorov, *The Fantastic: A Structural Approach to a Literary Genre*, trans. Richard Howard (Ithaca, N.Y.: Cornell University Press, 1975), pp. 59–60.
16. First published in *The New Statesman* on 23 October 1920; on which see Tom Paulin, 'Yeats's Hunger-Strike Poem', in *Minotaur: Poetry and the Nation State* (London: Faber and Faber, 1992), pp. 133–50. The poem was first collected in Yeats, *Michael Robartes and the Dancer*.
17. Todorov, *The Fantastic*, p. 33.
18. W. B. Yeats, *Last Poems and Two Plays* (Dublin: Cuala Press, 1939)
19. Yeats, *Michael Robartes and the Dancer*.
20. Yeats, *Last Poems and Two Plays*.
21. Ibid.
22. Ibid.
23. W. B. Yeats, *A Vision* (this edn., London: Macmillan, 1978), p. 300.
24. Ibid., p. 301.
25. Carmel Jordan, *A Terrible Beauty: The Easter Rebellion and Yeats's 'Great Tapestry'* (Lewisburg, PA: Bucknell University Press, 1987). Hereafter page references indicated in the text.
26. R. F. Foster, *W. B. Yeats. A Life: The Apprentice Mage, 1865-1914* (Oxford: Oxford University Press, 1997). Hereafter page references are indicated in the text.
27. W. B. Yeats, *The Autobiography of William Butler Yeats* (New York: Macmillan, 1965), pp.334–5.
28. Ibid., p 326.
29. W. B. Yeats, *New Poems* ((Dublin: Cuala Press, 1938).
30. W. B. Yeats, *Essays and Introductions* (London: Macmillan, 1961), pp. 43–4.
31. W. B. Yeats, *Uncollected Prose*, vol. II, ed. John P. Frayne and Colton Johnson (London: Macmillan, 1945), p. 141.
32. On this, see Stan Smith, *W. B. Yeats: A Critical Introduction* (London: Macmillan, 1990), pp. 48–9.
33. Marjorie Howes, *Yeats's Nations: Gender, Class, and Irishness* (Cambridge: Cambridge University Press, 1996), p.1.
34. W. B. Yeats, *Memoirs*, transcribed and ed. Denis Donoghue (London: Macmillan, 1972), p. 215.
35. W. B. Yeats, *Letters to the New Island*, ed. Horace Reynolds (London: Oxford University Press, 1934), p. 174.
36. W. B. Yeats, *Responsibilities: Poems and a Play* (Dundrum: Cuala Press, 1914).
37. Yeats, *Essays and Introductions*, p. 502.
38. W. B. Yeats, *A Full Moon in March* (London: Macmillan, 1935).
39. Yeats, *The Winding Stair*.
40. James Shirley, 'The glories of our blood and state', song from *The Contention of Ajax and Ulysses* (1659).
41. Yeats, *The Autobiography of William Butler Yeats*, p. 170.
42. Yeats, *The Tower*.
43. W. B. Yeats, *The Wild Swans at Coole* (London: Macmillan, 1919).
44. W. B. Yeats, *Words for Music Perhaps and Other Poems* (Dublin: Cuala Press, 1932).

III

Living to Tell the Tale:
Fallon, Clarke,
MacGreevy, Coffey

Doing Time: Padraic Fallon

The compounding and interpenetration of story and history is persistent in the literature of the first generation of Irish modernists. The deliberately contrived naivety of Padraic Fallon's poems, for example, allows for a constant elision between the two forms of narrative.[1] Behind many of them stands the figure of Odysseus, but an epic hero now in retirement, returned home to drowse out his last days on the periphery of things. Thus, in 'Painting of My Father', that 'yarning, true Ulyssean' is now, in old age, confined within the 'Eternal precincts / Of a huge present tense'. The old men, one-time sailors, of 'On the Jetty', are 'unhinged now from giant epics': 'What they made was rich / But has no history // And leaves nothing.' Fallon creates the myth of a world that lies apparently outside history, but he allows us to read, between the lines of his 'huge present tense', the tense historicity of the apparently timeless.

Nowhere is this more apparent than in those remarkable arguments with the rhetoric of Yeats. 'Yeats at Athenry Perhaps' starts from the likelihood that the great man must have changed trains at Fallon's home village of Athenry, since Ballylee is a mere fifteen miles away as the crow flies. In defiance of the Yeatsian grand manner, with its glamorising of peasant and what 'Letter from Ballylee' refers to sarcastically as 'some hard-riding nameless / Country gentleman', Fallon in 'Yeats at Athenry Perhaps' casts this parochial Ireland as 'a sightseeing place that had / Exhausted history'. 'I doubt', he says of Yeats, that 'He bothered with us, all his sight turned in'. Yet the text of the 'nunlike night... commit[ted]... in strokes / Of barbarous shorthand' was nevertheless something the two men shared, 'The same nightscript' that 'We could have read together'. It is a significant application of the writing/reading trope, picking up the play between poetic and physical feet in an earlier stanza, which contrasts 'That winged footprint' of Yeats's verse with 'The peasant metres of a street given over / To baker, grocer, butcher and / The treadmill of the till'. The image is developed in the closing stanza, with its picture of Yeats on the station platform writing a poem, not wanting to 'muddy a feathered foot', sitting 'by the line' (the word flickering in and out from railway to verse line), waiting for the train to take him to that 'great house… / Over in Coole' where aristocratic lines (lineages / stories) are spun – and baited, the throw-away parenthesis suggests, like ideological fishing lines to catch their man: '(He liked his heraldry alive, well baited)'.

Beneath the apparent simplicity of the expression here Fallon's Ireland enters into a complex ironic dialogue with the 'terrible and gay' Ireland imagined by this other, greater poet. In his own Raftery sequence, and in that other meditation on the Yeatsian sublime, 'Yeats's Tower at Ballylee', Fallon adopts a similar sceptical distance. The latter poem takes as epigraph Yeats's question in 'Blood and the Moon', 'Is every modern nation like the Tower / Half-dead at the top?' only to answer that 'this is a dream-structure', 'A boy's dream and the background of his rhyme', its fantasised Norman soldiery 'a score of bullies in black armour / Deflected and turned to phantasy / By the boy who brooded on book and paint / Long mornings in his father's study…'. For Fallon, the Tower is not a symbol of 'every modern nation' but an empty signifier, 'Useless as verse and as magnificent', and Yeats's 'bloody vision' is something that, in a pointedly political metaphor, 'usurped his eyes'. Yeats's vision, that is, is not his own at all. Rather, as Heaney might argue, it is *pre-occupied* by an ideological power which pre-empts and stains with blood every act of perception and intellection. Outside, meanwhile, 'Everywhere is the world' where, as Fallon says in 'Maris Stella', a different, impersonal looking presides, which casts a cold eye on all such ideological systems, and 'men with meanings / Inside … endure the wide stare of things'.

In 'Curragh, November Meeting', distance and time are both 'threaded over' with a spider's web of legend (the image itself recalls the Sleeping Beauty). Time condenses into a moment without any beyond, where all is compacted, unmoving, reduced to a tale spun about once-bright horses now bleached, of 'Jackets / And jockeys run / Out of pigment', event transformed into its figuration, reduced to the archaic residues of 'A caveman's scratches, a jostling script'. It may be that 'There's some time left / To use your magic on it, wish / The winner home', but the world depicted here is all retrospect, superseded, as the single-word sentence in the penultimate stanza puts it, active verb reduced to past participle, 'Gone'.

'It means nothing, nor should', the poem concludes. The Irishness fantasised by 'Suburban fathers' (parents or patriarchs) was always merely 'a mock-up', at most 'a slight / Affair with a trumpet blast', the starting trumpet transforming all to theatricality. Precisely this movement beyond the realm of signification (and therefore of sequence, causality, transit) takes up Fallon's world into the magician's realm of the spun tale, event turned into jostling script. But, like Yeats, Fallon acknowledges the prestidigitation involved in this 'magic'. The title of

'Fin de Siècle' ironically recalls a literary movement and moment which, defined in its historical transitoriness by the very phrase used to characterise it, believed it had nevertheless discovered a timeless aesthetics. The tradition of narrative which compresses time into co-presence, making the 'He' of the poem contemporary with Homer (as in Eliot's famous axiom), is nevertheless a particular way of living history, not an escape from it – an outdated attitudinising which has its own ideological function. The true storyteller has to elude history's murderous noise in order to tell his stories:

> Out on the periphery he put in the time;
> Achilles dead, and Hector, Ulysses flown....
> Who makes the rhyme
> Will have the resonance. Carefully
> He lived to tell the tale;
> Homer is he who survives the crumbling wall.

Batons and Blessings: Austin Clarke

Living to tell the tale amidst the contending interpretations led the post-Yeats generations to adopt a range of survival strategies, some of which drew, atavistically, on existing alternative traditions, others of which suggested a way beyond impasse in what was to be seen, retrospectively, as a postmodern relativising of cultures. The first generation of Modernist Irish poets sought a different ratio of parochial to universal from that espoused by Fallon, putting in the time on the periphery with varying success. Austin Clarke, for example, remaining stubbornly on home ground in Dublin, nevertheless sought to reconfigure traditional strategies, of religious and political allegiance, a polemic national historiography, at the interface of a class politics and the rhetorical opportunities afforded by an international modernist poetics.

'All poetry, as discriminated from the various paradigms of prosody, is prayer', Beckett wrote in a review of Thomas MacGreevy in 1934, adding that prayer is 'the only way out of the tongue-tied profanity'.[2] In the poetry of Austin Clarke, the interdependence of language and history is most originally and clearly grasped, through the metaphor not only of prayer but of all the other modes of language we create and endure.[3] 'Pilgrimage', the title poem of his 1929 volume, *Pilgrimage and Other Poems*, adds a new dimension to that opposition of speech and script.

'Pilgrimage' opens with a perception of a historic landscape which slips quietly, through metaphor, into language. This is a subtle reworking of the old concept of the Book of Nature, and fitting for the ancient Irish world it envisages. It suggests that there is no such thing as a 'clean' perception of things, that all our awareness is pre-structured by the history that has deposited us here, in this particular and evanescent moment. The beaching of the pilgrim's boat is a metaphor of an entry into history, as 'tying a wish on thorn' turns language into fact, tying the self down to an imagined future. In the same movement, we enter into closure, amidst rainfall 'as quiet as the turning of books / In the holy schools at dawn.'

The cloistered scholars of the second stanza, 'Whose knowledge of the gospel / Is cast as metal in pure voices', are agencies through which the provisional realm of speech becomes solidly material, not just as script but as the densely physical gilt illumination of a manuscript. The third stanza again sees intangible speech already structured into ritual ('The chanting of the hours, / White clergy saying High Mass, / A fasting crowd at prayer, / A choir that sang before them'). Beyond this lies the materialization of story into solid, abiding forms, which make even the mythical actual, as stained glass and carved dragons. At this point the solidifying of language into matter becomes explicit; the 'Great annals in the shrine' are not evanescent words, but 'embodied' script, which trace 'The noble forms of language– / Brighter than green or blue enamels / Burned in white bronze'.

Speech then becomes a desperate insurrection out of the enclosed world created from these fossilized embodiments, 'a sound / Of wild confession' rising from praying congregations. Prayer, in the last stanza, is equated with sailing away from material encumbrance, but not with *flight*. It involves a passage through the world, not a rising above it, hearing 'white Culdees pray / Until our hollow ship was kneeling / Over the long waves'. Language recruits the subject to an engrossing material history, not to something impalpable, but to a process as tangible as embossing, woven handicraft, lines on a page, or, when speech, to a material vibration in real air. But language is also pilgrimage, an active movement beyond the constricting givenness of things, the creation of new vibrations which leave the ship itself praying as it journeys: *laborare est orare*. Action itself becomes a form of discourse.

A repeated theme of Clarke's poetry is that the opposition between words and deeds, story and history, is not a valid one, but a stratagem of despair. Speech, print, script, are not only ways of distorting the world in our perception, but also ways of disturbing it, getting a purchase on it, as W. H. Auden wrote in his elegy for Yeats, 'A way of happening, a mouth'. There is always 'something to be done', and that doing cannot be simply separated from Beckett's questions, 'What have I said?' and 'what shall I say?', the interpretations we make of things. We are both historians and magicians, audiences and actors, collaborators in the storied histories we produce and reproduce.

'Inscription for a Headstone', from *Ancient Lights* (1955), seems initially to equate script with elegy and obituary, with the last word on a lost world of action and agitation. But it ends on a new point, that language is a form and means of action. It also seeks to displace questions of Irish identity from the level of nation to that of class, endorsing a politics that gives priority to social rather than national antagonisms. The political speeches and writings of socialist agitators such as James Larkin, it suggests – raucous, rabble-rousing – may appear to have been absorbed by time into the complacent murmur of dining-hall and study. But, as the final internal rhyme of 'page' with 'rage' suggests, inscription is not necessarily interment. The words 'Larkin bawled to hungry crowds' in the poem's first line can be translated into the enduring name 'Scrawled in a rage by Dublin's poor' on 'our holiest page' in the last. The poem itself, apparently a memorial recording a dead life, can be transformed from epitaph to incitement. Language is never finally dead, whether spoken or written. It is never just history, story, record, but also polemic, invective, critique, open, pointed at the future, struggling to grasp the present, in a world where speech turns into deeds and batons into 'blessings in disguise'.

From a Great Distance: Thomas MacGreevy

Austin Clarke hailed the appearance of Thomas MacGreevy's *Poems*[4] in 1934 as proof that 'the modernist revolt has at least reached the Irish Free State'.[5] MacGreevy had seen the workings of a capitalised 'History' at first hand in the Royal Field Artillery in the closing days of the First World War. For MacGreevy, it was the aesthetic which introduced distance, and thus a kind of liberation from an oppressive history, into experience. Writing to him in 1948, the American modernist Wallace Stevens foregrounded MacGreevy's manipulation of aesthetic distance by picking out three lines from 'Homage to Hieronymus Bosch' as an instance of his particular talent:

> High above the Bank of Ireland
> Unearthly music sounded,
> Passing westwards.

I thought about these lines of yours. Arranged as they are with the reality in the first line one's attention is focussed on the reality. Had the order been reversed and had the lines read,

> Unearthly music sounded,
> Passing westwards
> High above the Bank of Ireland

the attention would have been focussed on what was unreal. You pass in and out of things in your poems just as quickly as the meaning changes in the illustration that I have just used. These poems are memorabilia of someone I might have known and they create for me something of his world and of himself.[6]

It is the tribute of a major poet who is also an insurance broker to a minor poet with one slim volume who is an art critic shortly to become Director of the National Gallery in Dublin. Both men are aware of the co-presence of apparently opposed allegiances in a world where 'art' seems an 'unearthly music' in comparison with the banal demands of an administrative and bureaucratic 'reality'. Both alike know the need of the one for the other, and of their actual interdependence. But each poet also knows that these competing powers can only be reconciled by accommodation and evasion, that each in turn provides a critical and ironic dimension within which to see the other. MacGreevy's 'passing in and out of things', not just in the succession of his images or statements but within the supposedly unified syntax of a single sentence (so that in Stevens's example the real provides the context of the 'unearthly', but the 'unearthly' also reflects back upon and re-examines the 'real') is a technique which repeatedly provides the ironic frame of reference within which each item of experience is assessed. No moment is absolute, for MacGreevy: each in turn frames that which precedes and succeeds it. 'Experience' is a schema of receding frames, of successive bracketings in which no perspective is final, and in which the silence which surrounds the poem is the only (and then provisional) limit placed on the reverberations it creates.

'De Civitate Hominum', takes as its theme an insignificant episode of personal reminiscence from the Great War, and then exploits the contradiction between the triviality, the uneventfulness, of the memoir, and the actual enormity it encloses. There is a strange, dispassionate distance to the poem, which transforms the raw and absent violence it records with an antiseptic aestheticism that evacuates the human from its field of action. The opening setting depopulates the landscape, turning it into a painted scene, simply a 'Matisse ensemble'. To be visible in this landscape scarred by shell-holes a man has to be dead, or to risk death. In a washed-out world of whitened tree stumps, white bones and an ice-grey lake gleaming 'Like the silver shoes of the model', the unexpected personification reinforces the shell-shocked indifference of the speaker. Human reaction is itself framed, made redundant, by a movement which situates the subject as a function of the landscape and a function of history. The stillness of the model conceals her viciousness, of which the apparent master, the spectator artist, is really the victim and hopeless suitor. The chiaroscuro colouring is that of a memento mori. Death frames life as, in history, wars frame peaces and *vice versa*, and 'The model is our world, / Our bitch of a world'. The subject, in his shrivelled centre, persists, numbed, ostensibly superfluous; but this very superfluity then becomes an aid in setting up a picturesque canvas in which he becomes, in a play of bathos and pathos, simultaneously 'the famous brass monkey' and 'The *nature morte* accessory'.

It is 'still' not 'quick' life that lives, here, the poem adds, playing on the contrasting English and French terms, 'still life', '*nature morte*', to reinforce the irony of a scene in which to keep still is to survive, and motion betrays one to enemy fire. This leads on to a numb transcript of a death so remote from the recording subject that it can be seen in purely aesthetic terms, as a spectacle, an event in nature, without human consequence. 'Quick' draws the eye to the drone of an aircraft overhead, high over Gheluvelt, and those 'fleece white flowers of death / That unfold themselves prettily' around the plane. If the airman – whether he is friend or foe is irrelevant at this remove – is 'taking a morning look round', so too is the observer on the ground, from a vantage point equally distanced but, momentarily, safer, able to remark the silk and silver of the clouds and the blue of the sky. Casting a cold eye on this attenuated scene, the observer sees the moment of death simply as abstract spectacle, a matter of colour and line, where the invisible airman, developing the simile of the model with silver shoes, accepts the flowers of flak as an actress might receive a bouquet:

> I cannot tell which flower he has accepted
> But suddenly there is a tremor,
> A zigzag of lines against the blue
> And he streams down
> Into the white,
> A delicate flame,
>
> A stroke of orange in the morning's dress.

MacGreevy's insistent, painterly imagination (reinforced by the echo of Keats's Nightingale Ode, 'I cannot see what flowers are at my feet') shocks by converting the theatre of war into a theatrical performance. It is, after all, a real death he is describing, but the aestheticising remoteness of it all brings home just how depersonalised and depersonalising is the nature of modern warfare. The speaker of these poems inhabits a world of faltering energies, dwindling into stasis, finding 'freezing comfort' ('Fragments') in the Dantean thought that pity has to be dead for piety to live in Hell. The self is played-out, finished; it looks at its world as if from a great distance, even when contemplating, in 'The Six Who Were Hanged', the execution of Republican insurrectionists by the British authorities, at Mountjoy prison, in March, 1921. For all MacGreevy's Nationalist sympathies, this self is 'Tired of sorrow', 'Scarcely moved by the thought of the men to be hanged'. He can 'go from the epilogue' without apparent remorse, an evacuated subject in a world which has become all epilogue, refusing the role of Saint John, that chronicler of revelation and apocalypse who had the last word, in the final book of the Bible, about last things. But the poem's real testament to the nature of the crime of civil war is that very exhausted indifference, a kind of spiritual shell-shock.

'Seventh Gift of the Holy Ghost' salvages this mood from nihilism, by making it the final benefaction of grace. The desolation of reality rescues the self from caring, thereby (like the Aristotelian definition of art) teaching it humility in the purgation of pity and terror, 'The pity we had to learn' and 'The ultimate terror' to be imagined on a light-beaten plain. The individual subject is diminished by a vast, impersonal landscape which is itself beaten down as well as upon by the light. Grace here is the grasping of emptiness, of the vanity of things (Beckett significantly singled out this poem in his review), an apocalyptic vision revealed by the punning play, in reflecting on 'the end of love' as both goal and termination. Taking a cue from the title of one of the poems, Beckett wrote of this as 'the energy and integrity of "Giorgionismo", Self-absorption into light', 'uttering itself in the prayer that is a spasm of awareness'.

MacGreevy's poetry repeatedly presents landscapes stripped of emotion. 'Nocturne of the Self-Evident Presence' depicts a diminished self intimidated by a cosmos that towers over it in ascensions like the receding heights of Dante's Paradiso. The poem evokes the celestial perspectives constructed by the stagy foreshortenings of a Reubens or Domenichino only to supply the imagery of a lack. The pretensions of art, literature and religion, whether pagan or Judaeo-Christian, are mocked by an archly obsolete language which invokes Elijah's or Apollo's 'cars', and angels 'Plashing the silvery air', only to register their absence. There are no 'immaculate feet on those pavements, / No winged forms', as the poem puts it, with deliberate pedestrian bathos, 'Dashing about / Up there'. The poem's 'metaphysical bereavements' acknowledge instead that privation into which the soul must enter to grasp the fullness of God. Its chilly desiccation frames the self-consciously 'cultured', literary allusions with what another poem calls 'the without of glory'. The inhuman heavens of this poem testify only to the unresponding rigour of absconded deity: 'I see alps, ice, stars and white starlight / In a dry, high silence.'

Recession recurs in many of the poems: in 'Giorgionismo' as a retreat from the equal unreality of a film and its audience ('recessionalist lovers'), in 'Recessional' from 'the bright broad Swiss glare' to a wished-for burial in the remote west of Ireland, and 'tender, less glaring, island days'. This is the mood which Stevens's letter spoke of as a 'nostalgie du divin', but which, in 'Homage to Jack Yeats', MacGreevy was astute enough to recognise as a 'consecrated / Lie', tormenting the 'tired, tiresome body' with delusory 'proud stupidity'. A similar double vision pervades that largely unsuccessful attempt to write an Irish *Waste Land*, 'Crón Tráth Na nDéithe' (MacGreevy's own note tells us 'The title is an Irish equivalent for the German word *Götterdämmerung*'), which contrasts 'The brightness of brightness / Towering in the sky / Over Dublin' with 'The dark sloblands below in their glory / Wet glory'. The poem offers the 'dangerous occasions of beauty' of the Civil War as delusions of a 'reality [which] is but the lifted hand / Of oppression'. The promise of 'political absolution' is a fraud, 'an extra-real brightness', framed by the destroyed or damaged statuary, fountains and buildings of the eighteenth-century Dublin submitted to internecine modern violence. Again and again, the human subject is defined by the objects around him, in 'Anglo-Irish', for example, in the mode of Eliot's early poems of social observation, 'registering, unconscious / A London hat / And the gramophone starting / *Bach's Magnificat*', his 'gasping cry . . . lost' as 'The self-satisfied Lutheran music circled on'; or in the sharply-observed social satire of 'The Other Dublin' (which recalls Pound's *Hugh Selwyn Mauberley*) flickeringly aware of the discrepancy between the bric-à-brac of bourgeois normality and an unspecified, suggestive menace, represented by the gentleman 'resembling Conrad Veidt in *Caligari*', who solicitously hands around cups of tea.

Things are never as they seem in MacGreevy's poetry. The text of reality is always inscribed with its subtext, redefined by its context. Thus, in 'Breton Oracles' (a sequence recalled in Derek Mahon's 'Breton Walks'), the sea-beaten coast seems an inevitable metaphor of the beginnings and ends of things, bringing 'thoughts of cataclysm / At the world's first morning':

> A young world that was still to know;
> Then fears of other cataclysm
> And the world's last twilight –
> An old world known only too well.

Yet this sense of 'defeat', this 'nightmare' of being 'Shut out' from meaning, 'In the vast emptiness', is finally replaced by a strange touching 'daybreak', that answers the sparseness of a nature at its last gasp with the factitious full-ness of art, unexpected, out-of-place, in a 'half light' which reveals

> The dark green, touched with gold,
> Of leaves;
> The light green, touched with gold,
> Of clusters of grapes;
> And crouching at the foot of a renaissance wall,
> A little cupid, in whitening stone,
> Weeping over a lost poetry.

As in 'De Civitate Hominum', with its varying shades of white, the poem operates within a severely reduced colour spectrum. This deliberately restricted chromatic range produces what Wallace Stevens, in a poem addressed to MacGreevy, referred to, admiringly, as his 'thin-stringed music'. One poem, emphasising its posed artifice, is actually titled 'Arrangement in Gray and Black'. This stripped-down clarity of line and contrast is MacGreevy's special gift, situating each actual moment of perception within a frame of reference that repeatedly queries its absoluteness and offers it absolution, transforming inchoate personal feeling into consummately impersonal form.

'Gioconda' is one of the most successful of his poems in this mode, significantly, a meditation on art which becomes a surreptitious reflection on the human place in history. An evocation of Leonardo more convincing than Walter Pater's, it seizes not on the voluptuousness but on the otherworldly abstinence of the portrait. It begins, not with the figure of the Gioconda, but with her landscape: a terrain at once moving and static, in that paradoxical representation of motion achieved by the skill of the painter (so that, finally, the stasis can be imbued with the character of thought):

> The sun did not rise or set
> Not being interested in the activities of politicians.
> White manes tossed like spray.
> Bluish snakes slid
> Into the dissolution of a smile.

Time is suspended, the sun doesn't move for politicians (whose dimension is thus denied by art); yet what the painting enshrines is the moment of the Fall, of the human slide into 'dissolution', a word which takes up both the physical properties of the water everywhere in the landscape and the moral lapse associated with the decidedly *fin de siècle* snakes. The Fall is latent in that smile, as the painting inhabits the flux of which it is the unmoving record. This supension is a visitation of grace which catches the stillness of the soul at the moment of its entry into history, into the repeated falls and dissolutions of time.

The last poem in the *Collected Poems*, first published in *University Review* in 1962, reveals MacGreevy's sense of what that history is: the contingency of choice in a world of betrayals, where both faith and blasphemy involve denial, and the final choice is simply between repentance for moral failure and cold, dead defiance. The poem implicates the reader in its collective choices, speculating that we may 'like to think' that of the three men involved in a bombing, none would poison a well. The suggestion is that some apologists for political violence might regard the first, but not the second, as a 'principled' act, thereby requiring the reader to address the moral or immoral discriminations which 'liking to think' involves. The poem leaves deliberately unclear whether the bomb-throwing refers to a specific, contemporary Irish incident, or to some generic idea of terrorist atrocity. With a consummately understated irony in the use of the subjunctive, it adds that 'We may also choose to believe' that one of the men now knows whether he resides with Lazarus or with Dives, that is, euphemistically, in paradise or hell, presumably because the death penalty was imposed only on the actual bomb-thrower. But

MacGreevy's opening formula, referring to the *three* that threw the bomb, suggests that moral agency extends more widely than physical agency. This, perhaps, accounts for the sneaky zeugma which extends the verb 'knows' in the closing sentence from knowing his post-mortem location to knowing that the moral choice always remains between 'Peter who wept bitterly / And Lucifer who has no tears'. As so often in MacGreevy's poetic, it is the constrained, restricted nature of the choices available which strikes home, resonating here for the reader because it was the reader who was first invited to 'choose to believe'. The very title of the poem, calling attention to the kind of choices made when an ordinary Georgian peasant hardened and dehumanised himself into an agent of history, a 'man of steel', exposes the duplicity at the heart of the moral self: 'On the Death of Joseph Djugashvli *Alias* Stalin'.

The contrast between the modern theme and the traditional imagery of this poem reveals the paradox of MacGreevy's writing, succinctly picked out by Stevens. 'It is possible to see', he wrote, 'that you were ... a young man eager to be at the heart of his time' (by which he meant the obviously 'Modernist' nature of MacGreevy's style, its openness to the heritage of Joyce, Pound and Eliot). 'And yet all this is vitally attached to the sort of thing that Groethuysen speaks of', that is, 'the nostalgie du divin (which obviously is epidemic in Dublin)'.

The cosmopolitanism of MacGreevy's forms and sensibility nevertheless works to express a traditional, strangely anachronistic content. Along with Beckett's, this spiritual vision is one curiously stripped of consolation, austere, ascetic to the point of eschewing faith itself, casting emptiness as the precondition of grace. That both writers should need to return to such an unremittingly negative credo as the only viable realisation of the Christian vision is itself deeply related to the condition of the Ireland they knew. Caught in a stalemate in which neither the imagined world of 1916 nor a more prosaic, truncated 'reality' could be consolidated, built upon, the poet was transfixed in the hapless instant between two times. This is the ineffectual, dragged-out interregnum from which he cries, at the end of 'Crón Tráth Na nDéithe', with echoes of the confessional. Yet, out of this deadlock, as Wallace Stevens says in 'Our Stars Come from Ireland', 'These things were made', and 'The sound of him / Comes from a great distance and is heard'.

On Other Grounds: Brian Coffey

For that most experimental of Irish Modernists, Brian Coffey, displacement was both physical and linguistic, a re-inscription of the self in a new narrative of presence which nevertheless, like Joyce's, continually returns to the Ireland it has abandoned. For him too Wallace Stevens seems to have offered an alternative idea of poetry as a transcendence of the particular and parochial, which nevertheless could take that immediate material world as the *fons et origo*, the ground and foundation, of its 'supreme fictions'. A poet of the unintended diaspora, Coffey left Ireland in the 1930s to undertake chemistry research in Paris, spent the war years in Britain, and took up a post as assistant professor in Philosophy at St Louis University, Missouri in 1947, returning to Britain in 1954, living in Southampton and London. In the process he constructed, from the very casualness of his exile, a poetry which transcends the familiar categories of residence and expatriation. Coffey's stance is not the Joycean *non serviam* which, with its *frisson* of adolescent apostasy, implicitly subscribes to the allegiance against which it revolts. For Coffey, where one finds oneself is the result of an accumulation of circumstances, accidents and omissions, not a willed and single act of defiance or flight. And it is with one's circumstantial self that reckoning, for the poet, must always be made, as he concludes in his most ambitious and successful work, 'Missouri Sequence': 'No servant, the muse / abides in truth', for 'The true muse... / is a torment of oneself'.[7]

In Coffey's thought, with its undertones of Taoism and Christian neoplatonism, exile is not so much a social condition as an ontological given, the necessary ground of existence. An aside in 'Syllables for Accents' which speaks of 'the patient pale exiles, waiters, / Shells voided and beached by the sea' seems almost a joke at the expense of his seniors and contemporaries. Joyce's only play was called *Exiles*, while Sylvia Beach, who ran the Paris bookshop, Shakespeare & Co, which published *Ulysses*, helped Joyce financially throughout his career. Sartre observed that a waiter was only a man acting the part of a waiter, but Coffey, recalling Beckett's displaced persons in *Waiting for Godot*, recognises that the waiter, patiently or impatiently attending upon tables, is a symbol of the existential human condition, hovering between the registers of philosophic discourse and workaday experience. Coffey's phrase catches the contingency of being, the forfeit of autonomy that is paid in assuming a reductive and defining role. The waiter is, in his very choice of an occupation, other-defined, attendant on a social reality from which he stands back, deferentially. At the same time he is flotsam, casually cast up into this identity by a world that delivers him to his own emptiness. He exists merely to serve others, a shadowy presence hovering in the margins of their centre-stage dramas.

The stubborn ordinariness of Coffey's poetry, despite or because of its cryptic intonations, its inflections of cliché into oracular utterance, all insist on this interplay of the casual and the fictive. Conventions of speech are subverted in their very use, normal syntactic patterns are dislocated, displaced, cut short; the poetry abounds in anacoluthia; and what this indicates is a willingness to change direction, a refusal of linear progression, of the ruthless irrelevance of logic. Once a sentence's development is assured, and it moves inexorably to its predetermined goal, a moment of freedom has been surrendered, plenitude has been made over to necessity. Consistently, Coffey disposes of these expectations with a throwaway flourish.

The subversion of expectations is a central feature of 'Missouri Sequence', the four sections of which, in their reversals, circlings back and displacements, have a much more casual interdependence than the linear sequential logic their title implies. Section III, 'Muse, June, Related', suggests the primary principle of organization in the poem: 'related', that is to say, kinship, affinity, not identity. The double plane of narration on which this section operates, powerfully fusing a landscape and a woman's body into a single image of a muse, by unifying them in a linguistic field which describes both simultaneously, indicates another aspect of this structure. Statements about poetry become, by extension, statements about love, about relationship to others and to landscape: 'relationship', in its many forms, is the informing theme of the poem.

The sequence is a gathering together, briefly, of a tangle of threads which have converged and intertwined in this particular life. The dedications of the sections, suggesting in turn epistle, address, elegy and love letter, sustain a centrifugal impetus that pushes against the containing momentum, out towards a polycentric universe in which 'Many loves... / concur concretely' and 'Only in twisted man / does love scatter and disperse'.

The poem is about the attempt to hold together these tangential loves within the provisional unity of a life. 'Missouri Sequence' repudiates the musical rigour of Eliot's *Four Quartets*, avoiding any simple chronological or imposed schema. Though the first section, for example, moves from midwinter nightfall to perfected midnight, it immediately spills over, on the note of closure, into a proliferating displacement in time and space, first to tomorrow morning, when they will make lunches for the children to take to school, then beyond that, 'working out the week', to imagine an Ireland remote from this place, that native Achill where still the priest 'elevates / the Saviour of the World'.

Events are the shape we give to time, and the working out of the week is akin to the rituals which transmute the mundane into the sacred. The transposition from horizontal into vertical planes, here, as a deliberate human intervention, recurs in a variety of forms throughout the poem. But the cyclical myths we allow to shape our experience are gradually demonstrated to be a reductive attempt to impose symmetry on the open-ended exfoliating rhythms of a reality neither linear nor cyclical. It is introduced, at the beginning of the poem, as a child's strategy, a play of directedness which gets nowhere, which can assume meaning only within the invented space of a game or a house, as his children play Follow-my-Leader round and round through the rooms of the house, passing his desk once each minute.

Set against this, in the adult world, is a multiplication of relative perspectives where the self can drown – inside / outside, proximity / distance, from / towards – all of them functions of a particular point of view with no absolute hold on space, sensitive to the negativity and absences with which the present is pervaded, capable both of more and more minute discriminations of the particular (tree / branch / leaf), and of wider and wider margins of error, Canada, Ireland, the far bank of the river, the impassable road, all equally inaccessible:

> Inside the house is warm.
> Winter outside blows from Canada
> freezing rain to ice our trees
> branch by branch, leaf by leaf....
> I am distracted by comparisons,
> Ireland across the grey ocean,
> here, across the wide river.

To go west is restlessness, not return to the cradle. Every settlement was first a frontier and then a point of transit, before it lapsed into its proper autonomy. If they now live far from where his mother grows old, nevertheless, in nearby Byrnesville the cemetery is full of Irish graves. Over a hundred years ago, many people of diverse origin, Irish, German, Bohemian, drifted in off the river. The poem, however, contemplates a specifically Irish return: 'Many Irish souls have gone back to God from Byrnesville.' The line playfully converts the multifarious, horizontal displacements of emigration into an absolute vertical relation, a final going home to a pre-exilic source. What the poem actually records, though, is not exile, which presupposes some determining originary place in space and time, but a natural and inevitable vagrancy. Drifting together, drifting apart, men live – all settlements, of the spirit or of the body, provisional, a making over of the self in the making of a home. The demographic convergence, the movement of actual human history, which produced this particular place, with its comically hybrid name, is more than a mere metaphor for the genesis of personal identity. The self is not a rigidly fixed ego, but a precarious congruence of forces, discovering its bounds only in the encounter with resistance and incapacity. It is a 'settlement of walls', the poem 'How Far From Daybreak' suggests, because it is what one settles for, where one is, but it is also what one settles in, settles into, with the incipient fissures, cracks that may widen, the imminent collapse. Against the expansive movement to 'open fields' in that poem it would be easy to opt for the contrary movement of regression, the conserving of an established self which, initially protective, in the end seals the subject in its own labyrinthine desolation, a windowless monad. But Coffey's verse regularly resists such temptations.

Such a solution is indeed canvassed, and rejected, in the second section of 'Missouri Sequence'. The more frequent variant of this is that recoil of nostalgia, the flight from contingent being to the assurance of surrender, in return to an imagined, illusory 'homeland', 'the fictive form of heaven on earth, / the child's return to motherly arms... / flight from where one is'. But, though the poet here reaches in imagination to the hills behind Dublin, the parochiality of the soul has been subverted by a deeper sense of the relativity and contingency of all origins, and of affiliation as a disabling paralysis such as Joyce diagnosed, 'a love of Ireland / withering for Irish men'.

Asking whether it matters where one dies, supposing one knows how, the poem stresses just how much identity is a cognitive myth, a matter of what one happens to come to know, where and when one comes to it. Thus, knowing nothing of Ireland, his own children have grown American, learnt another set of images and imaginings, and, with them, a different narrative of cultural and personal identity. For them the extraordinary has become mundane. The learning of objects is a learning of love and loyalty, peculiar to its own place, whether chasing snakes, catching beetles and butterflies their parents didn't know existed, or paying homage to dead men with July fire-crackers, and eating turkey in November. The image of the cicada shedding its pupa, 'disrob[ing] for the short ruinous day', becomes a figure for this relation of self to place. For it is from what survives when the pupa of custom is shed – what the poem 'How Far From Daybreak' calls 'the residue / chance effects' – that the self can create its own proper grounds. Constructed in one place and time, its here and now can never be circumscribed by the externally given. A necessary tension impels self beyond all improvised allegiances, into a final schism. This last pain is that of shedding, not only what one has grown out of, but what one has grown into, the adopted ground. But there is a complementary movement, back to enclosure, as the free self is incorporated into the collaborative fiction of parenthood, the care of others.

This systolic / diastolic movement is characteristic of Coffey's poetry, which operates recurrently through a complex overlapping of rhythms of opening and closing, unfolding and infolding, rising and dispersal. The third section of 'Missouri Sequence', 'Muse, June, Related' opens with one such instant, the idiomatically American phrase 'school is out' catching a moment of closure which is also a liberation. The image of a house full of children gathered to burst beyond the husk where they have grown, casting janus glances backwards and forwards, is easily extended into a metaphor, or embodiment, of the momentum of human history, coalescing, uncoiling:

> All the passions meet at the dinner table,
> all men's history ever was or will be
> uncoils its features while we serve the food.

'March, Missouri' begins with a similarly expansive gesture, opening windows, allowing doors to swing, in response to the unseasonable mildness of the March weather, living at last at a liminal moment 'between times, charmed carefree', dreaming of spring's daffodils. The euphoric openness, with its expansive calm, its declaratory casualness, is cut short by the return of normative winter weather, its chiaroscuro candour, as the pun on 'candidus', the Latin for white, implies, as 'black wind wedged the candid snow', while the juxtaposition of 'home' and 'drifts' in successive line-endings reactivates the antithesis that pervaded the previous section, resonating through the reluctant accommodations with which the return of routine is greeted, half-heartedly facing winter once more.

'Missouri, Midsummer, Closure' is aware of the slipping moment, of once firm ground unsteady beneath the feet. There is a strange tension between the immemorial fixity of the place, locked in its own rhythms of renewal, and the transitory significance with which it is endowed by its tenants. The leisurely itemisation of the trees with which it opens implies both the diversity of the place and the attempt to hold on to a property that is merely rented, which is already sloping away into a different kind of distance. The trees are 'rooted', yet their composure is itself extempore, an illusory quiet at the intersection of chance and necessity, the 'casual fall of seed', the 'astonishing rise of sap', that causes them to flourish in the casually determined spot. Not accidentally, the passage recalls Yeats's 'chestnut tree, great-rooted blossomer', as 'the perfect leaves / compose... / the vivid temples poets contemplate'; for the next phase of the poem moves to the central preoccupations of 'Among School Children' and the 'Dialogue of Self and Soul', reflecting on the insufficiencies of both spontaneous natural growth and the 'struggle towards the exact muse' associated with Yeats in section I, and 'that perfect self sages praise', which 'grows mastering the unthought-of change' in section II. It evokes, in fact, Yeats in his most accomplished attitudinizing, in that 'monument to Celtic self-importance', the Preface to *Responsibilities*:

> Forty-eight years after my birth,
> tonight when faint heart counsels
> my concerning me
> with family cares and crises
> and decline, tonight
> I write verses at my desk.

The careful ordinariness here, the falling rhythms of doubt and decline, contrast forcefully with Yeats's rhetorical crescendos, which convert apologia into braggadocio, flaunting the unpoetic particularity of age in the daring exposure of rhyme ('Although I have come close on forty-nine'). Coffey mutes any sense of triumphalism with a guilty acknowledgement of having reneged on his responsibilities. The refusal to substitute a Yeatsian histrionic gesture for the fretful circlings of contrition carries the derelict self beyond decline, in the transformative act of writing.

The allusive richness of 'Missouri Sequence', evoking in the subsequent lines, by echoes of rhyme, image and theme, the concluding stanzas of the 'Dialogue of Self and Soul', modulates into a meditative abstraction reminiscent of *Four Quartets*, whose river imagery, as an emblemism of beginnings and endings, is here followed to its source, the Missouri of T. S. Eliot's birthplace. 'Missouri Sequence' is, in part, a poetry made out of a quarrel with the rhetoric of others, a polemic on the process of self-justification, on the modernist idea of art as a redemption, an excusing, of the fecklessness and failure of life, which disputes the self-abnegation of Eliot's Senecan Christianity as much as it rejects Yeats's invention of a strutting persona. The whole disjunction of art and life, 'Beauty' and 'Truth', is an aesthete's myth. If 'beginnings entrance us', the pun on 'entrance' as a way in, as well as a form of magical intoxication, suggests that the 'willing suspension of disbelief' is as much a prerequisite for participation in the 'supreme fiction' of 'reality' as of 'art'. The language recalls here Wallace Stevens's contemporary writings on this theme in both the verse of *Notes Towards a Supreme Fiction* (1942) and the criticism of *The Necessary Angel: Essays on Reality and the Imagination* (1951). Art is merely life grown to its most consummate fullness, not a dimension different from the 'real', but its epitome. When the poem says that 'Poetry becomes humankind' it does so in a double sense. It is both appropriate, becoming, to humanity, and in process of becoming human. It is the shape that will feature the human, a moment of communion where many loves concur, set against 'the habit of withholding love' which 'unfits us for poetry'. In contrast to Eliot, who wrote in *Four Quartets* that 'Humankind cannot bear very much reality', Coffey, pointedly deploying Eliot's unusual noun, insists that 'a poem born aright' offers us entrance into the real, precisely by entrancing us. The 'exact relation' between freedom and necessity, spontaneity and order, is one in which the perfection of utterance is the necessary fulfilment of that which is uttered, in which there is neither redundancy nor deficiency. Neither the internal emigration of the poet who 'dreamed himself / watched him go', nor Eliot's flight from self to the womblike reassurance of Tradition reaches this resolution, which is a moment of reconciliation and infolding, rooted in a mutual attentiveness, an acceptance even of loss and gracelessness, bearing the truth of all, attending freely on all, living 'whenever everywhere', and awakening, in true Walt Whitman fashion, 'when our / love says yes to all, accepts / even the viper vibrant in the vine'.

Such attendant readiness is that wisdom with which the poem credits the Chinese poet Su Tungpo in greeting adversity, who, at his due time 'fared forth gentle with reason'. Wisdom is a knowing how to deal with the adventitious, how to face the unexpected, a preservation of options which averts ruin at the moment that invites to closure and despair. If 'Fortune beyond their foresight / masters most with shifting wind', wisdom is no simple contrary growth to mastery over circumstance, but a skill called forth only occasionally, residing partly in the ability to decide when external 'questioning event' requires an inner and 'exact response', not a merely 'routine answer', and 'love alive alone proffers / love's unpredictable reply'.

Significantly, the running metaphor here is of speech, of some catechism of love in which there is a perfect adequation of question and answer. Such exactitude is not the consonance of two pre-existent parts, but a new, whole creation, a moment of closure and release. The world's body is the host to our self-creative, self-discovering enterprise, a fiction made true in that movement of question and response, twining and untwining, dispersal and convergence, which is the fundamental rhythm of biological and social life. To begin the journey is to ensure the outcome, for human beings are their own source, their destiny implicit already in their determination, 'bound to find / an eternal note of gladness' (contraverting the sea's 'eternal note of sadness' in Matthew Arnold's 'Dover Beach'), bound together, bound to find their own fit bounds, and, in the words of the song, 'bound away, 'cross the wide Missouri'. Despair, the poem says, was never imperative; we are never too old to start the journey, seeking both source and destination, 'the source whence they flow, / the ocean whither they go'. Such a source is not dependent on eventuality, on that accidental and incoherent life out on the periphery, where one puts in the time, but 'abides in truth', in 'loves true for men'. It is here, in the supreme fiction of human faith and love, whatever the location, that the poet faces 'a testing / based on other grounds than nature's'.

NOTES

1. All quotations from Padraic Fallon are from *Poems* (Dublin: The Dolmen Press, 1974).
2. Samuel Beckett, 'Humanistic Quietism', *The Dublin Magazine*, 1934, repr. as the 'Foreword' to the New Writers' Press edition of MacGreevy's poems (see note 4 below).
3. Quotations from Clarke are from the three-volume *Collected Poems*, ed. Liam Miller (Dublin: The Dolmen Press, 1974).
4. *Poems* (1934). All quotations in this section are from Thomas MacGreevy, *Collected Poems*, ed. Thomas Dillon Redshaw (Dublin: New Writers' Press, 1971). See also the next note.
5. See Susan Schreibman (ed.), *The Collected Poems of Thomas MacGreevy* (1991) *An Annotated Edition* (Dublin: Anna Livia Press; Washington, DC: The Catholic University of America Press, 1991), p. xxxii.
6. Wallace Stevens, *Letters*, ed. Holly Stevens (London: Faber and Faber, 1967), p. 596.
7. All quotations from Coffey's work are from Brian Coffey, *Selected Poems* (Dublin: New Writers' Press, Zozimus Books, 1971). The present section on Coffey substantially revises the discussion of 'Missouri Sequence' in my essay 'On Other Grounds: The Poetry of Brian Coffey', first published in *The Lace Curtain* 5 (Dublin, 1974), reprinted unchanged in Douglas Dunn (ed.), *Two Decades of Irish Writing* (Cheadle Hulme: Carcanet Press, 1975). The original essay contains discussions of Coffey's other poetry omitted from the present text. The argument developed here was extended in Stan Smith, 'Against the Grain: Women and War in Brian Coffey's *Death of Hektor*', *Etudes Irlandaises*, 8 (1983).

IV

The Course of Illegible Things:
Denis Devlin

Precarious Guests

Of the first generation of post-independence poets, Denis Devlin most acutely registers the dilemmas of a displacement at once physical, psychological and linguistic. Born of émigré Irish parents in Greenock on the Clyde, in 1908, Devlin spent little more than a third of his life in continuous residence in Ireland. He was indeed twelve before his family returned to Dublin, just as the independence struggle was about to mutate into civil war. Yet his relationship with the fledgling state, as its diplomatic representative for many years, was simultaneously the most intimate and the most public of involvements. In the 1930s, after three years of study in Paris and Munich, and two as a lecturer at University College Dublin, he joined the Irish Department of External Affairs. From 1938 he held a succession of diplomatic posts in Italy, the USA, England and Turkey. He died in 1959, a year after his appointment as Irish Ambassador to Italy. Significantly, he returned in his last weeks to die on 'home' ground in Dublin.

The choice of diplomatic career seems in retrospect a key to the enigmatic identity of the poet. The language of diplomacy, whether secular or spiritual, provides the 'other ground' upon which Devlin's relation to the actual state of Ireland was constructed. Like that other poet-diplomat whose work he successfully translated, St-John Perse,[1] Devlin saw himself, in the words of his translation of the latter's 'Snows', as essentially the 'Precarious guest of the moment, man without proof or witness', regretting, as his translation of 'Exile' puts it, that 'On too many frequented shores have my footsteps been washed away before the day'. Impelled to find in the impalpable community of language a home he could not locate in any specific time or place, he glimpsed there too the emptiness and evanescence of the forms on which the soul relies, as the translation of 'Snows' continues:

Those who, each day, pitch camp farther from their birthplace, those who, each day, haul in their boat on other banks, know better, day by day, the course of illegible things; and tracing the rivers towards their source, through the green world of appearances they are caught up suddenly into that harsh glare where all language loses its power.

This indeed is the central paradox for Devlin. If language is the tract on which the soul constructs itself from moment to moment, it is also an impermanent and treacherous ground. The temporising self, like its words, is easily erased. All utterance is pitched in the tension between allegiance and silence, where the restless spirit seeks a provisional coherence. In the words of 'Exile':

> And it is no error, O Peregrine,
>   To desire the barest place for assembling on the wastes of exile a great
> poem born of nothing, a great poem made from nothing...
>   I have built upon the abyss and the spindrift and the sand-smoke.
>   I shall lie down in cistern and hollow vessel,
>   In all stale and empty places where lies the taste of greatness.

St-John Perse's link here, between spiritual evacuation, as the precondition of poetry, and the weary personal renunciation of place, must have seemed an inevitable one for Devlin. This is the tenor of the assertion and parenthetical question, almost an afterthought, that closes the third section of 'Exile': 'You shall not cease, O clamour, until, upon the sands, I shall have sloughed off every human allegiance. (Who knows his birthplace still?)'

Absence is at the heart of Devlin's absolutes: an unaccommodating emptiness pursued by the stringently self-denying conscience, a greatness 'made from nothing'. Devlin's perpetual question is that set out in 'Galway', in *The Heavenly Foreigner*: 'How I might make my soul / In a freedom that might destroy it?'[2] But there is, too, a complementary quietism. In another poem in the same volume, 'Chartres', the 'protesting' self, striving to forge its own salvation, acknowledges a possible recusancy, in a gesture towards that mode of Christian resignation which equates activity with sin, ambition with insurrection:

> Like those who will not surrender a small liberty
> Which they cannot cultivate in any case.
> Rebellion is imperfection like all matter:
> Mirror without reflection, I am helpless...

Brian Coffey, the original editor of Devlin's poems, observed that 'I, for one, always associated with the seminary that mass of reserve of his, which struck so many people as noteworthy'.[3] Educated at Belvedere College, Dublin, the Jesuit institution which left such a mark on James Joyce's intellect, and at

Clonliffe, Devlin for a time intended the priesthood. The ascetic hauteur of Loyola's spiritual *corps diplomatique* probably appealed to him for complex biographical reasons.

W. M. Walker has discussed the state of mind of the Irish immigrant community in Scotland at the turn of the century. Walker attributes to the Scottish Catholic ghetto the 'siege' mentality of 'a community which ... feared for its reputation and for the preservation of its historically nurtured uniqueness'. Such a community sought refuge in a willed abstentionism, in the world yet not of it, which combined a canny, guarded superiority with defensive deference: 'Catholic social organization was inimical to free expression and suspicious of spontaneity. The training in self-effacement began in the home.'[4]

In 'Celibate Recusant', the double withdrawal implied in the title (from the flesh and from subscription to the civil power) uses the analogy with Catholic dissent to present Devlin's attitude as one of abstemious and even squeamish disengagement from an abandoned world, a stance summed up in the final terse exchange of the poem: '"Touch me not!"... "It's as you wish."' The mere fact of physical existence, of having a body, is enough to soil one with complicity. In 'Galway', in *The Heavenly Foreigner*, he speaks of 'My busy, alien lip and eye' as if the business of the world were something which estranged body from spirit, soul from self. Devlin is preoccupied with this tension between hypostatised Self and Other, in a way which leads him into innumerable paradoxes. For one's own body can become part of the Other, the 'fiery circle cataracting outerworld' of 'Galway'. Yet the Other is also the 'heavenly foreigner', one's own elusive soul which is also Christ and, in an extension which draws on Sufi mysticism and its troubadour variants, the Beloved who is *anima* and completion of one's own true being. The numinous is only revealed subversively, through the dangerous phenomenal forms of this material world, what 'Galway' calls the 'divine / Dissidence in river and wheat'. It is this intervention of which 'Irvine' speaks, in *The Heavenly Foreigner*:

> Something there was other
> Always at my elbow...
>
> When the foreign power intervened and made all the difference
> Between the bog and the road,
> Making the present, making life...
> The world glows with mortal divinity...
> O Heavenly Foreigner! Your price is high.

Characteristically, Devlin thinks of this negotiation between Self and Other in diplomatic terms, as if only protocol preserved that necessary composure without which self might be overwhelmed and its hard-won autonomy abolished. Devlin's position is, in fact, self-confessedly Jansenist, despite his early Jesuit training. In 'Jansenist Journey' the transition from guilt to innocence is associated with indifference and renunciation and, symptomatically, with distrust ('But I put no trust in him, no trust'). The goal is merely a continuation of the present in which pilgrimage is, punningly, a 'retreat':

> We entered cloisters with a priest,
> Sat on the stone wall, listening
> To his plans for our retreat,
>
> ...No rapture;
> The plain virtue of the chosen few.

Jansenism has been classically defined by Lucien Goldmann as the reaction of the seventeenth-century French 'legal nobility' to the decline of its social power. Potential leaders of the central bureaucracy, members of this class found themselves, instead, in the role of dispossessed administrative elite,

> economically dependent, as *officiers*, upon a monarchical state whose growth they opposed from an ideological and political point of view. This put them in an eminently paradoxical situation... where they were strongly opposed to a form of government which they could not destroy or even alter in any radical manner.[5]

Enough similarities exist between this experience and Devlin's own social dilemma to make Jansenism a fruitful source of analogies for him. The paradoxes are revealed in his 'Investiture of D'Artagnan' through a harshly convoluted language which in its unnatural inversions reproduces the spiritual tergiversations of which it speaks. D'Artagnan, reluctant servant and even embodiment of the State, preserves his self-respect through an aristocratic disdain for the mediocrity his squandered merit serves:

> With you is my last dignity in retreat from these the precise great.
> By Clio squandered, I have pacted with the times unworthy of my chance,
> ...first marshal of France
> Who should have ridden the times in spasm, have been I the State.

Clio, Muse of the historical record, may have driven his dignity into retreat. But principled withdrawal within an active life can be sustained by the conviction that the service of Caesar is a chastisement which may enhance worth:

> Foreclosed. Not to be captain conqueror of kneaded minds is my gift

> To resignation, smile to the King, Sire I cannot leave
> These lawns the hereditary breezes bevel, this soft life a reprieve
> From my intended life.

It is the dilemma of the poet-diplomat whose 'intended' vocation, as spiritual viceroy, has been twisted into this 'bitter' (line 9) secular parody. The resolution of these tragic paradoxes, within Jansenism, lay in a theology of grace as the interruption of the worthless material world by intimations of a nobler, juster dispensation ('the foreign power'), modest faith in a collective election substituting for loss of secular autonomy.

Huge and Foreign Universes

Such a theology is explored in that strangely anachronistic poem, 'The Passion of Christ', simultaneously part of the devotional tradition and a modernist critique of its assumptions, which sketches, in a series of vignettes, the whole of divine history from Fall to Transfiguration. Significantly, Devlin cannot avoid a surreptitious admiration for the figure of 'Pilate, the surgeon', who 'cleans his distant hands, / In sage disgust, praises the Good'. This silent diplomatic gesture preserves a self-absolving composure in an impossible colonial cul-de-sac. It is also sustained by a Stoicism with spiritual pretensions, his admiration for an abstract, capitalised 'Good' suggesting that a genteel Neoplatonism underwrites his contempt for the 'filthy wine-lit bands' who forgive Barabbas but bay for the blood of Jesus. But Devlin shows this to be bad faith, and sets against it the acknowledgement of Christ by the Good Thief. The latter's rueful self-criticism, aware of 'The huge and foreign universes round me', reverses Pilate's posture by remorsefully accepting guilty complicity. Ironically, however, he sees himself in terms which mimic Pilate's consular authority:

> It is not right for me to talk to You,
> To wait on You with ministerial bow...
>
> [M]y understanding less imperious...
> Loses whole continents where in my childhood
> I was Your Viceroy, and approved the Just
> And condemned my natural evil thoughts...

Devlin's recurrent antinomy of Justice and Nature is focused here in the orthodox belief that original sin is a fall from the state of grace into the state of nature. The poet's skill lies in playing up the statist metaphor to the point at which he can speak of the 'majesty of Christ' as that of 'God's Son foreign to our moor'. But Christ is also the supersession of the State, and 'The Last Supper' an initiation into this negativity, taking the self beyond the compromising loyalties and betrayals of a fallen political world:

> Outside the window, the world was still,
> Absence of principalities and powers:
>   The world His will,
> He broke bread and said He would be ours.

The characteristic supplication of the last line of 'The Passion of Christ', 'Oh, come, Unworldly, from the World within!', leaves the reader with an absence that can be filled only by faith, by the conviction of the Good Thief 'That You are there and are not there'.

    God is simultaneously absent from and immanent in creation, and this negative mode of divine presence is specifically that of the Jansenist Pascal's 'hidden God', a tragic theology salvaged from defeat and disillusion. Pascal's influence pervades Devlin's work. In 'Meditation at Avila' it is there in the idea of the 'saving presence' of a grace that is not habitual but momentary, which 'Is never a promise, comes without warning / Or, being most wanted, fails', yet is nevertheless sustained by a faith founded in the unanswering void which validates each 'doomed and sunny moment'.

    Christ's emissary, the Soul which is the precarious guest of an alien empire, is constructed by the mundane Self out of a dialogue in which one side is always silent. Yet the Self, like those 'Fountain waters' which 'Bloom on invisible stems', rides this apparent absence, its seed, sap and fruit:

> Magnificence, this terse-lit, star-quartz universe,
> Woe, waste and magnificence, my soul!
>   ...Soul, my dear friend,
> Welcome as always;
> Fibrous listener in the darks of mind
> Till my confession
> Articulate your silence...
>
> You shall see blue arches of emptiness marching into the horizon
> Over the yellow and black, the intolerant
> Excellency of the Castilian highlands....
> If I could not talk to you
> Fear would oppress me.

Devlin seeks to intercede between the two orders, between the intransigence of a material, political world, picked out by the enjambment which allows 'Excellency' a double meaning, and the 'impalpable' fluidity of grace. In sifting out the 'magnificence' from the 'waste', he rejects St Teresa's brutal dichotomy of spirit and flesh, which inverts his own terms:

> God being star-froze heaven
> And Devil, fluent earth
> O Santa, Santa Teresa,
> Covetous, burning virgin!
> Scorning to nourish body's
> Farmlands with soul's
> Modulating rains,
> You lost your eyes' rich holdings
> To rubble, snakes and swine
> And like the skeptical miser
> You lost the usufruct
> Of heaven, this floral life...

For Devlin, Soul transfigures this alien world with 'comfort'. The concept of 'usufruct' to redefine the parable of the good steward is apposite and precise. As a legal concept, 'usufruct' defines a ground which is not owned as property but simply used for pasture and cultivation by its transient inhabitants. But such comfort is rare and not to be presumed upon: the world easily falls apart into its discrepant antitheses. When Self 'call[s] in alien silence', out of the grief of a collective mortality, towards an infinite which looks mutely back, it confronts that eternal silence of space in which Pascal felt the terror of the divine. At the same time, as in a poem such as 'The Colours of Love', the world remains a 'fluent fantasy' that 'makes a mock' of the Self, tempting it to 'throw off [its] absolutist devices / And dissemble in the loose resplendent sea'. In 'The Colours of Love', Devlin's resolution is the Pascalian wager of faith:

> Yet, think on how, San Juan, bitter and bare,
> Wrapt in his drama, sent his cry above,
> And though, through layer on suffocating layer
> Nothing came back, he loved; and so I love.

As 'Obstacle Basilisk' indicates, the self must always be on guard against a world where the 'treacherous years' and 'each bandit landmark' of time and place threaten the careful distinction of the soul. The only proper stance is a 'scrupulous alarm' that keeps the 'mean groom' of the flesh at bay. The 'justified' self in this poem (in its theological sense, having been reconstructed in grace) fears that it may be assimilated into the alien, degrading universe around it. The anxiety sublated here is that of a recusant minority in a squalidly hostile environment, careful of a spiritual election which is also its guarantee of class superiority.

Embassies Not Understood

Dissolution, subversion, assimilation: it is this which appals the poet in 'Est Prodest', where 'Tablelands of ice', image of that 'identity' which is 'Other' ('He is me otherwise'), can easily thaw into the 'eternal horror' of the poem's middle section:

> Murmur of cities...
> Its voices, panic,
> Cataracting, bestial...
> The loosened universe flowing
> Loathsome, limpid...

It becomes clear, at this point, why Devlin's work is so dominated by the tone of the diplomat. In language alone can the anxious self be guaranteed a breathing space, a *cordon sanitaire* within which to conduct its negotiations with an alien and always potentially destructive world. That Devlin should describe the universe as 'cataracting' both here and in 'Galway' suggests a perpetual fear of that volatility that might engulf the self if it once let go of its stabilising protocols. This accounts for the peculiarly aureate, mannered quality of Devlin's language, its almost hieratic distance. Language is a specious resolution of antinomies for Devlin, the reduction of objective conflict to verbal paradox. The respectful rhetoric of the *amour courtois* tradition, which abounds in his love poetry, is finally admitted in 'Edinburgh Tale' to be a device for keeping down 'the ungovernable, scared birds of the heart and the blood risen'. The vocative mode of much of his poetry is an attempt to mediate between two worlds without being compromised by either, like those birds in 'Memoirs of a Turcoman Diplomat' characteristically seen as 'Imperial emblems', who 'in their thin, abstract singing, / Announce some lofty Majesty whose embassies are not understood'. Significantly, his second volume was called *Intercessions*.[6]

Islam, in 'Memoirs of a Turcoman Diplomat', seems almost a mirror image of Devlin's Jansenist Catholicism, a displaced discouse reconciling ascetic rigour with a worldly hedonism. The retired diplomat may reflect, with wry nostalgia, that the 'puritanic temperament's outgrown', but his casual rumination is qualified, given savour, by the inkling that this is not an absolute fact, but simply the reflection of a particular man no longer young. The evening's lapsing ('Evenings ever more willing lapse into my world's evening') is seen in the same way as the reflex of a merely personal acquiescence. The impermanency of residence in such a world is indicate by the title of the first memoir, 'Oteli Asia Palas, Inc.', admitting good-humouredly that one is a precarious guest in the hotel of the world. The old man casts himself as the emissary of a superseded past:

> [T]he yellow and blue skies changing place,
> I hold my stick, old world, the waiters know me,
> And sip at my European drink, while sunlight falls,
> Like thick Italian silks over the square houses into the Bosphorus.
> Ladies, I call you women now, from out my emptied tenderness,
> All dead in the wars, before and after war, I toast you my adventures with
> your beauty!

Time and place continually change, the only 'absolute kingdom' is 'far in the sky'. One is always left with the passing and accidental present. Such a realisation brings its own compensations. The slow assimilation of the volatile spirit of youth, that empty freedom which is all potential, into a shabby and specific actuality, a career and a past, may be a lapse from distinction to mediocrity. But it also brings the maturity, and the self-awareness, to see this and not be overwhelmed by it, an 'emptied tenderness' that does not equate transience with vanity:

> You are not what you thought, you are someone like all these,
> The most ardent young man turns, at the drop of a black hat,
> Into some rabbity sort of clerk, some heart-affairs diplomat,
> A John of the Cross into a Curia priest.
> It was years ago. It is not now like when the century began –
> Though, apple and peach lie brilliant on the dark,
> And mineral worlds on the dark sky shine,
> And the red mouth breathes in; thine is mine,
> And the careless Atlantic inhales the Thames, the Tagus and the Seine...

The syntax, hinging on that qualifying 'Though', suggests that the discrepancy is a subjective one, depending on point of view: there is no absolute change. The same awakening, the same fruitions and disappointments, go on for other lives, here and in other places. It is a salutary recognition.

'My father thought my feeling could take fire by the vibrant Seine / And a tough intellect be constructed in Göttingen'. But self is a construct not easily tampered with. The ceremonious distance of protocol may be a necessary way of endowing the transient with a more absolute dignity:

> In the Foreign Office, they humorously ask my advice,
> My father had money, I was posted from place to place:
> What can I tell them? even if I got it right?
> There would be protocol about the right time and the right place...

In reality, there is no such thing as the right time and the right place. Both alike in this poem are adjectival, fortuitous concurrences that speak always of elsewhere, attributes of the subject or its objects: 'my European drink', 'Italian silks', 'our salaried Levantine admirals', 'some international Secretary General', 'our Westernising dictator', 'the up-country captains', 'my Frankish Friend's one wife, / In a far Latin Villa'. The absurdity of the attempt to endow place with absolute value is disclosed by the nomadic ancestry of the Turks themselves, late inheritors of the residue of several empires, an experience crystallised in the title of the shortest piece in the sequence, 'The Turkish for Greek is Roman'. The Turkish name for Greece is 'Yunanistan', 'Yunani' being a corruption of 'Romani', referring to the inhabitants of the Eastern Roman Empire in Constantinople, a city renamed by conquest as a Turkish 'Istanbul', itself an eroded version of the Greek name.

The resolution of the poem is unusual in Devlin for its earthy colloquiality. The old man moves from nostalgia to opportunism, grasping at the compensations of a post-war world short of men and looking for paternal reassurance:

> Tuck in your trews, Johannes, my boy, be led by me,
> These girls are kind. And we're all the rage now, whiskey-
>   flushed men of our age
> The callow and the sallow and the fallow wiped off the page!

Asia seemed to offer Devlin a territory, beyond Christendom, in which he could relax his prickly defences. In 'Ank'hor Vat', for example, as if protected by his role as envoy, discreet, tactfully reserving his own opinions in the presence of an alien authority, he can face the flux of things with an unruffled equanimity. An ambassadorial *sang-froid* enables him to patronise the colonial deity, Buddha, with an easy deference, while taking notes on comparative anthropology, making a scholarly pun ('vegetative speed') and remaining quietly unperturbed by his ignorance of the local flora. A world of overflowing motions, of fecund disturbing energies, is thus contained by 'my mental distance from passion' which allows him to stand impassive and attendant. This is Devlin's version of that distance Stevens praised in MacGreevy, and it derives from the same source. Such a stance can translate even 'the lissome fury of this god' into the composure of script, 'quiet lettering on vellum', in a strategy similar to that which we have already encountered in Clarke.

Yet the consolation offered by this flexible quietism can turn to ashes in the mouth, for there is an immediate, urgent world, where Nature and Justice are inextricably intertwined, that will not easily be denied, that demands voice and commitment. At times Devlin, who shared the leftist political enthusiasms of the 1930s generation, seems to regard that very diplomatic discretion as his own particular version of the Sartrean *huis clos*. This at least seems to be the point of 'Tantalus', in which the charge laid against Pilate comes home to roost, as the diplomat now finds himself dumb, his hands tied, because 'Shame like an Alderman in Hell / Has broke me down till I have cried'.

Murderous Angels

One of those laments is 'At the Tomb of Michael Collins'. Both Collins and De Valera had been regular visitors of his parents in the young Devlin's Dublin home. The assassination in 1922 of the Free State leader by De Valera's anti-Treaty intransigents occurred at a key intersection of the personal and the public for Devlin, two years after his family had returned home to the emerging Irish state.[7] The poem links the birthpangs of the new state with the trauma of adolescence, its initiation into mortality and fallenness. There is an incipient oedipal dimension to the poem, which equates the Jesuit teachers of Devlin's youth with the 'voracious fathers' who bore Collins down, as if the suppression of the hero-figure were also, for the boy who identifies with him, a personal death imagined as a return to the state of unbeing before conception: 'He's what I was when by the chiming river / Two loyal children long ago embraced.' I take the 'two loyal children' to be Devlin's youthful parents, and the embrace to be that of his conception.

The nexus in which the persecutors meet is, significantly, literature. The news of Collins's murder is embedded, for the twelve-year-old Devlin, within other stories/histories of those in the past who were heroes in his mind, in particular a classroom reading of Whitman's poem on the assassination of Lincoln. Beyond this lies a whole tradition of pastoral elegy which reaches back through Milton's 'Lycidas', that poem read by Stephen Dedalus's pupils, to Theocritus. This literary tradition becomes a filter through which the monstrous event is simultaneously interpreted and controlled, kept at a distance. The poem records the deepening conviction on the young Devlin's part that we, the children, are accomplices of the 'voracious fathers':

> Then, Oh, our shame so massive
> Only a God embraced it and the angel
> Whose hurt and misty rifle shot him down.

The transferred epithets of 'hurt and misty rifle' suggest the general complicity. The assassination witnesses to a universal fallenness, to some original sin that makes a sacrificial martyr of its liberators. The analogy with Christ is implicit throughout, in a pastoral tradition where nature too is seen to be grieving:

> And sad, Oh sad, that glen with one thin stream
> He met his death in; and a farmer told me
> There was but one small bird to shoot; it sang
> 'Better Beast and know your end, and die
> Than Man with murderous angels in his head.'

Devlin is haunted by these equivocal angels, who lurk in the stony places of the soul. He is insistent that this is an Irish guilt ('No one betrayed him to the foreigner'), one more instance of that Irish tradition of keeping murder within the family. 'It is inside our life the angel happens', announcing that foreign power which is our own mortality and otherness. But there is no guarantee that such angel messengers are benign. The ending is richly ambivalent, framing the death with the poet's reception of it, in his own separate life, walking to Vespers at his Jesuit school, distinguishing the rawness of the immediate, unformed and inchoate response from its placing now, in an explicit act of retrospect which locates it as one more betrayal in a whole history of defections and dereliction. Whitman's exclamatory lament for Lincoln, 'O Captain, my Captain!', then becomes taken up in the young boy's grief, teaching a lifelong moral 'lesson' that transcends the afternoon's classroom lessons: 'How sometimes death magnifies him who dies, / And some, though mortal, have achieved their race.'

That final, outrageous 'Metaphysical' pun, recalling Dryden's elegy on Oldham but also Stephen Dedalus's ambition to 'forge the uncreated conscience of his race', suggests the homilectic purpose of this poem. Like Pascal, Devlin was preoccupied with the impossibility of Justice in a world divided by custom and state, convinced that of all possible evils, civil war was the worst. But achieving their race was the aim both of Collins's camp and that of his killers. The 'frightened antinomies' of Devlin's poetry transpose into a spiritual and personal dimension the whole condition of Ireland in the twentieth century.[8] The dissension is reproduced in the poetry as an internal schism in human nature, embodied in the oxymoronic construction which history unfolds as a paradox and truth: 'murderous angels'.

History in Devlin's work is always a recurrence of the same stories in new forms. He speaks, in *The Heavenly Foreigner,* of time 'volumed round me, thick with echoes', where the double meaning of 'volumed' recalls the young Stephen Dedalus's slippage from 'history' to 'the books of history'. That fine poem, 'Old Jacobin', centres on the way in which the self's participation in history is ideologically predetermined by the histories (and history books) it inherits, seeing 'the hero-selves that my imperium / Summoned from the *Odes,* the Roman *Lives*' as, finally, 'the antique stuff I wrapt my virtues in'. The poem combines the fervent political commitment of 'Michael Collins' with the poised and worldly relaxation of 'Turcoman Diplomat'. Like many of Devlin's poems, it specifies the civil war within the self in terms of a clash between past and present, fanaticism and scepticism, this-worldly and otherworldly values. Yet neither half of these binaries invalidates the other. Selfhood is the equilibrium that can admit, in Goldmann's words, 'the tragic teaching of Jansenism [which] insisted upon the essential vanity of the world and upon the fact that salvation could be found only in solitude and withdrawal', and yet seek that 'solitude and withdrawal' within the hectic arena of history. As Goldmann puts it:

> Prevented by the presence of God from ever accepting the world, but prevented at the same time by His absence from abandoning it altogether, he is constantly dominated by a permanent and fully justified awareness of the radical incongruity between himself and everything around him, of the unbridgeable gulf which separates him both from any real values and from any possible acceptance of the immediate reality of the ordinary external world. The situation of tragic man is paradoxical and can be explained only by paradoxes: for he is in the world and conscious of it from within, but refuses the world because of its inadequate and fragmentary nature.[9]

The poem is another retrospect, in which the Old Jacobin makes his reckoning with God and history, the slag of a life's sins washed away as he makes his soul 'In the light of innocence'. Those same sins are acknowledged as the necessary evils a man takes upon himself in trying to reform an unregenerate world. The discrimination is Jesuitical in its separation of intention and consequence, arrogant in its disdain for the venality of the *menu peuple* it intended to serve, delighting in its own Machiavellian pursuit of good intentions. He can claim that he never lied to the people, but admits that he did take advantage, in their best interests, of the fact that they lied to themselves, like a lover loving less than his beloved, who comforts her with lies.

That acknowledgement is crucial. The revolutionary cares *less*, that is, is more *disinterested*, than those he leads on, and in that fine carelessness lies the secret of his gift. For him, history is a drama, as for St John in 'The Colours of Love', an unreal plot to which the intending communicant, wearing 'the pandemonium of the heroes', must commit himself, signing away the men he loved, until his faith is vindicated, made real in the performance, as the Soul is constructed from the Self's dialogue with silence. Thus his histrionic shouting in the Assembly called out a complicitous response from the deputies, who 'Blushed in the drama', knowing along with him 'The Goddess Reason's treasonable trance'. What calls him to this sacrifice, of himself and those he loves, is a more pressing reality, the grief of others which is always real and absolute in a way that one's own never is, the ghosts of starving children and their weeping parents. To 'quiet the children's crying', he reflects, he would still give his 'one blood and heart'. Yet the closing mood of the poem moves beyond all this turbulence, into a strangely philosophic calm:

> ...nevertheless
> As the water bears the light equally
> As I will have no shame before my father
> I bear my life
> Without regret or praise.

The 'garden' cannot be restored in this world. The children still cry. But it was enough to try, to throw oneself unequivocally into the theatrical embarrassments of history. The repeated 'bear' gathers to it innumerable resonances. Life is a cross to bear, a bringing to birth, and an enduring which in the end is beyond 'regret or praise', a bearing of the self well; for, in the words of *King Lear*, 'we must endure / Our going hence even as our coming hither.' Precarious guest in the green world of appearances, the self must trace the rivers to their source, to 'that harsh glare where all language loses its power', where all allegiances are sloughed. But that glare can turn to grace, for it is precisely in these 'stale and empty places', amidst the 'bitter watercress' of disillusion, disappointment and defeat, that the self whose only pursuit was Justice can find its absolution. The fine balance of lyric plangency and ascetic rigour with which the poem ends catches the equipoise of chastity and charity which is Devlin's own particular gift, the precarious resolution of antinomies in a displacement which in the end takes the self beyond history and story, event and narrative altogether: 'Bitter watercress / Long water widening to where / There is but water and light and air.'

NOTES

1. St-John Perse, *Exile and Other Poems*, bilingual edition with translation by Denis Devlin (New York: Pantheon Books, Bollingen Series XV, 1953). See also note 3.
2. Denis Devlin, *The Heavenly Foreigner*, variorum edition, ed. and introd. by Brian Coffey (Dublin: Dolmen Press, 1967).
3. Denis Devlin, *Collected Poems*, ed. and introd. by Brian Coffey (Dublin: Dolmen Press, 1964), p. xi. Except where otherwise indicated, all the poems quoted subsequently are from this edition. Published more than a decade after the first version of this essay ('Precarious Guest: The Poetry of Denis Devlin') appeared in *Irish University Review* (vol. 8, no. 1, Spring 1978), J. C. C. Mays's fine edition of the *Collected Poems of Denis Devlin* (Dublin: The Dedalus Press, 1989) brings together all Devlin's volumes, including translations and uncollected poems, with helpful textual and bibliographical notes.
4. W. M. Walker, 'Irish Immigrants in Scotland: Their Priests, Politics and Parochial Life', *The Historical Journal*, xv (1972), pp. 649–67.
5. Lucien Goldmann, *The Hidden God*, trans. Philip Thody (London: Routledge and Kegan Paul, 1964), pp. 103–41.
6. Denis Devlin, *Intercessions* (Paris: Europa Press, 1937).
7. Edward Norman, *A History of Modern Ireland* (London: Penguin Books, 1971), pp. 296–7.
8. I have discussed this aspect of Devlin's work at greater length in 'Frightened Antinomies: Love and Death in the Poetry of Denis Devlin', in Brian Coffey (ed.) *Advent VI: Denis Devlin Special Issue* (Southampton: Advent Books, 1976).
9. Goldmann, *Hidden God*, pp. 55–6.

V

Plastering over the Cracks: Louis MacNeice

Manifold Illusions

'When the soul of man is born in this country', according to those much troped *obiter dicta* of Stephen Dedalus's from *Portrait*, 'there are nets flung at it to hold it back from flight', nets of 'nationality, language, religion'. Louis MacNeice's *The Poetry of W. B. Yeats* (1941) gathered in these cultural nets – nets of discourse – under the figure of paradox. 'Ireland', MacNeice perceived, is in reality a set of *discursive practices*. Its conflicted heterogeneity is, in the words of Yeats's sonnet 'Meru', only 'brought / Under a rule, under the semblance of peace / By manifold illusion'. MacNeice offered a familiar list of the contradictory ways in which Ireland has been so imagined:

> The Irish are born partisans [and] born puritans... Their character could best be expressed in a set of antinomies... We could say, for example: *The Irish are sentimental* (see any popular song book) but we could also say: *The Irish are unsentimental* (see *John Bull's Other Island*). Or again: *The Irish genius is personal* (see Yeats *passim* and the popular English conception of the Irishman as a 'character') and *the Irish genius is impersonal* (see almost any translations of early Irish poetry). Or again: *The Irish are formal* (witness the conventions of the peasantry, the intricacies of Gaelic poetry, the political technique of Mr De Valera) and The *Irish are slapdash* (witness the way they ruin their houses). Or again: *Ireland is a land of Tradition* (think of the Irishman's notorious long memory) and *Ireland suffers from lack of Tradition* (see Yeats's well-founded strictures in *Dramatis Personae*)... The Irish dialectic is best, perhaps, resolved by a paradox: Ireland, like other countries, has obvious limitations; these limitations, if rightly treated, become assets. I would suggest therefore as a final antinomy this: *It is easy to be Irish; it is difficult to be Irish.*[1]

These antithetical definitions, each of which can be backed up with persuasive examples, are the indisputable site of the ideological. *Antithesis*, the balancing of irreconcilable opposites, mutates into *paradox*, which holds together two opposing possibilities in an impossible union, to become the literary trope of a political and ideological dilemma. Paradox is a strategy for reconciling real, historical incompatibilities at the level of *discourse*, in a verbal device. Yeats's 'antithetical vision', MacNeice suggests, has its origins in an ideology of conflict only resolvable in this way. When Yeats delights in struggle and antinomy, one can see him using the possibilities of language, the fiction-eer's ability to tell the truth while lying, to resolve dilemmas of allegiance and belief which he cannot resolve in life without opting unequivocally for one cause or the other. Thus he creates linguistic, dramatic or imaginary resolutions of real and irresolvable conflicts. Yeats's creation in poetry of a verbal 'phantasmagoria', the transformation of 'the bundle of accident and incoherence that sits down to breakfast' into 'something intended, complete',[2] becomes the pattern of a larger set of political recuperations.

Spiritual Hyphenation

MacNeice himself deployed the 'ould antinomies' of his own hyphenated Anglo-Irishness as a complex strategy for establishing both distance and intimacy in relation to Ireland, maintaining in a largely English-dominated literary world what C. Day Lewis categorised as a 'humorous but armed neutrality'. MacNeice had other things to say on the cultural and political consequences of Yeats's antithetical vision which are relevant to this argument, speaking, for example, of

> the clannish obsession with one's own family; the combination of an anarchist individualism with puritanical taboos and inhibitions; the half-envious contempt for England; the constant desire to show off; a sentimental attitude to Irish history; a callous indifference to those outside the gates; an identification of Ireland with the spirit and of England with crass materialism. Even now many Englishman are unaware of the Irishman's contempt for England... the belief that the English are an inferior race.[3]

MacNeice certainly found it 'difficult to be Irish'. 'How can you mix with people who might be murderers without you knowing it?', MacNeice's father said in explanation of why, though he welcomed the creation of the Irish Free State, he refused to visit it.[4] It sums up, succinctly, the version of the national paradox MacNeice inherited as his patrimony. Like Yeats, MacNeice suffered for many years from sectarian dismissal of him as not an *Irish* poet, an objection based on his Northern, Protestant origins, his education and adult residence in England, and his work as a Classics lecturer at Birmingham University, for the BBC, and for the British Council. Only his Protestant provenance here, however, would differentiate him from any number of Southern Catholics, many of them ardent nationalists, who have lived, worked and voted for most of their lives in Britain. MacNeice's work has, in a sense, been perceived as 'extra-territorial', to use the word deployed by that other, rather more English Anglo-Irish poet, Robert Graves, an 'ambassador of Otherwhere', to the 'unfederated states of Here and There'.[5] As Tom Paulin could comment as late as 1984, 'For the English reader he appears to be Irish, while for certain Irish readers he doesn't really belong to Ireland.'[6]

In the last quarter of the twentieth century, the unravelling violence in the North, and the often polemically motivated rediscovery or re-invention by Republican intellectuals of the Protestant strands in the Nationalist tradition, seemed to have altered that perception for good. The case for MacNeice as essentially and representatively Irish, above all in his very expatriation and rootlessness, seems to have become normative. But such an interpretation veers too far in the opposite direction. For what is central to MacNeice's perception of himself, and the well-spring of all his writing, is neither the 'Anglo' nor the 'Irish' half of this equation, but the hyphen in between, something to which, as I shall argue later, Northern writers as different as Montague, Heaney and Ciaran Carson have also witnessed. That sense of social and cultural interstitiality MacNeice shared with his 1930s contemporaries, in particular with his friend and literary collaborator W. H. Auden, whose homosexuality and rejection of middle-class Englishness constituted a similar kind of discursive displacement. Auden summed up this condition, in the American title of the first volume of poetry published after he departed for the United States, as that of *The Double Man* (1940). MacNeice's lifelong friendship with the art critic and Cambridge don, subsequently the knighted curator of the Queen's Pictures, finally exposed as a British / Soviet double agent, Anthony Blunt, is suggestive in considering this psychological and social 'doubleness'. Suggestive enough, in fact, for the Irish novelist John Banville to have created in *The Untouchable* (1997) the portrait of a spy which merges the characters and histories of Blunt and MacNeice, seeing each as the site of contradictory, irreconcilable loyalties resolved by the assumption of a subversive, clandestine and ironic distance. Banville's title is expressive. If an 'untouchable' is a social pariah, he is also someone who eludes capture or encapsulation: he can't be touched. He may also be, like Elliot Ness and the FBI 'Untouchables', the 'G Men' of America's Prohibition era, a semi-secret agent outside or above the law. Such a status certainly accords with that antinomian streak that underlies MacNeice's secularised, God-forsaken version of Calvinism.

In his ground-breaking and still essential study, *Louis MacNeice: Sceptical Vision* (1975), Terence Brown elucidated such a cultural (dis)location by reference to the moderate 'Ascendancy' nationalist Stephen Gwynn's account of the identity crisis precipitated by the accelerating pace of the independence process:

I was brought up to think myself Irish, without question or qualification; but the new nationalism prefers to describe me and the like of, as Anglo-Irish. A.E. has even set me down in print as being… the typical Anglo-Irishman. So all my life I have been spiritually hyphenated without knowing it.[7]

Writing before the advent of postcolonial theory and the concept of 'cultural hybridity', Brown, himself, significantly, the Peking-born son of Dublin Quaker missionaries, recovered in the concept of spiritual hyphenation a key to interpreting Northern Irish writers, whatever their cultural and denominational backgrounds.

The Medusa's Gaze

In personal as well as cultural terms, MacNeice was doomed to paradox. The son of the Church of Ireland rector of Carrickfergus, later a Bishop, who espoused the cause of Home Rule in a fiercely Loyalist congregation, he soon learnt to negotiate that intercalated and imaginary region with what Brown called a 'self-protective reserve . . . a fundamental distrust of experience, of relationships'[8] which could only have been reinforced by the early death of a loved mother. MacNeice indeed attributed his own prevailing melancholy to that event, writing in 1940 in the poem 'Autobiography', 'When I was five the black dreams came; / Nothing after was quite the same'.[9] If MacNeice's recurrent mood was that of muted paranoia, less hysterical than Yeats's, it had similar sources in an equivocal cultural patrimony. Brown saw the question of ambivalent nationality as central, writing of MacNeice's 'blend of dismay and ineradicable love' for a country which seemed to shrug off his advances with a mixture of obloquy and sly neglect. It seemed that, whenever MacNeice tried to speak to Ireland, in the words of 'Autobiography', 'Nobody, nobody was there' to reply. This sense of an unreciprocated attempt at dialogue invites parallels with Denis Devlin's unequivocally Catholic and 'Irish' preoccupation with Pascal's unresponsive *deus absconditus*, and suggests that Devlin's experience, as a child of the Irish-Scottish diaspora, might also have an implicit politico-cultural dimension.

Ontologically insecure, 'afraid… of being spilled', as his Oxford friend John Hilton wrote of him in an appendix to *The Strings are False*, MacNeice sought in *form* a displacement of the lived contradictions of a world torn between extremes of fixity and flux, allegiance and exile. As Brown demonstrated, his poems reveal him to be a perpetual gazer through windows that interpose a protective glaze between rawly vulnerable consciousness and a rawly unregenerate world. His language itself, replete with paradox and irony, antithesis and oxymoron, and a parenthesis-laden syntax, calls attention to its own mediating intervention in the encounter of self and world. Images fade and merge into each other without finality, reminding the self of its own factitiousness and finitude, dissolving its most cherished absolutes in a pervasive epistemological scepticism. The reassuring caducity of the scene presented by cinematograph and train-window, those recurrent tropes of the always-travelling self, paradoxically exacerbates and relieves the anxiety of the excluded, recasting the special fate into a universal dilemma. 'We cannot cage the minute / Within its nets of gold', he wrote in 'The Sunlight on the Garden', in *The Earth Compels* (1938), cannot, in the nature of things, transfix the moving picture in its artificial frame.

MacNeice's stance was that of the quizzical Kantian, interrogating the void between the evanescent moving film of phenomena and an unknowable *Ding-an-sich* lurking within the menacing surfaces of sea and land and people, and the wind prowling around the house in a poem such as 'House on a Cliff'. The divided nature of the self here, registering internally a displaced, subjective echo of the external violence, is figured in images in which external events and their subjective appropriation are simultaneously joined and distinguished in perception: 'Indoors the sound of the wind. Outdoors the wind.' One of his most anthologised poems, 'Snow' casts this interface of inner and outer in initially more positive terms, seeing the interior of the room 'suddenly rich' in the juxtaposition of pink roses inside and 'Spawning snow' outside its bay-window. Yet, though 'collateral', the two images are also 'incompatible'. The world may be 'Incorrigibly plural', and the self may feel momentarily elated by 'The drunkenness of things being various'. But such plurality is also menacing, catching the self unawares, 'suddener than we fancy it', 'crazier', with 'more of it than we think'. It is not surprising therefore that by the last stanza it is the antithetical contradictoriness of a world 'more spiteful and gay than one supposes' that prevails, leaving the self anxiously transfixed, like the window-pane, between snow and roses, all the organs of sense, tongue, eyes, ears, hands, themselves the disputed, intercalated, displaced place between inner and outer. For the world of phenomena is founded in a terrifying emptiness – silence, absence, death. The wafer-thin film of appearances conceals murderous depths. MacNeice knew that the window-glass could crack, to let in 'What looms behind / The fragile fences of our mind' ('Letter from India'). He toyed with that horror, fascinated with the nightmare within the commonplace, which erupts when 'The lid is off', and recounting, with a strange exhilaration, for example, the liberating destruction of the Blitz; but he kept the lid firmly on.

Expelled from 'the blessedness of fact' ('Ode') by his sceptical intelligence, he was driven by a perennial nostalgia to seek that plane beyond the quotidian which would make sense of what *Autumn Journal* calls 'All this debris of day-to-day experience', on tiptoes 'hankering after Atlantis' ('Leaving Barra'), after 'what was lost when the ballet curtain fell' ('Autumn Sequel'). Yet he remained stubbornly convinced of the immanence of value, struggling pragmatically to 'Conjure value in passing and out of the passing', and finally finding in death and denial themselves the ultimate validation of life. Even his choice of the parable as a mode reflects this conviction, creating a world of placid empirical surfaces with unplumbed allegoric depths.

MacNeice saw the ego as both gift and perplexity, reiterating the everyday discovery that selfhood cuts one off from the rest of the universe. Death became, thus, 'a necessary horizon', and, in a striking echo of Devlin's Jansenist attitudes, that peculiarly Calvinist inflection of humility, a business arrangement: 'I fully admit my rent is due.' If the world snatches away happiness, descending darkly at moments of isolation and exposure, it is nevertheless a world with which he seeks reconciliation, for 'we lose ourselves / In finding a world outside'. The desire for that murderous indifferent world, for some deeper communion with it, lies as the nagging Irish residue within MacNeice's itinerant cosmopolitan scepticism, an unfulfilled aspiration after grace which was, in one sense, a longing to come home. One of his most powerful poems, in part because it seems to contain unresolved, unresolvable personal material, is 'Perseus', about which he wrote in his study *Modern Poetry* (1938):

> I am describing a mood of terror when everything seems to be unreal, petrified – hence the Gorgon's head, which dominates this poem... In such a mood, both when a child and when grown-up, I remember looking in mirrors and *(a)* thinking that my own face looked like a strange face, especially in the eyes, and *(b)* being fascinated and alarmed by the mysterious gleams of light *glancing* off the mirror. And, lastly, a mirror is a symbol of nihilism via solipsism.[10]

That last paradoxical binary says it all: nihilism, the total expunging of all value and of objective existence itself, is reached via solipsism, the total absorption of everything external into a voracious subjectivity. The poem itself operates through a structural confusion of self and other, subject and object. The mirror is 'full of eyes, / The ancient smiles of men cut out with scissors and kept in mirrors', evoking ideas of castration, the fathers, the generations of defeated sons – with that punning play on 'sun' – the living fullness of being reduced to flat two-dimensional simulacra. What strides out of the mirror, however, towards the threatened subject, is its own omnipotent reflection, become a party to that Other and its castrating agent:

> Ever to meet me comes, in sun or dull,
> The gay hero swinging the Gorgon's head,
> And I am left, with the dull drumming of the sun, suspended and dead.

The doubleness here, in which omnipotence and impotence coalesce, speaks of what T. S. Eliot in a different context observed of *Hamlet*, that play about fathers and sons, murderous patrimonies and parricidal filial obligations, that it is 'dominated by an emotion which is inexpressible, because it is in *excess* of the facts as they appear', 'the buffoonery of an emotion which can find no outlet in action... The intense feeling, ecstatic or terrible, without an object or exceeding its object... which every person of sensibility has known'.[11] A poem such as 'Perseus' reveals what happens in the psyche when the verbal displacements no longer work, when paradox as a verbal strategy comes face to face with the violent, irreconcilable actualities of a riven culture. The way out, then, seems to lie in that petrifaction which is the curse and blessing of the Medusa's gaze, so that to remain 'suspended', in abeyance between two worlds is also, almost thankfully, to be emotionally dead.

Defying the Sirens

There is an early poem of MacNeice's, little more than an exercise, which Geoffrey Grigson chose to place beside one by Auden at the start of the first issue of *New Verse* in 1933. 'Upon this beach' is, in cadence and idiom, pure Auden, its last line a give-way ('And boarding bus be jolly') and its antepenultimate vocative ('Turn therefore inland, tripper') an echo of Auden's recently published 'Who stands, the crux left of the watershed', with its command, 'Go home, now, stranger, proud of your young stock'.[12] Itself a moment of passage like that of which it speaks, it reveals how one poet can mediate another back to himself, throwing considerable light on the incestuous intertextuality of the 'Auden group'. For 'Upon this beach', also points forwards three years to the poem that was to provide both the English title, *Look, Stranger!* and the American one, *On This Island*, for Auden's massively influential 1936 collection, 'Look, stranger, at this island now'.[13]

Almost in direct refutation of MacNeice's poem, Auden took up the challenge of its middle stanza, which laments the inability of any artist in any medium to represent by any device the sound of the sea, to demonstrate that here at least was *il miglior fabbro* who could pull off the trick. When it comes to describing the indescribable, Auden's poem is all hands-on, calling up 'the pluck / And knock of the tide' with onomatopoeic bravura, superbly confident of its virtuoso ability to represent the sea's falling wall with all the devices at its command, including a word-splitting enjambment ('the suck- / ing surf'). Supremely sure of his Faustian power to arrest the moment, the poem's speaker, who may also be its addressee, is not some casual tripper but the monarch of all he surveys, come to claim his inheritance, standing stable before a world subordinate to his youthful mastery, where the leaping light exposes the whole scene for his delight alone. In Auden's poem, the provisionality and momentariness are all out there in the world of objects. The subject pauses not hesitantly but in leisurely assurance in order more fully to enjoy what is rightly his, now and in the future, in order that 'the full view / Indeed may

enter / And move in memory'. In contrast with MacNeice's poem, the changing world is appropriated to an imperious consciousness that saunters through
it like the ships of the last line, that verb indicating the difference between
Auden's upper middle class assurance and MacNeice's sense of his own – as
he saw it – anxious lower middle class provinciality, a mere 'day tripper' in a
world where he has to urge himself to 'be jolly'.

And yet, is all this diffidence really genuine? Another, more substantial
poem of MacNeice's, 'Train to Dublin', in 1934 repeated the motif, opening
characteristically with the poet moping that 'I can no more gather my mind up
in my fist' than the shadow of the train's smoke on the grass. But it moves on
to a more complex proposition. All over the world, he says, people are toast-
ing the king, but 'I give you the incidental things which pass / Outward
through space exactly as each was'. The last clause leaves ambiguous whether
it is the passing outward or the giving which is exact. This is no mere verbal
laxity, for one of the things the poet gives, in toast or benefaction, is that previously unrepresentable sea:

> And I give you the sea and yet again the sea's
> Tumultuous marble,
> With Thor's thunder or taking his ease akimbo,
> Lumbering torso, but finger-tips a marvel
> Of surgeon's accuracy.

We might wonder just whose finger-tip accuracy is celebrated here. Is it the
Norse father-god, an image shared with Auden and shortly to be visited at home
in the trip they made together, to produce the poems of the jointly authored
Letters from Iceland (1937) and of MacNeice's *The Earth Compels* (1938)? Or is it
the supposedly ineffectual poet himself, recalling that 'surgeon's idea of pain'
Auden set up as a model in the 1932 poem which was to become the 'Prologue'
of *On This Island*? MacNeice may go on to say, in conclusion, 'I would like to
give you more but I cannot hold / This stuff within my hands and the train goes
on', but the duplicity of this posture has been signalled in an earlier stanza, with
its guarded confession, half exonerated by the raffish candour and the generalising 'we':

> At times we are doctrinaire, at times we are frivolous,
> Plastering over the cracks, a gesture making good,
> But the strength of us does not come out of us.

MacNeice, in fact, is pretty good at plastering over the cracks with artful
gestures. All those rueful confessions of verbal inadequacy, of inability to
'cage the minute / Within its nets of gold', scarcely dissemble a consummate
mastery in turning the world of appearances into the fool's gold of poetry.

'Our God Bogus', an essay MacNeice wrote for the second and last issue of *Sir Galahad*, the Oxford journal he edited, picked up the 1920s neologism, 'bogus', redolent of fashionable post-bellum disenchantment and cynicism, to defend that world against the assaults of a positivist science:

> Easily down-cast, over-ridden by scepticism, we are told 'The apple you are eat-
> ing is mere appearance excepting the pips; *they* are the reality'; and the apple
> promptly loses its flavour for us. Yet we should have got past judging things by
> their cores or intestines or origins or atoms. We should say rather: 'No doubt you
> are right and those things are the real. So much the better for the apparent, the
> superficial, the conventional… Thank God for Make-Believe.' [14]

The image deployed to refute such crude reductionism pointedly begs the question. Lurking like a worm at the core of this analogy, possibly, is that scientific illuminator of nature and nature's laws, the alumnus of Anthony Blunt's Trinity College, Sir Isaac Newton. Auden was shortly to use the image of Newton's apple 'falling towards England' more positively, making gravity a metaphor for the 'eternal tie' of an ineluctable patriotism, in the 1932 poem which was to become the 'Prologue' to *Look, Stranger!* In the politically disaffected 1930s, the concept of the 'bogus' was recruited to a specifically leftist discourse by those MacNeice dismissed, after a boozy visit to a Blunt who 'had now gone Marxist', as infantile fantasists of the Left. Cambridge, he wrote in *The Strings Are False* about this visit, 'was still full of Peter Pans but all the Peter Pans were now talking Marx'.[15] Judging things by their cores had turned into self-satisfied and superior taunts which contrasted superstructural illusions with the realities of the material base. Since, for MacNeice, poetry, love, and all that made life worth living subsisted in that 'superstructure', the 'bogus' remained for him the true element of human existence. The poem 'Passage Steamer', recalling that Thirties leftist rebuke about rearranging the deck-chairs on the Titanic, acknowledges the effective power of that 'material base':

> Upon the decks they take beef tea
> Who are so free, so free, so free,
> But down the ladder in the engine-room
> (Doom, doom, doom, doom)
> The great cranks rise and fall.

Even here, though, art transforms the materialist critique in that splendid onomatopoeic parenthesis. The poem ends with the world made grey and vacuous not by Marxist dialectic but by the absence of the beloved. The lost boys still needed their Wendys.

Throughout the 1930s MacNeice seemed to be engaged in continuous argument with some internalised pseudo-Marxist voice of conscience and reproach. While he was always ready to concede his own compromised position as a petty-bourgeois intellectual, waiting as in 'June Thunder' for the cleansing downpour that would 'Break [...] the blossoms of our overrated fancies / Our old sentimentality and whimsicality', he usually got the better of the argument. Jon Stallworthy was probably right in his 1995 biography[16] to suggest that Auden is the addressee of the 1933 poem 'To a Communist' (though Blunt might be another candidate). It reads like a direct response to Auden's 'A Communist to Others', published in *The Twentieth Century* the previous autumn. MacNeice sounds sure enough of himself here, speaking of the Communist's thoughts like snow engrossing and unifying all the petty particulars of grass and stones, but like snow rapidly vanishing. His closing advice has an almost patronising assurance, underlined by the camp vocative, 'my dear': before announcing the millennium his Communist should consult the barometer, for 'This poise is perfect but maintained / For one day only'.

The falling barometer is one of MacNeice's most personal metaphors, from one of his earliest poems, 'Glass Falling', written in 1926, a year in which the General Strike presaged stormy times to come ('the frown / Is coming down of heaven / Showing a wet night coming'), to the notorious prophetic conclusion of the satiric 'Bagpipe Music' in 1937: 'The glass is falling hour by hour, the glass will fall for ever, / But if you break the bloody glass you won't hold up the weather.' The contrast between the accurate subjective monitoring of events and the powerlessness of that subject to affect them by what MacNeice elsewhere called smashing the aquarium is symptomatic here. The retrospective remarks in *The Strings Are False* are instructive:

> The strongest appeal of the Communist Party was that it demanded sacrifice; you had to sink your ego... I had a certain hankering to sink my ego, but was repelled by the proggishness of the Comrades... I joined them however in their hatred of the *status quo*. I wanted to smash the aquarium.[17]

It is MacNeice's rather than Auden's (or even more, Blunt's) 'poise' / pose which has stood the test of time. In hindsight the deft and conscientious diffidence with which his poetry records what 'An Eclogue for Christmas' in 1933 called 'all these so ephemeral things... somehow permanent like the swallow's tangent wings' seems like a vindication of the tentative liberalism it affirms. In this, it seems to be in sharp contrast to the doctrinaire confidences of Auden's political verse and subsequent 'defections', and Blunt's internal emigration as Soviet agent and establishment guru. MacNeice's is certainly a good trick. The fine poem which provides the title for *The Earth Compels*, 'The Sunlight on the Garden', may acknowledge in that eponymous phrase, 'The earth compels', the truth of the materialist claim that existence precedes essence. It may ruefully acknowledge that 'Our freedom as free lances /

Advances towards its end', but the self-criticism of the self-styled rentier intellectual, so sneered at by 1930s Communists, is worn with a certain dash. MacNeice wrote in 'Poetry To-day' that 'the common assumption that English poets have always been free lances is a gross misrepresentation. Those who admire the "freedom" of the free lance should take a course of Spinoza; the best English poets have been those most successfully determined by their context.' But, he added at once, 'The context must be a suitable one'. He thought, in 1935, that 'The English context is now more congenial to poets than it has been for a long time', and this, he had just suggested, was in part because 'The best poets of to-day belong to, and write for, cliques', ones which 'lately, have not been purely literary', but 'identify themselves with economic, political or philosophical movements', an identification 'more fruitful when it is voluntary'. [18]

Nevertheless, a few pages later he made it clear that he had 'no patience with those who think poetry for the rest of the history of mankind will be merely a handmaid of communism', though 'This intoxication with a creed is, however, a good antidote to defeatist individualism'. [19] He is, then, in this poem, as always, having it both ways, 'not expecting pardon', in fact 'Hardened in heart anew' to cling to his heartfelt illusions. For, after all, 'The sky was good for flying', defying alike the church bells and 'every evil iron / Siren and what it tells' – defying, that is, both uncritical faith in the status quo and the same dialectical sirens of rejection and revolt which, in the opening line of Auden's 'A Communist to Others', had been a clarion call for the 'Comrades, who when the sirens roar...'. The factory sirens of the modern world are for MacNeice the classical scholar also, and primarily, the sirens of Greek myth, whose barely resistible, haunting voices tempt the mariner to his doom.

Empty Boxes

In an uncollected poem, MacNeice wrote that 'I remember the illusion of Persons. / There is no person. / I live in an empty box full of frauds'. [20] His prefatory note to the book-length sequence *Autumn Journal* speaks, defensively or combatively according to how we read it, of the poem's 'over-statements and inconsistencies' and of how 'In a journal or a personal letter a man writes what he feels at the moment; to attempt scientific truthfulness would be – paradoxically – dishonest'. [21] But what impresses most about the poem is the consistency with which a narratorial persona holds together all the evanescent, conflicting, 'paradoxical' and, no doubt, sometimes fraudulent moods and motives, effortlessly locating them in the contexts of personal and public life with a sure sense of their importance and their abidingness, in a way which makes it still one of the most illuminating accounts of how people really thought and felt in the 1930s, as accurate and authoritative in its way as Mass Observation. (With characteristic Bloomsbury myopia, Virginia Woolf dismissed the book in her essay 'The Leaning Tower' as 'feeble as poetry' but 'interesting as autobiography'.)

'It is the nature of this poem to be neither final nor balanced', MacNeice wrote in that prefatory note, in what amounts to the declaration of a whole poetic: 'For this reason I shall probably be called a trimmer by some and a sentimental extremist by others' – once again positioning himself at the impossible interface of irreconcilable interpretations. The concession, withdrawn as uttered, takes on in advance some inner voice of marxisant rebuke, insisting that 'poetry in my opinion must be honest before anything else and I refuse to be "objective" or clear-cut at the cost of honesty'.[22] But the apparent conflict here, between 'objectivity' (or '"objectivity"') and 'honesty' is an ideologically conditioned one, growing out of that Stalinist identification of the 'objective' with whatever was the current Party line, and of the 'subjective' with any deviation from it, particularly in the name of that 'illusion of Persons' to which bourgeois intellectuals were regularly prone. MacNeice tried, inevitably, to reconcile these murderously actual as well as discursive conflicts (life-and-death conflicts, and not mere conflicts of terminology) by paradox, just as in his study of Yeats or as, in his last and unduly neglected critical work, *Varieties of Parable* (1965),[23] he deployed the concept of a 'double-level' writing, not only parable but symbolism, allegory, fable, fantasy and myth, to reconcile truth claims with the 'illusion' of the aesthetic or of personal experience. He may have called his autobiography, with a coy admonitory smile to the reader, *The Strings Are False*, but the confession itself is disarming, persuading us of the sincerity and urge for the truth of this petty-bourgeois who recognises his own boxful of frauds. Not for nothing was Anthony Blunt his oldest friend. But what emerges from a comprehensively documented biography such as Jon Stallworthy's, through all the emotional upheavals, the career shifts, drinking bouts and moral tergiversations, is the sheer consistency of the personality gathered together in the box called 'Louis MacNeice'.

As for MacNeice's sense of his own social and cultural determinations, he is more acute than most Thirties marxists in setting the socio-economic scene for his own stage entrance as the archetypal liberal intellectual, full of the bad faith of his spiritual hyphenation and interstitiality, keen to demonstrate that he has been there before them. The sense of cultural betweenness that pervades the poems is set out programmatically with some sophistication in the potted autobiography of 'Carrickfergus', the strategically placed opening poem of *The Earth Compels*:

> I was born in Belfast between the mountain and the gantries
>   To the hooting of lost sirens and the clang of trams:
> Thence to Smoky Carrick in County Antrim

> Where the bottle-neck harbour collects the mud which jams
> The little boats beneath the Norman castle,
>   The pier shining with lumps of crystal salt;
> The Scotch Quarter was a line of residential houses
>   But the Irish Quarter was a slum for the blind and halt.

What is most striking in these artful antitheses is the balance of inclusions and omissions. There is the country and the industrial city, implicitly naturalised and, as Stallworthy points out discussing its sequel, 'Carrick Revisited', given a familial gloss as his mother's 'pre-natal mountain' and his father's sea. And there is the metropolitan and the parochial. But though the latter has a rustic charm, its myth is in turn deconstructed by industrial pollution (brooks running yellow with effluence) which ironises the self-congratulation of those upper class 'residential houses'. Scotch (i.e. Unionist) salubriousness is juxtaposed with Irish (i.e. Nationalist) squalor but both are placed under the thumb of the imperious foreigner (once Norman, now English), while across the lough is the really privileged poshness of Bangor, looking down on them all. Beyond all this lies the European war, figured by the prison ship full of Germans in the harbour. But the final displacement undoes the lot, moving out from between the Anglo-Irish antitheses to a mainland that puts them all in parenthesis. At school in Dorset, the parental world 'Contracted into a puppet world of sons'. This derealising reduction cuts in both directions, estranging the subject both from the world he has left, distanced, belittled, and from the world he has joined, 'Far from the mill girls, the smell of porter, the salt-mines / And the soldiers with their guns' – the last two phrases turning memory into a sly prolepsis of a 1930s which updated both these images. As 'Carrick Revisited' says, he was 'Torn before birth from where my fathers dwelt, / Schooled from the age of ten to a foreign voice'. It is not in these originary places but in the uprootings from them that the reality of the rootless subject can be found. He is not the 'topographical frame' in which he is 'dumbfounded to find myself', but the congeries of displacements that emerges from the succession of superseded frames, always passing on, passing through, speaking in a voice whose foreignness is the guarantee of his freedom as a freelance. The box may be empty, but it may be that it also contains Schrödinger's cat – not that we can ever know.

The chronicle of MacNeice's life is a biography of betweens, as if he really were that vagrant scholar gipsy whose persona he adopts in so many poems. The poems 'Belfast' and 'Birmingham', where he was for some years a lecturer in E. R. Dodds's Classics department, are juxtaposed in Dodds's edition of the *Collected Poems* as if the Scylla and Charybdis between which this Anglo-Irish Ulysses must slip. But *Autumn Journal* recalls an altogether more slippery passage, observing

> That having once been to the University of Oxford
>> You can never really again
> Believe anything that anyone says and that of course is an asset
>> In a world like ours,
> Why bother to water a garden
>> That is planted with paper flowers?

Not an obvious or necessary conclusion to draw from an Oxford education, but one inevitable, perhaps, if the poet is both to have his cake and bite the hand that feeds him. The pose, making disclaimers equally in both directions, is one that suited MacNeice down to the ground. It produced some of his finest and his most symptomatic poetry, justifying the assertion of an Auden himself about to turn, in 1941, that 'poetry might be defined as the clear expression of mixed feelings', which is what makes the poet inevitably, in Auden's term, a 'double man', sheepishly acknowledging his trade-offs between trimming and extremism, the doctrinaire and the frivolous, the archetypal – Joyce's phrase – gay deceiver.

The charm and the achievement of the man, as of the poetry, are best captured in Auden's elegy for MacNeice, 'The Cave of Making'.[24] Self-confessedly an 'egocentric monologue', the poem nevertheless offers an anthropological biography as much Auden's as MacNeice's. Both men, the poem says, became self-conscious at a moment when

> the Manor still was politically numinous:
>> both watched with mixed feelings
> the sack of Silence, the churches empty, the cavalry
>> go, the Cosmic Model
> become German, and any faith if we had it, in immanent virtue died.

For the pre-war MacNeice, the bourgeois subject constructed as a fantasy projection of selfhood was simply plastering over the cracks of a crumbling manor. In the post-war era, it was more often a question of getting plastered. Increasingly, those cracks turned out to be not structural at all, but merely the signs of settlement. MacNeice could write, a year before his death, in 'Memoranda to Horace', of how the monuments of poetry were 'Weaker and less of note than a mayfly / Or a quick blurb for yesterday's detergent'. But Auden's shrewd memento, implicating MacNeice in his own youthful indiscretions, tells a different story, going one better on MacNeice's Oxford disenchantments: 'we shan't', Auden wrote, 'not since Stalin and Hitler, / trust ourselves ever again: we know that, subjectively, / all is possible'. A whole history of mixed feelings and double dealings is encapsulated in that weasel word 'subjectively', a year after MacNeice's death, and it goes to the heart of his writing. For if the word warns on the one hand against confusing subjective wishes with the horses of a real and objective history, it reminds on the other that the Stalin and Hitler who murdered the 'merely subjective' in the name of history's iron objectivities, had themselves, by 1964, vanished into what Auden called 'History's criminal noise', while the truest feignings of poetry survive:

> especially here, where titles
> from *Poems* to *The Burning Perch* offer proof positive
> of the maker you once were, with whom I
> once collaborated, once at a weird Symposium
> exchanged winks as a juggins
> went on about Alienation.

MacNeice himself offered a less grandiose, more troubling image for the subject's self-deluding persistence. The poem 'Budgie' provides the title to his final volume, *The Burning Perch* (1963). Its cage a stage, the bird dotes on its own image in the mirror, at once self-absorbed and unaware that its loved object is merely its own reflection. Beyond, galaxies are banked on galaxies; here, the perch is burning beneath him. Selfhood, however, requires that each self this day does its duty, stands firm at the post of itself:

> But the budgerigar was not born for nothing,
> He stands at his post on the burning perch –
> I twitter Am - and peeps like a television
> Actor admiring himself in the monitor.

Except, of course, that, unlike the budgie, the poem, ever so gently mocking us with that boy – call him Louis MacNeice – who stood once on the burning deck, gives a knowing wink.

NOTES

1. Louis MacNeice, *The Poetry of W.B. Yeats* (London: Faber and Faber, 1941), pp. 45–6.
2. W. B. Yeats, 'A General Introduction for My Work', in *Essays and Introductions* (London: Macmillan, 1961) p. 509.
3. MacNeice, *Yeats*, p. 47.
4. Louis MacNeice, *The Strings Are False* (London: Faber and Faber, 1965), p. 226.
5. Robert Graves, 'From the Embassy', *Poems 1953* (London: Cassell, 1953).
6. Tom Paulin, *Ireland and the English Crisis* (London: Faber and Faber, 1984), p. 75.
7. Stephen Gwynn, *Experiences of a Literary Man* (London: Butterworth, 1926), p. 11; cited in Terence Brown, *Louis MacNeice: Sceptical Vision* (Dublin: Gill and Macmillan, 1975), p. 10.
8. Brown, *Louis MacNeice*, p. 8.
9. Louis MacNeice, *The Collected Poems* (London: Faber and Faber, 1966). Except where otherwise indicated, all the poems cited here can be found in this volume.
10. Louis MacNeice, *Modern Poetry: A Personal Essay* (London: Oxford University Press, 1938), pp. 174–5
11. T. S. Eliot, 'Hamlet', in *Selected Essays* (London: Faber and Faber, 1951), pp. 145–6.
12. W. H. Auden, *Poems* (London: Faber and Faber, 1930).
13. W. H. Auden, *Look, Stranger!* (London: Faber and Faber, 1936).

14. Louis MacNeice, 'Our God Bogus', in *Sir Galahad* 2 (14 May 1929), pp. 3–4.
15. MacNeice, *The Strings Are False*, p. 156.
16. Jon Stallworthy, *Louis MacNeice* (London: Faber and Faber, 1995), p.154.
17. MacNeice, *The Strings Are False*, p. 146.
18. Louis MacNeice, 'Poetry To-day', in Geoffrey Grigson (ed.), *The Arts To-day* (London: The Bodley Head, 1935), pp. 30–31.
19. Ibid., p. 44.
20. Published in *This Quarter*, vol. 4 (June 1932), pp. 610–11.
21. Louis MacNeice, *Autumn Journal* (London: Faber and Faber, 1938), p. 7.
22. Ibid., p. 8
23. Louis MacNeice, *Varieties of Parable* (Cambridge: Cambridge University Press, 1965).
24. W. H. Auden, *About the House* (London: Faber and Faber, 1966).

VI

Periphery of Incident:
John Montague

Going Home or Passing By

The agenda set by Douglas Hyde's address to the National Literary Society in Dublin in 1892, for creating 'an Irish nation on Irish lines' instead of an anglicized one 'imitating England and yet apparently hating it', continued to haunt Irish poetry throughout the twentieth century. For Hyde, speaking of 'The Necessity for De-Anglicizing Ireland', the recovery of the Gaelic tongue was the only way to expel the English from the soul of Ireland. Until this had happened, the Irish consciousness would remain a colonised one, the very language in which it found self-definition betraying it to its enemy. The project failed, of necessity, like all utopian fantasies, but the trope of an occupied language persisted. Stephen Dedalus takes his cue from Hyde when, tapping his forehead in *Ulysses,* he proclaims 'In here it is I must kill the Priest and the King'. So, too, did Yeats in 1901, distressed at the upper class writer's choice 'not to express but to exploit his country', when he contemplated a similar symbolic parricide, in which the son turns in Oedipal revolt against the false father of the language which has adopted him: 'Moses was little good to his people until he had killed an Egyptian; and for the most part a writer or public man of the upper classes is useless to this country till he has done something that separates him from his class.'[1]

Despite the work of such poets as Michael Hartnett, that linguistic revolution was never really on the cards as a majority choice. But its ghost has continued to walk abroad. Indeed, it could be argued that, at the level of style as well as theme, it has provided some of the key strengths and insights of twentieth-century Irish poetry, inserting a troublesome but productive disturbance into what might otherwise have become the complacent self-congratulation of a partially successful political transformation. The language of these writers has been, as it were, haunted by the ghostly presences of an older and forfeit tongue. Joyce and Yeats both testify to the power and authority of this disturbing presence, in a writing which recurrently explores and embodies in the very contradictoriness of its language the contradictions of a divided Ireland.

Historically, the Irish poet has imagined him or herself fretting out, in the shadow of a usurper's language, the contradictions of an unresolved cultural and political identity. Displacement as a physical and demographic condition has been a recurrent theme of Irish poetry, as of its criticism. Less attention has been given to the idea of language as itself a locus of displacement, in Freud's sense of the word: a terrain or tract where the writer seeks the imaginary resolution of real conflicts, but is reinstated in the very process in the same closed circuit of discourse. Yeats's antithetical vision provided the paradigm for one version of this kind of displacement activity, transforming the contradictions of an historical world – political dissension, class conflict, civil war, religious division – into rhetorical strategies and a dramaturgy of conflict that made a virtue of necessity, but at the same time constituted an absolute horizon of thought.

Denis Devlin recognised the problematic nature of this strategy when he spoke of the 'frightened antinomies' of Irish identity, recognisably kin to MacNeice's 'ould antinomies'. Joyce in *Ulysses* had sought to move beyond the simple binaries of such a vision, but that novel remains dominated by an implicit, reductive dialectic (Dedalus: Bloom: Molly), though this is repeatedly subverted by the actual multiplicity and polyphony of the text, as in the 'Wandering Rocks' sequence. The intuition of *Finnegans Wake* that escape from the nightmare of history lies in the *jouissance* of an incorrigibly plural language ('Here Comes Everybody'), is repeatedly rescinded by the return of the repressed binary (Adam and Eve, Ham and Shem, etc). Nevertheless, Joyce had grasped the essential problem: a language of antithesis, dialectic, confrontation has been the untranscended ideological boundary of Irish thought. The rhetoric of antithesis becomes the metaphor which not only transcribes but underwrites a political deadlock.

Joyce's literal emigration from Ireland becomes, then, the figure of an alternative linguistic strategy to Yeats's internal displacement. In order to forge an uncreated conscience, the ideological frontiers of a language and a culture have to be examined from the outside. This is the movement, for example, of Heaney's *Station Island*, where Joyce, in the last sequence of the title poem, appears as an admonitory and exemplary ghost, stretching out a 'helping hand' in 'alien comfort'. The advice he offers harks back explicitly to that encounter in *Portrait* with the old English Dean which provokes Dedalus's reflections on a language which is 'his before it is mine', what this poem jokingly alludes to as 'The Feast of the Holy Tundish'. The advice is unequivocal:

> 'Who cares,'
> He jeered, 'any more? The English language
> belongs to us. You are raking at dead fires,

a waste of time for somebody your age.
That subject people stuff is a cod's game,
infantile, like your peasant pilgrimage.

      ...Keep at a tangent.
When they make the circle wide, it's time to swim

out on your own and fill the element
with signatures on your own frequency,
echo soundings, searches, probes, allurements,

elver-gleams in the dark of the whole sea.'[2]

It is the whole sea of language, that leitmotiv of Joyce's writing from *Portrait* to *Wake*, adding a nautical edge even to the idea of the wake's verbal and performative celebration, which the poem prescribes, not a single shrunken river. This 'old father' speaks not just as a spokesman of the Liffey but as a cosmopolitan 'voice eddying with the vowels of all rivers', the voice of a distinctively postmodern heterogeneity. That sea represents an uncontainable plurality outside the circle of a prescriptive and proscriptive language, the self-congratulatory myths ('stuff' is powerfully dismissive) of a self-styled 'subject people'. One can relate creatively to that circle only at a tangent – an image which refuses closure, which heads off into unknown territories. That 'whole sea' cannot be foreclosed upon, but only sounded, searched, probed, its mermaid allurements and elver-gleams not finally graspable, but witnesses to a totality of language in which closure is always necessarily deferred.

Responding to this fecund plurality, the poet may 'fill the element / with signatures on [his] own frequency', but that word 'element', echoing through Heaney's work, makes it clear that such a filling does not issue in a fullness, a stuffed plenitude like that of 'That subject people stuff', which puts an end to difference. Rather what Joyce represents here, as Heaney himself observes in the lecture *Among Schoolchildren*,[3] is a patient attempt to 'deconstruct the prescriptive myths of Irishness'. Joyce rather than Yeats has attracted most attention from the post-structuralist criticism of the last few years precisely because, unlike the poet's, his work resists closure. Even the circle which a single 'riverrun' sentence draws around the *Wake* actually expands in a widening gyre, or runs off at a tangent into unfamiliar horizons, listening to the 'tale of distant nations', evading those nets spread to ensnare the soul. Heaney appears to have grasped the point that a deconstructive method, drawing on Derrida's warning against the deforming, constricting contours of the binary, can offer a language in which to theorise the break with the inheritance of Yeats.

In the last quarter of the twentieth century, poets, particularly in the North, have returned to this disputed border region – the topographies of

Irish politics constituting an inevitable model for conceptions of the self – increasingly with the conviction that such a predicament no longer constitutes an enabling disturbance, but has become what Medbh McGuckian calls an ideological 'traplight'. Foremost among these poets, its elder statesman, is John Montague, his own particularly conflicted linguistic 'birthright' a suggestive paradigm of a situation reflected in the work of many Northern writers. 'I happen to live in a country where the poet *has* a relationship with society, and has always had', Montague has said in interview: 'In the case of Ulster, to state the problem, to define the disease, to diagnose the disease, is at least helpful.'[4] His own writings record a lifetime's struggle to state, and diagnose, that problem.

In *The Dead Kingdom*[5] John Montague summarised the dilemma of an Irish poetry still fretting in the shadow of Yeats, speaking in 'The Plain of Blood' of the writer's temptation to romanticise conflict, in an 'evasive fiction', as a legendary, primordial feud, rather than 'wise imperial policy / Hurling the small peoples / against each other'. But it is not so much the pithy juxtaposition of literary and historical clichés here which goes to the root of the matter, as the subtle overlaying of cadences with which he concludes 'Wintry Dawn':

> Do pale horsemen still
> ride the wintry dawn?
> Above Yeats's tomb
> large letters stain
> Ben Bulben's side:
> *Britain, go home!*

Whatever the historical appositeness of the graffito, for Montague, as a Northern Catholic nationalist born in Brooklyn, it remains an Irish side which it stains, as the boar's tusk of the legend gashed the thigh of an Irish hero. And if 'Fionn's hand was stayed / by a poet, from slaying / the snoring MacMorna', it is the ghost cadence of a poet's last words, Yeats's epitaph (*'Horseman, pass by!'*), which here resonates within the Nationalist slogan. Beneath the engaged aggressivity of the writing, that is, lurks the siren voice of Yeats's aristocratic indifference, abstentionism and withdrawal. A cadence may be enough to arouse 'the indomitable Irishry', as Yeats had observed earlier in 'Under Ben Bulben', where this epitaph appears, with his reference to Mitchel's prayer, 'Send war in our time, O Lord!' Yeats repeated this bellicose call as a reproach to England, at a time when the contemporary British mantra, in the face of Hitler's expansionism, was Chamberlain's defeatist 'Peace in our time'. But here the idiom even at the level of its cadence has itself become an ideological traplight. Displaced into verse, as Yeats had recognised clearly enough in 'The Man and the Echo', what Montague calls, in the poem 'Red Branch', 'the iron circle of retaliation', here returns to plague the inventor.

Cultures of Constraint

There is something tight-lipped about John Montague's poetry, revealed even in the terse titles of his volumes and the repeated use of a short, abrupt line, where enjambment projects the reader into sudden peripeties and reversals, and the shifts of pace and meaning have the effect of a clipped, curt rebuff. Yet, within these constraints, the poetry can flower into an unexpected, lyric generosity. Not many poets, for example, could carry off successfully the Anglo-Saxon bluntness of 'Love, A Greeting', when it speaks of 'the strange / thing' that inhabits a woman, listing, in a very postmodern blazon, face, breasts, buttocks, and 'the honey sac / of the cunt'. [6]

It is the puritanical tautness of Montague's speech that can bring off such large gestures. Constriction is his native ground, admits the sequence 'Home Again' in *The Rough Field*.[7] Narrowness runs as a theme through his work, an expression of that bare past and 'bleak economic future' shared, as he has written, by all such peripheral and remote areas of Europe as Ulster, Brittany, the Scottish Highlands. It is this which marks him out clearly as a Northern Irish poet, despite the casual displacement of his Brooklyn birth. The 'Narrow huckster streets' of Belfast, 'All this dour, despoiled inheritance', together with the heritage of sectarian hatred, in 'a culture where constraint is all', have in 'Home Again' a precise, socio-economic origin: 'narrow fields wrought such division'. The 'Rough Field' which gives the name to this major collection is not just a translation of the Gaelic name for his native village, Garvaghey, but – in the words of an Afghan proverb which provides his epigraph – the summary of an historical destiny: 'I had never known sorrow, / Now it is a field I have inherited, and I till it.' This in turn, in 'The Bread God', he sees reproduced in 'the lean parish of my art.' Deracination, eking an existence on the peripheries, has been a major theme for Montague, from his first volume, *Forms of Exile* (1958), through to his latest work.

'A Lost Tradition', in *The Rough Field*, lamented the physical expropriation that went with the loss of the Gaelic language, for which no amount of 'school Irish' could compensate:

> The whole landscape a manuscript
> We had lost the skill to read,
> A part of our past disinherited.

The entire volume explored the consequences of this uprooting, spanning several hundred years of Irish history, while always relating the public events to the particular lives of individual people and families, including his own forebears. 'A Grafted Tongue' saw the linguistic loss not just as a metaphor for this larger dispossession, but its key event: 'To grow / a second tongue, as /

harsh a humiliation / as twice to be born.' The image, though, as we shall see later, has peculiarly personal implications for Montague.

In *A Slow Dance*[8] Montague moved away from history into the shadowier and more dubious realms of Celtic myth to explain the current violence of the North, resurrecting that ancient 'Black widow goddess' whose 'love-making / is like a skirmish' and who wears 'a harvest necklace of heads'. The move brought with it a loss of precisely that kind of acute historical particularity which distinguishes his best verse. It remains nevertheless an impressive volume. The 'slow dance' of the title is an atavistic ritual in which 'we move slowly / back to our origins', where fertility and massacre are intimately linked, uniting human and elemental cycles, pagan and Christian Ireland. If the poet is cast as 'the lucky dancer on thin ice' by news of his composer friend's impending death in 'Ó Riada's Farewell', there is a sense in which the dance is the 'sad, awkward / dance of pain' of all living on the grave of all the dead, in 'A Graveyard in Queens', and, ultimately, in 'Lament', the last poem in the volume, 'a lament so total / it mourns no one / but the globe itself / turning in the endless halls / of space'. Yet a leitmotiv is no substitute for an argument. When Montague imagistically links 'The whole world / turning in wet / and silence, a / damp mill wheel' in 'Sweeny' ('Sweeney' in the *Collected Poems*) and the 'sun's slow wheel' in 'Almost a Song' with the wheels of an overturned army lorry in 'Wheels Slowly Turning', there is an illicit collapsing of natural rhythms and human destructiveness which issues in that exasperated image of Irish history as a 'treadmill of helplessness' in the sequence 'The Cave of Night'.

'The Cave of Night' condenses Irish history into a series of vignettes in which the primitive human sacrifices of the ancient fire festival Samhain coexist with and explain the violence of the Falls Road. 'In dark November, / when the two worlds near each other', ordinary temporality is overthrown as the supernatural powers of the Sidhe invade the human world, to abduct mortals into their own realm, 'A land I did not seek / to enter. Pure terror'. In section II of the poem, time is telescoped. A levelling bathos defines the absurdity of the pagan blood-letting to the Cromm Cruaich:

> Here was raised
> a tall idol of savage fights…
>
> Well born Gaels lay prostrate
> beneath his crooked shape until
> gross and glittering as a cinema organ
> he sank back into his earth.

The suggestion that this is all some kind of home-made entertainment is given a macabre twist in section IV, in which the slow-motion unfolding of an explosion, stretching instants to eternity, reveals an unreal time stilled and yet still proceeding, beyond belief, from cosiness to atrocity. The punning play on 'trying', 'part', and 'separating' is gruesomely effective:

> A friendly hand places
> a warm bomb under
> the community centre
> where the last evacuees
> are trying a hymn.
> Still singing, they
> part for limbo, still
> tucking their blankets
> over separating limbs.

Yet it is not that 'brooding tumulus / opening perspectives beyond our Christian myth' in 'The Errigal Road' which is the real source of 'the violence troubling these parts'. There is a sense in which Montague's myth-making itself endorses the curt logic of those for whom 'A burst of automatic fire / solves the historical problem' ('Heroics'). The elegy 'Ó Riada's Farewell' sums up this perennial ambiguity. It is the composer's own Promethean 'playing with fire', with 'the darker harmonies' of section V ('Samhain'), which has released the demons of section VI ('Hell Fire Club'). He 'has / called them from defeat'; now, dying, 'a lucid beast fights against / a blithely summoned doom'. In its balancing of agency and evasion, that oxymoron is crucial: the dark fatality of events is a human choosing.

Montague has, in fact, a shrewd historical sense, as in the subtle discrimination of absences in the diptych 'Homes', where the 'soft flute note of absence' of 'Famine Cottage' redefines the 'Tennysonian solitudes of cliff / and waterfall' of 'Victorian Ireland', contrasting forced emigration with the privilege of the hunting lodge's absentee landlord. The irony is deliberate. In 'All Souls', repudiating Yeats's urbane fantasising in 'All Souls' Night', a family reunion of 'the dead and their descendants / Share in the necessary feast of blood'. All alike, the dead and the living, are revenants, framed by the poet's distancing vision 'in the chill oblong / Of the gilt mirror'. In 'At Last', in *The Dead Kingdom* (1984), that volume of recovery and renewal in the face of death, it is as the 'disembodied voice of 'a broadcast I had done' that the successful poet can 'at last' welcome a prodigal father home from America to Ireland. The abstractive distance of the returned expatriate father in such poems as the same volume's 'A Muddy Cup', recalling the poet's own Brooklyn childhood, lies behind both the mythic myopia and the anguished historical scepticism of Montague's middle period, epitomised by *A Slow Dance*.

Beginning Again

The love poems of Montague's volume *The Great Cloak* (1978) returned to the lucid, melodic airs of *Tides* and *A Chosen Light*, but the atmosphere had been darkened by the intervening, public violence, which now found its correlative in personal life. These poems are as much concerned with loss, jealousy, marital breakdown, and its humiliations and shames, as with the lyric celebration of love – 'that always strange moment / when the clothes peel away / (bark from an unknown tree)', as 'Do Not Disturb' puts it. The violence spoken of as inseparable from love in such a fine early poem as 'The Same Gesture' (*Tides*) is now felt more urgently, and as a greater threat. Only briefly, in the sequence of poems which explore the consciousness of the estranged wife, is any connection explicitly acknowledged between personal disintegration and the larger violence of the North, in 'She Writes'. But throughout Montague is groping towards a new understanding of the interdependence of the personal and the political, and their common roots in a harsh and souring history.

Such a quest can bring him desperately close to the unspeakable, to silence, shamefaced and appalled, as 'No Music' recognizes:

> To tear up old love by the roots,
> To trample on past affections:
> There is no music for so harsh a song.

The Dead Kingdom charts a journey north, along 'minor roads of memory', from Cork to Fermanagh, summoned by his mother's death to traverse a landscape dense with personal, historic and mythic associations. The volume itself is a 'dead kingdom', preserving in print 'things that are gone,' as 'Gone' puts it, sardonically accepting its own ultimate disappearance, like the library of Alexandria before it, and more recent 'substantial things / hustled into oblivion', down the maw of Spenser's 'goddess Mutability, / dark lady of Process, / our devouring Queen'. When individuals die, a unique 'world of sense & memory' vanishes with them. Races and nations, recalling *Ulysses*, are alike 'locked / in their dream of history,' subjective realms as 'fragile /as a wild bird's wing', bulldozer and butterfly alike ephemeral forms. Even the archaeological relics of ancient Ireland are now torn up by the mechanized peat-cutters that destroy the bog wholesale. Yet, as 'A Flowering Absence' suggests, the poet's own childhood experience of exile and fostering compels him to fill that emptiness, urged by a 'terrible thirst' for knowledge and love 'to learn something of that time / Of confusion, poverty, absence'. Thus the journey upstream to the source is also, as the last poem, 'Back', indicates, a journey to his own death. 'There is no permanence', one epigraph informs us. But another speaks of the need to discover the 'Source of lost knowledge', and, in the penultimate poem, 'A New Litany', it is the impulse to name which

94

provides those 'frail rope-ladders / across fuming oblivion' that offer 'A new love, a new / litany of place names', and allow the poet to return home, to 'a flowering presence'.

Return is also a motif of the volume *Mount Eagle* (1988),[9] which opens with the image of one salmon which 'returns, / a lord to his underwater kingdom', and of another dying, abdicating a polluted planet. This ecological lament runs through the volume, providing some of its most powerful writing. But the book closes in another, more hopeful return of the salmon in 'Survivor', where the old bare earth reappears, promising that 'Life might begin again' after all that human poison has been purged, and Fintan, a recurrent presence, finds himself turning into a salmon that returns from the ocean bottom to reclaim its own, recalling the legendary Finn who tasted of the salmon of knowledge.

The returns of this book are not mere nostalgia trips back to the origins. On the contrary, in a volume that is shot through with the hope of renewal, it is the *past* which returns to the *present*, sustaining and vivifying it. The cricket in 'Hearth Song' strikes up again as in his childhood. In 'A Real Irishman', a boyhood friend from across the religious divide turns up in a Belfast pub to save the embattled poet from 'A swirl of trouble' with two off-duty UDR men. A childhood memory in 'Turnhole' of a squat, coarse Jim Toorish caught splashing naked in a pool returns redeemed, cleansed of giggling prurience, in 'a satyr, laughing in / the spray at Florence'. And, in a sequence of sensually charged love poems celebrating the conjunction of May and September, Wordsworthian memories of youth's glad animal movements restore the ageing man, disclosing 'Secret wellsprings / of strength',

> those long, lovely
>
> leaps in the dark
> returning now to steady
> my mind, nourish
> my courage as
>
> No longer young
> I take your hand.

Growing a Second Tongue

'To be always at the periphery of incident / Gave my childhood its Irish dimension; drama of unevent', Montague observed in his 1993 sequence *Time in Armagh*. Montague's margins are in one sense the inevitable Irish ones: an early poem in *Forms of Exile* (1958) spoke of 'this island, at the sheltered edge of

Europe'; while 'Northern Lights' in *The Dead Kingdom* defined those margins more precisely as 'A stranded community, / haunted by old terrors' in a North 'neither Irish nor British', its natural hinterland / severed by the border'. Elegies for a recently dead mother, 'marginally living ... obsessed with dying, / now finally managed', these poems redefine that sense of margins, while ostensibly turning their back on 'this narrowing world / of bigotry and anger'. Yet what one notices, here as in the earlier poem, is that demonstrative, 'this' (so unlike Yeats's haughtily distancing 'that'), appropriating affiliation even as it denies it. And indeed *The Dead Kingdom*, as the title indicates, is as much about 'our dark island ... our sad land' in both its historic and mythic dimensions, as it is about his mother's death or the childhood and family histories that death calls up.

Montague knows intimately the politics of such severances, writing eloquently here as in *The Rough Field* of 'the embittered diaspora of / dispossessed Northern Republicans ... / a real lost generation' like his own father who, 'Stele for a Northern Republican' records, chose exile in a Brooklyn slum rather than 'a half-life in this / by-passed and dying place', returning home only in old age. Montague himself, however, born in New York to a mother who, unable to cope, fostered him out to real (and symbolic) wet-nurses, was soon shipped back to 'an older country, / transported to a previous century', forced to do time at the boarding school whose petty, marginal deprivations and brutalities are recorded in *Time in Armagh*.

'A Flowering Absence' in *The Dead Kingdom* attributes to this early maternal rejection 'that still terrible thirst of mine, / a thirst for love and knowledge'. Traditionally opposing absolutes are here paired, as in that Eros and Psyche motif which lay behind *The Great Cloak*'s terrible requiem for a broken marriage, in which an adulterous carnal lyricism joins an unlovely floundering self-pity, to exorcise the shade of a faithless mother by abandoning a faithful wife. But that rejection accounts, equally, for 'the stereoscopic lens / of a solitary childhood' which, in *The Dead Kingdom*, 'This Neutral Realm' (the same affectionate and dismissive demonstrative adjective) brings to bear on the 'divided allegiances' of an Ireland caught between 'a mock and a real war'. Driven Northwards, in his own image in 'Upstream', like a salmon pulled back to the source, Montague seeks in many of these poems that 'Source of lost knowledge' at the heart of dispossession, striving, in 'A Flowering Absence',

> to learn something of that time
> of confusion, poverty, absence.
> Year by year I track it down...
> seeking to manage the pain –
> how a mother gave away her son.

Echoing the immediately preceding 'Northern Lights' with its image of the mother managing her dying, 'manage' reminds us that the salmon returns to the source not only to spawn but also to die; and the poem too finds in uncovering 'the travail of my birth' only another cold trail:

> There is an absence, real as presence...
> All roads wind backwards to it.
> An unwanted child, a primal hurt.

In the same way, in 'Northern Lights', the seven-year-old child found in separate identity not liberation but a mortal wound, lying awake and singing to himself '*I / am I, and I must die*; / recognizing the self as / I feared the end of it'.

Taunted by an Irish schoolmistress for his 'outlandish accent', publicly hunted down to 'near speechlessness', as 'A Flowering Absence' records, the young Montague found language itself a barely crossable frontier, the real periphery of incident, reduced to 'Stammer, impediment, stutter' in a shadowy border country between Armagh and America, North and South, Britain and Ireland, his tongue for 'two stumbling decades' become 'a rusted hinge, until the sweet oils of poetry // eased it and grace flooded in.' Similarly, in 'Deo Gratias' in *Time in Armagh*, hounded for his stammer by a sadistic Dean, his unfaltering adolescent singing at high mass offers the shift of modality from speech to song as a metaphor for a more general transcendence. 'A Grafted Tongue' in *The Rough Field* had early made the connection between his own schoolboy ordeal and the condition of an Ireland forced

> To grow
> a second tongue, as
> harsh a humiliation
> as twice to be born.

The salving grace of poetry becomes, in 'A Flowering Absence' as elsewhere, the metaphor of a talking cure for the ravaged realm of Ireland itself, healing the 'Soft flute note of absence' of 'Famine Cottage', or exorcising the 'evasive fiction' which in 'The Plain of Blood' hurls the small peoples against each other in 'blind rituals of violence'. But 'Cassandra's Answer' in *Mount Eagle* reveals that it is not as easy as that, her unheeded prophecies that the small towns will burn falling from a thick tongue that 'longs / for honey's ease', in a world where 'a street will receive its viaticum // in the fierce release of a bomb'.

As this poem recognises, 'Roots are obstructions / as well as veins of growth'. *The Rough Field* had opened with a sequence called 'Home Again': but the Epilogue of that volume acknowledges that you can't go home again, that 'all my circling [is] a failure to return / to what is already going / going / GONE', the nationalist myth of 'man at home / in a rural setting' now a 'lost dream' under the auctioneer's hammer. *The Dead Kingdom* takes as epigraph a passage from the ancient Babylonian *Book of Gilgamesh*: 'There is no permanence. Do we build a house to stand for ever, do we seal a contract to hold for all time?' The subsection 'A Flowering Absence' finds in John Donne epigraphic consolation for this provisionality, a kind of renewal in annihilation itself: 'I am rebegot / Of absence, darkness, death: things which are not.' In such acknowledged absences, in the gaps between certainties, rather than in any dream of return to an originary presence, Montague locates that transitory home which alone may save us from the neighbourly murders recorded in A *Slow Dance*, where 'jungleclad troops / ransack the Falls' and that ironically 'friendly' hand places its convival 'warm' bomb under the community centre. Set against the pure terror of this 'land I did not seek / to enter', 'The Cave of Night' envisages a mythic 'final place' where a solitary being begins again its slow dance, not the supernatural realm of the Sidhe but some elemental, residual place of human existence.

The periphery of incident is not necessarily a bad place to be. 'Edge', the final poem of *The Great Cloak*, had spoken of finding 'a sheltering home' right on the margin, concluding that 'on the edge is best'. Montague's *Collected Poems*[10] ends with a hitherto uncollected 1995 sequence, 'Border Sick Call', about a winter journey along the Fermanagh-Donegal border, visiting patients with his doctor brother. 'Hereabouts, signs are obliterated', the poem begins. Not only the road signs, but the very processes of signification itself seem under erasure. It soon becomes clear that it is not just the recent snow but a more long-term violence that has done the obliterating: the Customs Post they pass through has been blown up twice. But on foot, their car snowbound, 'For hours... adrift from humankind', they may well have gone backwards and forwards across that sundering but undetectable border many times. An old man, their momentary host, tells them: "Sure we don't know where it starts / or ends up here'", the 'it' ambiguously referring as much to events in time as demarcations in space. The poem's, and the whole volume's, last words then ask the most pertinent question, poised, on the periphery of incident, between history and, it might seem, some timeless otherworld of snow-dazed enchantment: 'But in what country have we been?' But this, Montague might argue, is not where we end, but where we begin, yet again.

NOTES

1. W. B. Yeats, 'Samhain: 1901', in *Explorations* (New York: Macmillan, 1962), p. 83.
2. Seamus Heaney, *Station Island* (London: Faber and Faber, 1984).
3. Seamus Heaney *Among Schoolchildren* (Belfast: John Malone Memorial Committee, 1983), pp. 10–11.
4. John Montague, interview with Shirley Anders, *Verse*, 6 (1986), pp. 35; 37.
5. John Montague, *The Dead Kingdom* (Portlaoise: The Dolmen Press, 1984).
6. John Montague, *Tides* (Dublin: The Dolmen Press, 1971).
7. John Montague, *The Rough Field* (Dublin: The Dolmen Press, 1972).
8. John Montague, *A Slow Dance* (Dublin: The Dolmen Press: 1975).
9. John Montague, *Mount Eagle* (Dublin: The Gallery Press, 1988).
10. John Montague, *Collected Poems* (Oldcastle: The Gallery Press, 1995).

VII

Ghost Writing:
Seamus Heaney

Familiar and Foreign

Seamus Heaney first deployed Stephen Dedalus's reflections on his encounter with the old English dean, 'How different are the words "home", "Christ", "ale", "master" on his lips and on mine', as epigraph to 'The Wool Trade' in his third volume, *Wintering Out* (1972).[1] But the poem also attempted to deconstruct that mythic encounter, taking its own innocent title apart, to reveal a whole history of economic transformations, the social conflicts they generated, and the processes by which language inscribes the double dispossession Dedalus lamented.

Attributed to an unidentified speaker from Yeats's and MacNeice's background – that of the Protestant mercantile classes – the phrase seems to ramble 'warm as a fleece / Out of his hoard'. But it presumes an order of social and economic exploitation beyond its pastoral pleasantries, speaking to the Catholic Heaney not of soft names such as Bruges and merchants returned from the Netherlands, but of all those parishes where hills, flocks, streams, in Wordsworthian pastoral mode, 'conspired / To a language of waterwheels, / A lost syntax of looms and spindles'. Rural hamlets, transformed in the late eighteenth century by an emerging capitalist economy into thriving centres of production, were then plunged back into poverty again by the British embargo on wool exports, leaving as deposits an accumulated capital in the hands of a Protestant ascendancy, a rural hinterland locked in stagnation and marginality, and a language which preserves a history of power and oppression in every turn of speech.

The urban middle class Protestant's 'word hoard' outlived these losses, gaining from them. But, as, the subsequent poem 'Linen Town' and the sequence 'A Northern Hoard' make clear, for someone like Heaney, from the Catholic rural working class, the innocuous phrase bespeaks a more compelling economic necessity, as the closing lines of the poem indicate, in which the poet finds himself compelled or required (the word 'must' allowing either possibility) to speak of tweed, 'A stiff cloth with flecks like blood'. What Heaney grasps, in this early poem, is the extent to which language is preoccupied by politics, but also *displaces* the preoccupations of a larger political world. The struggle to come to terms with this displacement is a key impulse not only of his own but of much Northern poetry over the last forty years. The key to such a dilemma lies in the double-take, which Heaney has spent thirty years unravelling, contained in Dedalus's reflections on a language at once 'so familiar and so foreign', which 'will always be for me an acquired speech'.

Pinioned by Ghosts

The central premise of Seamus Heaney's first collection of literary essays, *Preoccupations: Selected Prose 1968–1978*, and of some of his earliest and now canonical poems, is that language, like the landscape, is always preoccupied: someone's been here before us. The much-anthologised 'Digging', the first poem of his first volume, *Death of a Naturalist* (1966),[2] initiated an originary analogy between spadework and writing, both forms of manual labour, in the process digging up Yeats's haunting image from 'Under Ben Bulben' of spades which 'thrust their buried men / Back in the human mind again'. 'Bogland', the last poem in *Door into the Dark* (1969),[3] Heaney later wrote in *Preoccupations*, 'set up – or rather, laid down – the bog as an answering Irish myth'[4] to that of the American frontier. In the process it also transformed Yeats's image by opening a frontier downwards, making the landscape as text an endless palimpsest of replacements, displacing all easy assumptions of an originary centre:

> Our pioneers keep striking
> Inwards and downwards.
>
> Every layer they strip
> Seems camped on before.
> The bogholes might be Atlantic seepage.
> The wet centre is bottomless.

That this is, like Yeats's, an image charged with an Oedipal anxiety about one's relation to the past is confirmed by Heaney's comment in *Preoccupations*, complete with its final Oedipal pride in recuperation, that

> What generated the poem about memory was something lying beneath the very floor of memory, something I only connected with the poem months after it was written, which was a warning that older people would give us about going into the bog. They were afraid we might fall into the pools in the old workings so

they put it about (and we believed them) that *there was no bottom* in the bog-holes. Little did they – or I – know that I would filch it for the last line of a book. (p.56)

That the Yeatsian echo is part of the unconscious of the text is confirmed by the paragraph which immediately follows, in which Heaney speaks of his poem 'Requiem for the Croppies', in the same volume. The poem, he says, looked back through the Easter rising of 1916, 'the harvest of seeds sown in 1798', to that earlier rebellion:

> The poem was born of and ended with an image of resurrection based on the fact that some time after the rebels were buried in common graves, these graves began to sprout with young barley, growing up from barley corn which the 'croppies' had carried in their pockets to eat while on the march. The oblique implication was that the seeds of violent resistance sowed in the Year of Liberty had flowered in what Yeats called the 'right rose tree' of 1916. I did not realize at the time that the original heraldic murderous encounter between Protestant yeoman and Catholic rebel was to be initiated again in the summer of 1969, in Belfast, two months after the book was published. (p. 56)

In the archaeology of Heaney's texts, however, that recognition, with all its sense of guilty complicity, was to issue in the harrowing images in *North* (1975)[5] of fossilized bodies exhumed from the Danish peat-bog, and staring up, reproachfully textualised, from the pages of P. V. Glob's *The Bog People* under such names as Tollund and Grauballe Man. This return of the repressed, conflating Viking ritual slaughters with 'each neighbourly murder' of present-day Ulster, gave a new and sinister twist to Yeats's image, and was to haunt Heaney's subsequent poetry. Stilled epitomes of violence, fossilised into symbolic indictments, these figures stir rich, ambiguous feelings, as with the nameless beheaded girl, outstaring 'axe / And beatification' alike, and 'What had begun to feel like reverence', in the unrhymed sonnet 'Strange Fruit' from *North*. The reference to Diodorus Siculus' confession of 'gradual ease' with such scenes, like the titular allusion to the Billy Holiday blues song about lynched Negroes in the American South, cools and distances atrocity. A language which objectifies and generalises the murdered girl into 'the likes of this' permits the poem to slide effortlessly, it would seem, through beatification to reverence. But this drift is pulled up short at the last minute by the uncertainty and incompletion of the last line, which reflects back on and opens up, harrowingly, the reproachful gaze of the victim in that repeated 'outstaring'. The tension between supposedly 'civilised' ease and a guilt which is not archaic but distressedly modern, the guilt of the 'artful voyeur' of 'Punishment', recurs throughout a volume obsessed with murdered and exhumed corpses. Some of these, like Baudelaire's 'Digging Skeleton', suggest the basic consanguinity of the live and the dead body, digger and dug, the almost comic medical textbook image of the flayed corpse and its reality. 'Bone Dreams' goes so far as to envisage poetry itself as a kind of necrophilia, pruriently pushing back, 'past philology and kennings', to a primal crime, 'where the bone's lair is a love-nest in the grass', unearthing 'a skeleton in the tongue's old dungeons'.

These dungeons are, in a sense, the executive suites of what Heaney in the title of a later essay collection was to dub the 'government of the tongue',[6] the places where language is imprisoned and simultaneously imprisons its speakers. In looking forward to that other dungeon which was to haunt his later work, the one where, in Dante's *Inferno*, Ugolino and his sons are starved to death, until the patriarch, at his sons' invitation, kills and eats them, 'Bone Dreams' opens a door into some of the darkest places of Heaney's poetic imagination. The mediating link is that series of Goya paintings in the Prado which are evoked in one of the most guilt-ridden sequences in *North*, 'Singing School'. In this sequence, 'Summer 1969' juxtaposes presence and absence, seeing the poet sweating his way through 'The life of Joyce' (that is, a biography of Joyce, a written displacement of actual life), 'suffering / Only the bullying sun of Madrid' while, elsewhere, the Royal Ulster Constabulary were providing cover for the Loyalist mob firing into the Falls Road – the events referred to in 'Feeling into Words', the *Preoccupations* essay cited above. The connection with 'The Wool Trade' is made by the poem's unexplained simile of 'the reek off a flax-dam' and the gleam of dead fish in 'flax-poisoned waters'. Television pictures arrive 'from where the real thing still happened'. But 'the original heraldic murderous encounter between Protestant yeoman and Catholic rebel' recorded in 'Requiem for the Croppies', 'initiated again in the summer of 1969, in Belfast', finds now only an aesthetic, 'heraldic' displacement in 'the cool of the Prado: in Goya's painting of two berserks clubbing each other to death 'for honour's sake', in his 'Shootings of the Third of May', with its firing squad and dying rebel, and, most potently, in his astonishing images of Saturn devouring his children and of the reign of that Chaos which is always the fruit of civil war.

The poem speaks of an unknown interlocutor, much like those accosting ghosts in Dante and Eliot which are refigured repeatedly in his work hereafter, in a poem such as 'Casualty' in *Field Work* (1979) or throughout *Station Island* (1984), urging him to '"Go back... try to touch the people"'. This is not so much an *unheimlich* visitation as a Faustian temptation, to sink back into that Yeatsian fantasy proclaimed in 'The Municipal Gallery Revisited', with its conviction that all inspiration 'Must come from contact with the soil'. Such 'diamond absolutes', the last poem of this sequence and of *North* suggests, invite to the massacre from which he feels he has escaped. They are related, that is, to Yeats's stone that troubles the living stream in 'Easter 1916'. The poem's title, 'Exposure', is deeply ambiguous. This 'inner émigré', weighing his 'responsible' but unresponsive *tristia* (the title of exilic volumes by both Ovid and Mandelstam) has no clear idea of what or whom he would write for, even if he went back: 'For the ear? For the people? / For what is said behind-backs?' He fears, nevertheless, that he may have missed 'The once-in-a-life-time portent'. His 'exposure' might be that of honourable exhaustion, like that of the fleeing wood-kernes Edmund Spenser had observed. But it could instead be a matter of being exposed either as an 'informer' and collaborator or, antithetically, as a committed partisan, to be interned for his republican loyalties. Lurking as a possibility is a guilty sense even of over-exposure, as, already, 'Famous Seamus', posed in the exposure of a publicity photograph. It might even, negating all these, be exposure as a fraud. Instead, the poem represents a third way, a different kind of exposure, like Yeats's 'enterprise / In walking naked' in 'A Coat', exposing the poet as one standing indeterminately in that space between allegiances, in a textual limbo which is at once 'extra-territorial' and a free-fire zone.

Throughout *North*, in a discourse of rootedness which is both populist, and potentially reactionary, and elegantly manipulated into radical opportunities, language is equated with the rich secretive loam of the Irish bog, which engulfs and preserves, but can also be kindled again and again, as peat, into a fire of meaning. It is a powerful and ambiguous image of the poet's complicity in his linguistic and political inheritance, but it also constitutes, in its conversion of history into geography, time into space, other grounds than one's culture on which to make a provisional stand. Language perceived as landscape is both an inescapable patrimony and a place of internal emigration, as for Stephen Dedalus. All poetic composition requires, as its very premise, the material decomposition of the culture it both records and moves beyond, the dead men thrusting up out of the ground to be transformed in what Yeats called a 'mirror-resembling dream'. The title poem of *North*, in a moment of wilful return to the long strand of a fabulous Viking past, calls up ancestral 'ocean-deafened voices' of warning, 'lifted again / in violence and epiphany'. What 'The longship's swimming tongue... buoyant with hindsight' advises, however, is just what the poet wants to hear:

> It said, 'Lie down
> in the word-hoard, burrow
> the coil and gleam
> of your furrowed brain.
>
> Compose in darkness...'

The whole volume identifies the troubles of poetic composition with the fratricidal decomposition of Ireland's 'Troubles', finding a romanticised analogy in antithesis. Heaney is struggling to overcome the Yeatsian rhetoric, but in the process he repeatedly reinstates the anger and exasperation of the later Yeats. Death and love, poetry and politics, converge in necrophilous union in poem after poem. 'Ocean's Love to Ireland' presents the amorous Raleigh of Aubrey's anecdote (the maid backed up to a tree) as the soldier-poet who laid waste to Ireland: 'Smerwick sowed with the mouthing corpses / Of six hundred papists, "as gallant and good / Personages as ever were beheld"'. The elaborately extended foreplay of 'Act of Union' makes the same punning correlation, while the Viking landings on the Liffey in 'Viking Dublin' require a simile which fuses copulation and interment.

It is the condensations of pun and metaphor, fusing tenor and vehicle, which allow for this compacted overlaying, displacing language away from culture into the irresistible givenness of nature. For Heaney in this volume Ireland is a series of violent matings, explosive copula, whose spawnings are everywhere in the language. 'Belderg' probes Norse, Celtic and Plantation English for the etymology of 'Mossbawn', which turns out to have alternative but incompatible etymologies in Irish and English. 'Viking Dublin' reveals the name of the city as itself a 'spined and plosive' Norse name. 'Bone Dreams' pushes back through dictions, Elizabethan, Norman, Provençal, Church Latin, to an ancient violence at once linguistic and martial, 'the scop's twang, the iron / flash of consonants / cleaving the line'. In 'Kinship', 'bog' is itself spelt out in a series of riddling contradictions, as in Anglo-Saxon runes:

> Insatiable bride,
> Sword swallower,
> casket, midden,
> floe of history...
>
> This is the vowel of earth
> dreaming its root...
> a windfall composing
> the floor it rots into.

But if, as Heaney says, 'I grew out of all this', there is another side to him: a déraciné intellectual, whose 'dithering, blathering' constitutes a fretful questioning not easily reconciled to a 'mother ground... sour with the blood / of her faithful'. For the 'inner émigré', 'neither internee nor informer', of 'Exposure', growing out of something means not only recognising the soil from which one springs, Antaeus-like, but also abandoning it, as one outgrows a youthful fashion or passion. From the start, Heaney has been aware of his ideological function as an 'Irish poet', locked inevitably in a symbolic posture, and aware all the more, therefore, of his responsibilities. When, in *North*, he identifies with Hamlet, or inevitably, with Stephen Dedalus evoking *Hamlet*, he is not simply the cunning deviser of literary tropes, but a poet who comes to consciousness, finds matter for his parables, by jumping into graves, as in 'Viking Dublin: Trial Pieces':

> skull-handler, parablist,
> smeller of rot
>
> in the state, infused
> with its poisons,
> pinioned by ghosts
> and affections,
> murders and pieties.

This double-edge involvement is significant. When Heaney speaks of the poet's 'complicity', he is recalling Dedalus's home truth about language, that we are all born in its shadow, 'pinioned by ghosts', our very ability to think pre-empted by its rituals and routines. It is thus that we are 'infused' with the poisons of the state, familiarised, made to feel at home in its murderous domesticity, that language at once foreign and familiar that holds us all at bay.

Speaking in Riddles

Such claustrophobic imprisonment lies at the heart of the double-binds and double-speak of the poem 'Whatever You Say Say Nothing' in *North*, the wry Irishism of the title phrase itself a riddling slogan with a compromised and duplicitous history. Language does not simply diffract history into the phantasmagoria of the imagination – at least, not in a land 'Of open minds as open as a trap', where even one's 'Christian' name nominates a sectarian lineage, and 'Norman, Ken and Sidney signalled Prod / And Seamus (call me Sean) was sure-fire Pape'. What we see in *North*, in retrospect, is the thickening of a Yeatsian rhetoric to the point at which its contradictions clot into something quite different, the 'stuff' of a self-styled 'subject people' to be renounced in *Station Island* (1984). Language here becomes a compost so dense it has to be turned over again and again before it can produce anything new. Indeed, there is another image Heaney deploys in the volume which transforms the relationship of speech and soil. Part I of *North* opened with a celebration of Antaeus, the autochthonous giant whose strength was constantly renewed by contact with the soil. The analogy is deliberately Yeatsian in its resonance, echoing that claim about the Irish Literary Renaissance made in 'The Municipal Gallery Revisited':

> All that we did, all that we said or sang
> Must come from contact with the soil, from that
> Contact everything Antaeus-like grew strong.

Part I closed, however, with the poem 'Hercules and Antaeus', and it celebrated the giant's defeat by that sky-born hero who weaned the 'mould-hug-
ger' 'out of his element, / into a dream of loss / and origins', bequeathing the
'cradling dark' to elegists. The last ambiguous line, seeing Antaeus as 'pap for
the dispossessed', leaves the actual outcome obscure. But this struggle to find
origins in loss, by drawing the subject of language 'out of its element', became
the project of Heaney's work throughout the subsequent decade. As Heaney
put it in interview with John Haffenden:

> To me Hercules represents another voice, another possibility; and actually
> behind that poem lay a conversation with Iain Crichton Smith, a very fine poet
> but essentially different from the kind of poet I am. He's got a kind of
> Presbyterian *light* about him. The image that came into my mind after the con-
> versation was of me being a dark soil and him being a kind of bright-pronged
> fork that was digging it up and going through it... Hercules represents the pos-
> sibility of the play of intelligence... That kind of thinking led into the poetry of
> the second half of *North*, which was an attempt at some kind of declarative
> voice.[7]

Heaney here deconstructs the binaries of North and South, Catholic and
Protestant, at the very moment that he deploys them, by moving tangentially
towards the distant voices of another, at once familiar and yet alien culture.
But the gravitational pull of a new binary (Ireland / Scotland) is deconstructed in advance by the displacements of the Greek myth, and in context is even
more variously deconstructed, since *en passant* Heaney also takes the opportunity to distinguish Borges and Neruda, writers in the same language from
two very different post-colonial nations, Argentina and Chile, both of which,
however, in the previous decade had seen democratic systems overthrown by
US-backed military juntas.

In his later work Heaney has pursued this other voice as political metaphor
and metonymy through to its source, to a recognition of language as both place
of necessary exile and site of a perpetual return home, of *nostos*. *Station Island*[8]
is a volume full of departures and returns, its title sequence of 'dream encounters with familiar ghosts' set on that island in Lough Derg which is a traditional place of pilgrimage and penitence, but moving, as we have seen, to an
imaginary dialogue of renunciation beyond all that fiddle. The book explores
the guilt of such meeting with the dead, returning from a remove to make
peace with that which has been abandoned, but it also wilfully moves out of
its element, into a clearer air. Displacement is here seen not as exile but as

freedom, whether in the wide-blue-yonder of America or the poetically licensed otherworlds of Dante's *Divine Comedy*.

The loving fidelity of the émigré who is nevertheless just 'visiting' that which he's left behind is the motive force for the volume. A poem ironically entitled 'Away from it All' acknowledges that you can't go home again by deploying the most bathetic figure of all for the émigré poet, a lobster taken out of its tank in a restaurant. At the end of the poem the lobster is the 'hampered one, out of water, / fortified and bewildered'. The poet too, though he doesn't finally share the fate of being cooked and served up to his consumers, cannot clear his head of all those lives he has left behind, 'still in their element'. And this awareness lies behind the 'rehearsed alibis' earlier in the poem, in which he speaks of himself *'stretched between contemplation / of a motionless point / and the command to participate / actively in history'*, the flabby phrasing of which calls up the abrupt, brutal response: 'Actively? What do you mean?'

Eliot's abstentionism and Auden's bad faith that 'poetry makes nothing happen' here jostle with that agonising but also self-aggrandising question Yeats asked in 'The Man and the Echo', which Heaney variously summons up in his writing, and specifically in that essay in *Preoccupations*, 'Yeats as an Example?' This essay opens with a quotation from Robert Lowell about a 'collaborating muse' (p. 98) that had plotted perhaps too freely with his own life and the lives of others. Yeats's notorious question Heaney had attempted to rephrase in the rueful reproach of a familiar ghost in 'Casualty', in *Field Work*, an old father-figure boozing companion accidentally 'blown to bits' because he failed to observe a Provisional curfew:

> How culpable was he
> That night when he broke
> Our tribe's complicity?
>
> 'Now you're supposed to be
> An educated man,'
> I hear him say. 'Puzzle me
> The right answer to that one.'[9]

If Yeats is present here in the recollection not only of 'The Man and the Echo' but also of his mythicised, imaginary icon of Irish virtue, 'The Fisherman', the more sceptical Hamlet is not far away, evoked in that resonance from the start of the play when Marcellus, prefiguring the Prince's prevarications in the face of patriarchal ghosts, passes the buck to one more intellectually qualified: 'Thou art a scholar, speak to it, Horatio.'

The Goyaesque threat that 'participation in history' means being devoured for an alien's pleasure is an anxiety which pervades *Station Island*. It explains Heaney's identification in the third part of the volume with the legendary

Sweeney, 'transformed into a bird-man and exiled to the trees by the curse of St Ronan', finding in madness a relief from remorse, but also a liberating escape from (in the title of one poem) 'The Old Icons', taking flight like Superman ('up and away') or the birdman Dedalus in the final poem of the volume, 'On the Road'. That this escape is a question of another kind of transformation, a displacement of the poet and his contradictions into language, is revealed in a poem such as 'The First Gloss', which opens the sequence 'Sweeney Redidivus', and echoes back to that initial break with the paternal lineage, which is also presented as a continuation, in 'Digging', the very first poem of Heaney's first volume. The multiple puns of 'The First Gloss' ('subscribe', 'justified line', 'margin') sum up in miniature the delicate relation between independence and immersion in one's native element, when that element is as much a language as a way of life.

This textualising of experience gives a significant new resonance to the topos of Irish marginality. Heaney subscribes to a poetic line and lineage at the moment that he takes that step beyond Ireland's margins and injustices. I take him to be attempting here, in a poem which overlays manuscript with map, what he speaks of in 'Yeats as an Example?' Yeats offers the practising poet, he says, 'an example of labour, perseverance', because 'he bothers you with the suggestion that if you have managed to do one kind of poem in your own way, you should cast off that way and face into another area of your experience until you have learned a new voice to say that area properly' (*Preoccupations*, p. 110). But the question mark in his title is significant. Heaney admires Yeats's restlessly self-transforming activity. But if Yeats worked towards stylistic innovation by following the logic of a changed content, and his content was changed by experiments with form which generated their own new perceptions, Yeats's example to Heaney in the end is a negative one, of rejection – the casting off of old mythologies. As Heaney says, Yeats encourages us 'to experience a transfusion of energies from poetic forms themselves, reveals how the challenge of a metre can extend the resources of the voice' (p. 110). The persona of Sweeney is important to him, Heaney explains in the Introduction to *Sweeney Astray* (1983), because 'insofar as Sweeney is also a figure of the artist, displaced, guilty, assuaging himself by his utterance, it is possible to read the work as an aspect of the quarrel between free creative imagination and the constraints of religious, political, and domestic obligation.' But he goes on, in what he calls 'a more opportunistic spirit', to deconstruct these Irish antitheses by talking, with a silent nod to Crichton Smith's example, of Sweeney's 'easy sense of cultural affinity with both western Scotland and southern Ireland as exemplary for all men and women in contemporary Ulster'.[10]

In *Station Island*, Heaney moved away from the determining ventriloquisms of that 'subject people stuff' precisely by pluralising and diversifying his voices, taking in Ovid, Chekhov, Mandelstam and Dante, Crichton Smith and many more in addition to Joyce, as writers of a real and tangible exile. By stepping into the margins, he, like them, had also drawn a line. No wide-eyed innocent abroad, he has his tongue in his cheek when he turns the tables on a series of cosmopolitan readerships. Heaney, like the jocoserious Joyce, has here taken serious refuge in the comedy of justified margins, remaking himself as a story which speaks of Ireland only in transcending its ideological antitheses:

> incredible to myself
> among people far too eager to believe me
> and my story, even if it happened to be true.

'Traditionally an oracle speaks in riddles', says Heaney in 'Feeling into Words', 'yielding its truths in disguise, offering its insights cunningly. And in the practice of poetry, there is a corresponding occasion of disguise, a protean, chameleon moment when the lump in the throat takes protective colouring in the new element of thought' (*Preoccupations*, p. 49).

Presences

The cover of Michael Parker's book, *Seamus Heaney: The Making of the Poet*[11] offers the close-up of an affable middle-aged Heaney, holding before his face a blurred object, clutched between finger and thumb, which might be either a squat but unresting pen or a hand microphone. The ambiguity (with all its phallogocentric blurriness) is apt, for Heaney's poetry has always hovered between the carnal intimacies of voice and the dispassionate distance of writing. I have only once seen Heaney perform live, at the Roundhouse during the London Festival of the Irish Arts in 1980. His North London appearance, like the apparition at Knock or those ghostly intimations, whether of persons or texts, which manifest themselves throughout the poetry, was rich with the rhetoric of presence. Here was the authentic voice of the Northern tragedy, in the flesh (too, too solid), delivering oracular, sometimes sibylline *sortes Heaneyianae* to a congregation that came to worship, wanted to be possessed, and squirmed in its seats with scarcely suppressed ecstasis at every turn of a voice that was familiar, seductive, and well and truly there, a presence among them.

Parker's immensely thorough study stalks Heaney's progress through the poetry and prose from *Death of a Naturalist* to *Seeing Things*, sharing the same hushed reverence in the presence of what is clearly more than a merely local genius. It genuflects to the oeuvre's universalist standing and its increasingly globalist standpoint, looking down as in 'Alphabets' like an astronaut on the 'lucent O' of 'all he has sprung from'. But it also roots down the necromancer's auraed figures in the loam of place and personal history. If, at times, as we follow Parker's relentless plough down the furrowed *versus* of poem after poem, the effect is claustrophobic, much of this is to do with that mythology of origins cultivated by Heaney's cunning muse, seen at its most taunting in the image of the lobster in 'Away from it All', 'the hampered one, out of water, / fortified and bewildered'. Not easy to think of Heaney as bewildered, though. He reads like a poet whose very unconscious has a game plan, with every innuendo and nuance orchestrated to the last detail to produce the effect of a significance both here, abiding our presence, and yet, as in 'Bogland', always striking inwards and downwards, every layer stripped carrying the traces of previous occupation, down to the bottomless centre.

Such literary self-consciousness owes a lot to a good singing school, and Parker is illuminating in charting the effect of school and university, Belfast and Berkeley, and other, less formal ministrations, as well as an early autodidactic impulse, on the development of Heaney's talent. Heaney's poetry, like Auden's, is full of the imagery of the schoolroom, and not just because for most of his adult life he has been a teacher, first in secondary and then in higher education here and in the United States. It is not just homage to Yeats that leads him to call one of his most revealing lectures 'Among Schoolchildren' – 'Here's two on's are sophisticated', as he wrote to Seamus Deane in 'The Ministry of Fear', calling up ghosts from *Hamlet*.

Parker's book is full of the language of presence, its critical *fons et origo* that same Leavisian / Ricardian tradition of 'practical criticism' that, under the influence of Philip Hobsbaum's Belfast 'Group', shaped Heaney's own writing (and reading) practice. The ultimate figure of unmediated presence, of the immediate and tangible as the truth of things, is for Parker the water pump at Mossbawn, Heaney's original place, lovingly reproduced in the book's first photographic plate as if its represented ordinariness were the heart of the mystery as well as the navel of the world. This, Parker says, discussing 'A Drink of Water' in a language dense in oxymoron, is one of the Mossbawn poetry's 'most potent presences... *the omphalos*, a transcendent, ever-present, unseen being which "stands" and will remain standing long after all these... will have passed away' (pp. 158–9). In the poem 'Sunlight', we have been told earlier, the pump, 'like its human counterpart, Heaney's Aunt Mary, is realised in the poem as a physical and mythic entity... It embodies cast iron reality, occupies, literally, a concrete place within the Mossbawn scheme of things, yet also serves as a symbol or ikon for the subterranean energies of the place and its people.' Likewise with Mary Heaney, 'Her presence is made immediate to us... and dramatically conjured for us by means of the accumulation of visual, sensual detail' (p. 127).

Yet as Parker's own words unwittingly reveal, this is far from unproblematic immediacy. Mediation (mediumship, even, to continue the tone of hushed oracular revelation the passage espouses) is apparent in that verb 'made', followed so rapidly by the even more explicit 'dramatically conjured'. And indeed, Parker himself has unconsciously registered the paradox, observing already that the poem opens 'with a mystery, with the illumination of an "absence"', seeking now to recuperate 'the original "sunlit absence"' with the poet's 'sense of fullness, not of loss', of a love 'tangibly "here" in the present tense'.

Presence, of course, everywhere carries absence as its melancholy verso. All that words can conjure up is the illusion of presence, the very act of writing putting a distance between the referent and the signifiers which point at it, as Heaney himself spelt out in his account of how the second Mossbawn poem for Mary Heaney ('The Seed Cutters') came to be written, cited by Parker on the very next page: 'The more exactly I described what I remembered, the further and further away it became and it went so far away it turned itself into a sonnet.' Indeed, Parker actually acknowledges that this poem of presence 'ends in elegy', acknowledging absence: 'The shelter was once there but is there no longer' (p.128).

Throughout his work, Heaney uses members of his family, father, wife, and, in the powerful elegiac sequence 'Clearances' in *The Haw Lantern*,[12] his dead mother, as touchstones of the lost referent, that original reality forever forfeited on entry into the Symbolic, for which all our empty signifiers continue to mourn. In the last sonnet of that sequence, self-presence itself is converted into the idea of a radical absence, speaking of a chestnut tree planted at his birth in the hedge of what once was home, now uprooted by Mossbawn's new tenants, leaving 'a space / Utterly empty, utterly a source', 'a bright nowhere'. Heaney knows exactly what he is doing in such poems, 'neither internee nor informer', as he had described himself in 'Exposure' (a poem as much about literary over-exposure as about other forms), 'An inner émigré, grown long-haired / And thoughtful'. When he described himself there as 'a wood-kerne / Escaped from the massacre, / Taking protective colouring' from his native ground, he played sly, teasing games with the metropolitan English culture that had taken him up as its latest pastoral 'find', like those Irish predecessors patronisingly transfixed in Robin Skelton's Introduction to his *Six Irish Poets* (1962), which according to Parker (p. 36) supplied 'exemplars' and was 'an act of confirmation for Heaney'. According to Skelton,

> Irish poetry can still base itself firmly upon what might be described as 'natural resources'. It is interesting because in England there appear very few poets indeed with this kind of awareness of their nationality, this sense of belonging, however rebelliously, to a social or ethnic group.[13]

'I hate how quick I was to know my place', Heaney wrote in 'Station Island'. The artful double-take identifies that intimate knowledge of his original place, for which English critics first praised him (to be echoed here by

Parker) with his 'biddable' readiness to accept his place as a subaltern warbler of native woodnotes in the metropolitan scheme of things. 'Sweeney Redivivus' in the same volume speaks of having become 'incredible to myself, / among people far too eager to believe me / and my story, even if it happened to be true.' But such incredulity is a necessary condition of all discourse, lurking bashfully and abashed in the spaces between secondary 'story' and originary 'truth'. The wide-eyed pastoralism of such storytelling had received its death-blow as early as the dedicatory poem to *Wintering Out*, which drily sent up all the folksy patter of walking out in the morning dew, speaking instead of a 'dewy motor-way' from which one sees 'the new camp for the internees', and ending with a rather different version of pastoral: 'we hug our little destiny again'.

The Making of the Poet in the end seeks to domesticate its subject, perpetu-ating the patronising metropolitan icon with its assumption, discussing the 'Glanmore Sonnets', that dialect, 'the intimate native tongue of Mossbawn', is somehow closer to the referent than 'the more formal, extended register of language acquired at St Columb's and Queen's' (p. 169). Parker's account of 'Making Strange' (*Station Island*) contrasts Viktor Shklovsky's *ostranenie* with the 'Hiberno-English' of Heaney's 'first dialect', where '"to make strange" means "to be unfriendly", "to draw back in fear", "to react defensively"'. According to John Banville, it has in addition a touch of the *Unheimlich*, which would give a more specific edge here to Heaney's negotiations with his patri-mony: 'The Irish say, when a child turns from its parents, that it is *making strange*; it comes from the belief that fairy folk, a jealous tribe, would steal a too-fair human babe and leave a changeling in its place.'[14] Heaney's anxiety, that he may have simply been caught in another, bigger net, rather than freed from the trammels of a contingent and parochial 'identity', is powerfully figured in this equivocal phrase. The poem's own 'cunning middle voice', pun-ning on the Socratic sense of 'dialectic', urges the poet to be 'adept' and 'dialect', to "Go beyond what's reliable / in all that keeps pleading and plead-ing"'. Parker however relocates the poetic voice undialectically within its 'native' dialect, finding only closure and a return to 'poetic roots... in preserving native speech, private and parochial experience... able to recover his country, rediscover its familiar features and figures by means of metaphor and allusion that "make strange"' (p.189). Heaney's double register works in fact in quite the opposite direction, opening up to strangeness and the uncanny, in that fraught passage between the abstract music of the signifiers and the unknow-able swayed body, 'reciting my pride / in all that I knew, that began to make strange / at that same recitation'.

Yeats's 'Presences' in 'Among School Children' dance in that same middle passage, spirits unappeased and peregrine between two worlds, between the order of signification and that of the immanent, absent referent. Parker's study keeps collapsing that distance in Heaney's poetry, yet it is everywhere the very premise of his work. This is what makes him such a master of the uncanny. In the epigraph to his final chapter, Parker quotes John Montague as saying that, 'when you write about the dead, you are expiating your connection with them, you're cleansing it. And that means that they are also present. Even if they're not there as spirits, your own mother and your father... are actually present inside you and therefore you must come to terms with them.'[15]

That repeated 'present' is crucial. The secret of all literary presence is contained in Yeats's ambiguous usage. For 'Presences' is another way of speaking about ghosts, whether those ghostly intertexts speaking through the language of the living, at once present and absent (and no poetry is more artful than Heaney's in its interweaving of such alien, familiar voices); or those family ghosts, at once intimate and strange, who haunt so many of his lines. And these are not only familiar (in 'Casualty' , indeed, over-familiar, taking liberties, in the implied rebuke to the poet), but, like the revenants of 'Funeral Rites', 'Station Island', 'Clearances', or countless other poems, 'familiars'. The textual ancestors of Heaney's ghosts haunt the shadowy passages of Homer, Virgil and Dante, Yeats, Auden and Eliot. But they figure those absences which invest all discourse, making the familiar strange, all the way back to our first world, from which we were irredeemably excluded by the entry into language. Or, as Heaney wrote in 'A Migration' (*Station Island*), of that first exodus which spilt us into separated being, into a world of ghost stories:

> Familiars! A trail
> of spillings in the dust,
> unsteady white enamel
> bucket looming. Their ghosts,
> like their names, called from the hill
> to 'Hurry', hurry past,
>
> a spill of syllables.
> I knew the story then.

Going On

In *The Redress of Poetry* (1995) Heaney wrote of poems that are 'about the way consciousness can be alive to two different and contradictory dimensions of reality and still find a way of negotiating between them', adducing as one exemplar Hardy's 'bewitching' poem 'Afterwards', a putative auto-epitaph for 'a man who used to notice such things'.[16] The volume *Seeing Things* (1991)[17] was centrally concerned with such doubletakes and negotiations, signalled in the polyvalency of a title that hovered between mere observancy, visionary insight, and delusion verging on hallucination or haunting. But so, too, was

The Spirit Level,[18] the first collection to follow his Nobel Prize. Here, though, the seeing went further, so that the book might equally well have been called *Seeing Through*, an ambivalent phrase in which seeing through illusions, the refusal to go on being fooled, is counterbalanced by a readiness to see things through, to sustain, clear-sightedly, those same illusions, in full knowledge of what one is doing.

Such undeluded double vision is what the poem 'Keeping Going' celebrates in the poet's brother Hugh. At the end of his tether sometimes amidst the farm's diurnal round and the quotidian slaughter (the killing, 'That morning like any other morning', of a part-time reservist), Hugh exemplifies the 'good stamina' needed to 'stay on where it happens' and see things through. The poem opens with a childhood memory of Hugh pretending, with whitewash brush for sporran and a kitchen chair over his shoulder for bagpipes, to be a piper, 'keeping the drone going on / Interminably, between catches of breath'. The 'keeping going' with which the poem ends, however, involves a stubborn pretence the other side of disenchantment, one that lays claim to (*pretends to*, like any piping Jacobite Pretender) the everyday world of which those neighbourly murders would dispossess us.

Heaney's own yea-and-nay-saying in *The Spirit Level* takes the form of Frostian parable in 'The Flight Path'. Opening with memories of his father's conjuring of a toy boat from folded paper, an 'ark' from which, every time, the young Heaney's heart soared like a dove with admiration, the poem reveals him an already disingenuous accomplice in illusion, knowing the boat 'every bit as hollow / As a part of me that sank because it knew / The whole thing would go soggy once you launched it'. Such double bluffs prepare for that moment of refusal and affirmation later when, playing to himself the role of returning exile ('Standing-in in myself for all of those / The stance perpetuates'), he is challenged on a train by a red-eyed Ciaran Nugent, a revenant fresh out of Long Kesh and the Dirty Protest: '"When, for fuck's sake, are you going to write / Something for us?"' Eyes that last he saw in dreams, inviting him with a wink to plant a neighbourly bomb, here drill their way through rhyme and image 'Like something out of Dante's scurfy hell'. Another one of those ghostly and over-familiar interlocutors that beset Heaney's verse, buttonholing the poet with his 'responsibilities', Nugent elicits a sheepishly defiant, artfully 'righteous' response (with the insinuation of 'self-righteous') – the hand-washing of one who has only half seen through, half said goodbye to all that: '"If I do write something, / Whatever it is, I'll be writing for myself."'

The moment of real illumination comes later in the poem, 'Out of the blue', recalling another, earlier episode in which he climbed alone to the hermit's eyrie above Rocamadour, addressing his own solitude like Stephen Dedalus refusing to serve, and self-consciously setting it down in his tables, translating the place's name to his own satisfaction:

> Eleven in the morning. I made a note:
> 'Rock-lover, loner, sky-sentry, all hail!'
> And somewhere the dove rose. And kept on rising.

The exaltation of this is undercut, though, not only by its adolescent theatricality but also by the curious echo of that moment in *Macbeth* where the conquering hero is interpellated to his doom by the witches. And indeed, that very scene had been evoked a few pages earlier, when 'Keeping Going' spoke of a haunted Macbeth, 'helpless and desperate / In his nightmare', adding complicitously: 'I felt at home with that one all right.' Perhaps denial, rejection, are the true path of flight: off into the blue. But the dove ascending testifies to an older, unbroken covenant, winging back to the ark in his father's hands at the start of the poem, held 'like a promise he had the power to break / But never did'.

It may be that in 'The Flight Path', as in Robert Frost's 'Directive' (which Heaney reads in *The Redress of Poetry* (pp. xiv–xv) as a parable about poetry's 'games of make-believe'), the 'quester has been led beyond everything familiar' to 'a locus of knowledge, a scene of instruction and revelation' on a deserted mountainside. But the unbroken promise with which it opens recalls, I would suggest, another Frost poem which turns down the cold pure enchantments of poetry for what *Redress* calls 'the world of social speech'. 'Stopping by Woods on a Snowy Evening' can be read as a counter-parable which refuses the lovely, dark and deep enchantments of poetic make-believe, chastening the exultant spirit with the social responsibility of 'promises to keep, / And miles to go before I sleep'. According to 'A Sofa in the Forties' (*The Spirit Level*), with its memories of the Heaney boys playing at trains on the family sofa, it was through such make-believe journeys that 'We entered history and ignorance / Under the wireless shelf', seduced by 'The sway of language and its furtherings' so that 'We occupied our seats with all our might'. But 'The Flight Path' knows in advance that the flight from history, across the frontier of writing, is nothing more than a charming ideological sleight-of-hand, a paper ark.

'The Errand', which gives *The Spirit Level* its title, enshrines a brief and trivial exchange in which his father tried to send the young Heaney on a fool's errand, telling him to run and ask his mother for 'a bubble for the spirit level'. The boy, however, has already seen through the joke, and the grown man knows in retrospect that his father was glad when he stood his ground, trumping his smile, 'Waiting for the next move in the game'. It was a slight poem on which to hang Heaney's first post-Nobel volume, but its resonances grow, as one might expect, hinting, with the involvement of the mother, at that Oedipal triangle in which the spirit level itself stands in for the riddling sphinx. That standing of his ground becomes a rite of passage, turning the edge on the phrase 'his fool's errand' by making the fool not the son but the fooling-around father.

Growing up and growing out of, but returning, as here, to negotiate a new understanding which sets the spirit level, levels with the past, but also takes one, like Odysseus in Hades, on to the level of the spirits of the dead, has been a theme of Heaney's poetry at least since *North*, where an Oedipal Hamet observed with wry *double entendre* of the massacre from which he hoped to escape: 'I grew out of all that.' Such returns are at the heart of this volume, in, for example, that retake of one of his most famous sequences from *North* in the penultimate poem, 'Tollund', which reflects gravely on the fame now acquired by both the poet and his subject-matter, the once obscure Jutland bog where these dark age corpses were interred. The fame in part derives from the celebrity his poems have conferred on the spot, now transformed into 'user-friendly outback', well signposted for tourists in mock runic script in Danish and English. The landscape has itself become a parallel text, 'Hallucinatory and familiar', overlaying, as in Hardy's late elegies, memories of that earlier visit with a shifted present where even a standing stone has been 'resituated and landscaped'. After twenty years of public exposure in a heritage culture, 'Things had moved on' quite literally for both megalith and poet. Photogenic, repro, the place now might be 'a still out of the bright / "Townland of peace"', a poem of dream farms past contention. Footloose now, 'at home beyond the tribe' (which recasts the 'lost, / Unhappy and at home' of *North*'s 'Tollund Man'), revisiting their olden haunts like the late Hardy, these revenants also recall Hamlet's father's ghost, doomed for a certain term to tread such Danish levels of the spirit:

> More scouts than strangers, ghosts who'd walked abroad
> Unfazed by light, to make a new beginning
> And make a go of it, alive and sinning,
> Ourselves again, free-willed again, not bad.

The closing poem of *The Spirit Level* likewise turns on a reprise, a 'Postscript' to some unspecified prior act of writing, not necessarily this volume, which begins with the instruction some time to make the time to drive out west. The words recall, perhaps, Joyce's closing story in *Dubliners*, where the literal west is also symbolically the realm of 'The Dead'. The rest of the poem actually constitutes that return in imagining it, in a prolepsis that is not so much the prelude to, as the realisation of, that imagined visit, in a ghostly border country between writing and event, where

> You are neither here nor there,
> A hurry through which known and strange things pass
> As big soft buffetings come at the car sideways
> And catch the heart off guard and blow it open.

This book is full of returns and recurrences, making strange as it renders known in the retelling. In the opening line of 'A Brigid's Girdle', the simple repetition of two words clarifies the act of writing as perpetual repetition: 'Last time I wrote I wrote from a rustic table / Under magnolias in South Carolina.' In the same way, one place repeats another, the rustic American South mirroring but also displacing the rustic Irish North. Simile doubles and plaits the world beyond disentangling, a 'Flight of small plinkings from a dulcimer' seeming 'Like feminine rhymes migrating to the north', in a poem which is itself a Brigid's girdle woven with feminine rhymes, 'As strange and lightsome and traditional / As the motions you go through going through the thing'. That closing repetition, echoing the opening one, goes through the motions but in the process makes strange the whole act of going through with things, seeing them through to the end even when we've been there already.

Repetition is the key motif and formal strategy of *The Spirit Level*, whether verbal (anaphora; the sestina of 'Two Lorries'), or narrative (familiar myths estranged in the retelling, as in 'Mycenae Lookout'), structural (translations which re-create the worlds to which they advert, as in 'A Dog Was Crying Tonight in Wicklow Also'; the revisionary retreading of his own earlier poetic terrains), or thematic (the reiteration of old themes *passim*). Indeed, *The Spirit Level* is, in Heaney's complex sense of the word, pre-occupied by its immediate predecessor *Seeing Things*, re-running most of its topoi, but without the emotional pressure or formal innovation that made that book a major volume. In the words of Walt Whitman: 'Do I repeat myself? Very well then I repeat myself.'

Marking time, all the poems in *The Spirit Level* have the professionalism and assurance we have come to expect, but sometimes they come too pat, or occasionally, as in 'Two Stick Drawings', set down Glanmore a little too close to the literary acres of Cold Comfort Farm. But if the spirit seemed to have levelled out in this volume, *Electric Light*[19] has subsequently demonstrated that it would have been a mistake to assume Heaney's spirited talent had now found its level. 'Postscript', one of the best poems in *The Spirit Level*, was as much a prescript and prologue of what was yet to come, those 'big soft buffetings' out of the murderous innocence of the sea promising to blow wide open the whole poetic vehicle. Laurels of one kind or another have been the death of many a poetic talent, but a postscript is not an epitaph. Heaney's capacity not only to go on but to go on changing has astonished us in the past, and poems such as 'The Little Canticles of Asturias' and the 'Sonnets from Hellas' in *Electric Light* break new ground in terms both of content and form. Still negotiating between two dimensions on the frontier of writing, his 'ultimate achievement', as he says of Hardy in *The Redress*, repeating Eliot repeating Shakespeare, is 'to transform the familiar into something rich and strange', laying claim to his title as 'one who had an eye for such mysteries'. Heaney himself remains that kind of familiar, a ghostly presence lurking in absences and omissions of his postscripted, always-already written 'life', 'neither here nor there, / A hurry through which known and strange things pass'.

There he is, going on again.

NOTES

1. Seamus Heaney, *Wintering Out* (London: Faber and Faber, 1972).
2. Seamus Heaney, *Death of a Naturalist* (London: Faber and Faber, 1966).
3. Seamus Heaney, *Door into the Dark* (London: Faber and Faber, 1969).
4. Seamus Heaney, 'Feeling into Words', in *Preoccupations: Selected Prose 1968-1978* (London: Faber and Faber, 1980), p. 55; hereafter page references are indicated in the text.
5. Seamus Heaney, *North* (London: Faber and Faber, 1975).
6. Seamus Heaney, *The Government of the Tongue* (London: Faber and Faber, 1988).
7 . John Haffenden, ed., *Viewpoints: Poets in Conversation* (London: Faber and Faber, 1981), pp. 69–70.
8. Seamus Heaney, *Station Island* (London: Faber and Faber, 1984).
9. Seamus Heaney, *Field Work* (London: Faber and Faber, 1979).
10. Seamus Heaney, *Sweeney Astray* ((London: Faber and Faber, 1983).
11. Michael Parker, *Seamus Heaney: The Making of the Poet* (London: Macmillan, 1994); hereafter page references are indicated in the text
12. Seamus Heaney, *The Haw Lantern* (London: Faber and Faber, 1987).
13. Robin Skelton, ed., *Six Irish Poets* (London: Oxford University Press, 1962).
14. John Banville, *The Untouchable* (London: Picador, 1997), p. 198.
15. Parker, p. 211. The interview, with Shirley Anders, can be found in *Verse*, 6 (1986), pp. 33–8; this quotation at p. 34. Montague has just cited Auden to the effect that 'poetry is breaking bread with the dead'.
16. Seamus Heaney, *The Redress of Poetry* (London: Faber and Faber, 1995), pp. xiii, xvi–xviii.
17. Seamus Heaney, *Seeing Things* (London: Faber and Faber, 1991).
18. Seamus Heaney, *The Spirit Level* (London: Faber and Faber, 1996).
19. Seamus Heaney, *Electric Light* (London: Faber and Faber, 2001).

VIII

The Distance Between:
Heaney Again

A Place to Come From

Perhaps Seamus Heaney's commonest critical mannerism is the teasing out of
innuendoes and ambiguities in some ordinary locution, as for example in his
comments in *The Government of the Tongue* on Robert Lowell, whose poetic
'resources proved themselves capable of taking new strains, in both the musical and stressful sense of that word'. [1] Heaney's device doesn't always take the
strain, sometimes seeming more a tic of rhetorical routine than a necessary
complication. As with his recurrent arguing from etymology, too much of the
argument's strain can be taken up in a verbal play which substitutes for logic
and demonstration. Most notorious perhaps is the schoolboy double entendre
of that lecture given at the Royal Society of Literature in 1974, 'Feeling into
Words', which effectively exposed Leavisian pieties by touching up their
lower parts as a discourse of sexual displacement. [2] But it is evident even in
such apparently innocuous items as his 1977 lecture at the Ulster Museum,
'The Sense of Place', a phrase which he glosses as 'our sense, or better still –
our *sensing* of place'. [3]

Nevertheless, the linguistic strategy is deeply symptomatic. It effects a
kind of destabilisation on the ground of language itself, unsettling what he
calls the 'sovereign diction' (*Government*, p.137) with alternative, subversive
voices. This is apparent in the slant light cast on the 1977 lecture by a later
one given at the Wordsworth Summer Conference at Dove Cottage. *Place and
Displacement: Recent Poetry of Northern Ireland* makes it clear, in terms of a
Saussurean binary, that place is impossible to define without displacement.
Displacement, one might say, is the necessary ground upon which to find or
found one's place.

> 'I hate how quick I was to know my place.
> I hate where I was born, hate everything
> That made me biddable and unforthcoming',

the poet mouths at his 'half-composed face / In the shaving mirror' in a moment of confessional self-loathing in 'Station Island'. If the shaving mirror recalls Joyce's image of Irish art, the 'cracked looking-glass of the servant', the 'half-composed face' seems to be an unconscious echo of Yeats's image for the textual afterlife in 'Nineteen Hundred and Nineteen', 'The half-imagined, the half-written page'. But really knowing your place means refusing to settle for being put in your place, whether it is your own people or an occupying presence (Joyce's Haines) which is doing the placing – means learning, in the ghostly ventriloquism of 'Station Island', '"that what I thought was chosen was convention"'.

The subtitle of this lecture significantly speaks of poetry *of* Northern Ireland, not *from* it, and a whole world of difference can hang on such a preposition. In *The Haw Lantern*,[4] four parables give a precise twist to this topographic insistence: 'From the Frontier of Writing', 'From the Republic of Conscience', 'From the Land of the Unspoken', 'From the Canton of Expectation'. The preposition in one sense simply indicates the place of origin of the missive (as in 'A Postcard from Iceland'). But 'from' carries more weight than this. In the first poem he *writes* from the frontier. But as the last three stanzas indicate, he also experiences a sense of release at having *come away from*, escaped across it:

> And suddenly you're through, arraigned yet freed,
> as if you'd passed from behind a waterfall...
>
> past armour-plated vehicles, out between
> the posted soldiers flowing and receding
> like tree shadows into the polished windscreen.

The prepositions do much here in effecting the sense of relief in passage, 'passed from behind... past... out between... receding... into'. That 'through', a preposition turned adverb and then colloquially a verb complement, takes on a heavy freight of meaning. If it 'concentrates an identity in a heave of renewal' it also 'disperses it in a blast of evacuation', a process which *The Government of the Tongue* (p.168) finds 'morbid' in Sylvia Plath's 'Daddy' – where, though he does not remark on it, the word acquires a similar duplicity:

> So daddy, I'm finally through.
> The black telephone's off at the root,
> The voices just can't worm through...
> Daddy, daddy, you bastard, I'm through.[5]

Working it through, getting through, may mean saying you're through with it for ever. This poem Heaney disapproves of (though he nevertheless calls it a 'brilliant... *tour de force*'), is apposite to the frontier of writing. Heaney too is not only through the roadblock. He is also through with that country: with its exposed positions, with having to justify himself, with perpetual interrogation. In the light of Plath's usage, 'through' picks up the resonance of that 'spent' applied to the self earlier – spent, that is, like a used cartridge, or a life 'spent' by an over-itchy trigger finger; for all the time, as the sergeant transmits data about him, he is half aware of the marksman with his rifle trained down upon him out of the sun, and the prepositions themselves relentlessly train *down out of upon* the subjugated, obedient self, held in its place down the sights of 'cradled' guns.

That the preposition is a key resource in Heaney's poetic armoury is confirmed by his remarks,' in 'The Sense of Place', on a line of Kavanagh's:

> And the same vigour comes out in another little word that is like a capillary root leading down into the whole sensibility of Kavanagh's place. In the first line, 'the bicycles go by in twos and threes'. They do not 'pass by' or 'go past', as they would in a more standard English voice or place, and in that little touch Kavanagh touches what I am circling. He is letting the very life blood of the place in that one minute incision. (*Preoccupations*, p. 138)

'Pass by' may be a sly dig at Yeats's horseman. Heaney, *at* the frontier, we note, is *suddenly through*, as if by magic without any apparent act of transit, only in a simile passing from behind, passing out between. The 'From' of the poem's title takes up but also takes *on* the title of W. H. Auden's play *On the Frontier*. In 'Sounding Auden', the second lecture of *The Government of the Tongue*, Heaney remarks on the oddity of the preposition 'between' at another frontier of decision in Auden's verse:

> Who stands, the crux left of the watershed,
> On the wet road between the chafing grass
> Below him sees... (p.118)

Similarly, in analysing the effect of 'chafing' (p.123) he tunes in, finely, on its inbetweenness: 'disturbed by a lurking middle voice' between active and passive, it 'occupies' (a loaded word for Heaney, here redoubled in significance before the Popean noun phrase) 'a middle state between being transitive and intransitive, and altogether functions like a pass made swiftly, a sleight of semantic hand which unnerves and suspends the reader above a valley of uncertainty'. When he writes of 'This deferral of a sense of syntactical direction', Heaney is indicating some of the preoccupations of his own poems in *Station Island* and *The Haw Lantern* which also, like early Auden, turn upon 'the necessity of a break, of an escape from habit, an escape from the given... only to expose their ultimate illusory promise' (p.110).

121

If Auden's poems 'sound back' to earlier ones, Heaney's own poem here resounds with this earlier source in Auden, coming out 'from behind a water-fall / on the black current of a tarmac road'. Auden's advice to the stranger, 'frustrate and vexed', is to 'Go home', or find himself equally emptied and subjugated by a land, which 'cut off, will not communicate'. Heaney's poem inhabits an occupied 'middle state' and 'middle voice' full of spoken and unspoken communications (the 'intent' of the rifles, the atmosphere of 'pure interrogation'), of knowledges of the self withheld from it (what the sergeant exchanges with HQ on his on-off mike), and of the silent messages of fear, obedience and power that grow from the barrel of a gun. In 'The Mud Vision' this is identified as that state of Irish paralysis in which, once, 'We sleep-walked / The line between panic and formulae', unable to 'dive to a future'. 'Terminus', recalling his variously divided childhood, takes a more balanced position – between rural and urban, agrarian and industrial, active and passive, transitive and intransitive, weighing pros and cons. If baronies and parishes met where he was born, so that he grew up 'Suffering the limit of each claim', these 'limits' are not only passively borne (suffered) as limitations on the self, but also tolerated, in a learnt and active sufferance, as limited claims, which can be put in their place because they are limited. Coming to understand such limits can then offer insight: 'Two buckets were easier carried than one. / I grew up in between.' Second thoughts thus become the first fruits of thinking itself, and the poem's second thoughts, moving out from between, end at a watery margin which is also a crossing point, a place of negotiation between opposing forces which figures the stance of one whose end is peace, 'in midstream / Still parleying, in earshot of his peers'.

Whereas the early Auden stands repeatedly transfixed 'Upon this line between adventure', caught 'Between attention and attention', ordered to 'Turn back' before he reaches any frontier by a man with a gun, because 'There is no change of place', Heaney's prepositional space is a different one, not transfixed but moving 'with guarded unconcerned acceleration' from 'out between'. In 'Station Island' the ghost of William Carleton speaks of his own hardness in a hard time as maybe containing a lesson for the poet, '"whoever you are, wherever you come out of"'. Freedom may be found in displacing oneself. But, in the words of Carson McCullers cited in 'The Sense of Place', 'to know who you are, you have to have a place to come from'.

Sounding Out Through

For such 'an earnest of the power of place' this essay returns to the world of Heaney's own childhood:

The landscape was sacramental, instinct with signs, implying a system of reality beyond the visible realities. Only thirty years ago, and thirty miles from Belfast, I think I experienced this kind of world vestigially and as a result may have retained some vestigial sense of place as it was experienced in the older dispensation. (*Preoccupations*, pp.132–3)

The Celtic Twilight, for all its naiveties, was 'the beginning of a discovery of confidence in our own ground, in our place, in our speech, English and Irish', a discourse 'that would bind the people of the Irish place to the body of their world'. This bodiliness of a world 'instinct with signs', I shall suggest, is important. Heaney's model here is Patrick Kavanagh's assertion that 'Parochialism is universal; it deals with fundamentals... now that I analyse myself I realize that throughout everything I write, there is this constantly recurring motif of the need to go back'. Kavanagh's 'sense of his place involves detachment, for it is only when one is fully *in* and *of* a place that one can feel fully Kavanagh's need to be "detached, remote... take part but ... not belong"'. As with Wordsworth, these native places are 'influential in the strict sense of the word "influential" – things flowed in from them'. As Heaney elaborates the argument, the prepositions once again pre-position the preoccupied subject, in this 'middle state' where things *flow in from* and *flow out to*. Etymology is summoned to explain this relation at the beginning of the Plath lecture in *Government*, speaking of a Yeats

> less concerned in his criticism to speak about the actual tones and strains of poetic language than to evoke the impersonal, impersonating, mask-like utterance which he takes all poetry to be. We are reminded of how *persona* derives from *personare*, meaning 'to sound out through', how the animation of the verb lives in the mask's noun-like impassiveness. For Yeats, the poet is somebody who is spoken through. (p.149)

'Sounding back' in the discussion of Auden has its corollary in this 'sounding out through'. 'Through', as we have seen, is another little word fraught with ambivalence. 'Poetry makes nothing happen', Auden said famously, in what is clearly a direct response to Yeats's fretful questions about poetic responsibilities in 'The Man and the Echo'. But it is nevertheless, in a less frequently cited line, 'A way of happening, a mouth'. This is what Heaney argues in the opening, title lecture of *The Government of the Tongue*, quoting the Polish poet Anna Swir on the poet as 'an antenna capturing the voices of the world, a medium expressing his own subconscious and the collective subconscious':

> Poetry's special status among the literary arts derives from the audience's readiness to concede to it a similar efficacy and resource. The poet is credited with a power to open unexpected and unedited communications between our nature and the reality we inhabit. (p.93)

Heaney's habit of ringing all the possible changes on an equivocal word or phrase comes from a refusal to be pinned down prematurely in a fixed place, a wish to keep open those channels of communication which allow all the ambivalences of his Northern Irish provenance to sound through. As 'From the Republic of Conscience' indicates, dual citizenship as an Irishman and an Ulster Catholic has its poetic equivalents. To *come back from* is to carry no baggage of duty-free allowance; but, as the comic circumlocution makes clear, it does carry the duty to be oneself, and to speak conscientiously, and without relief, as an ambassador of this freedom:

> I came back from that frugal republic
> with my two arms the same length, the customs woman
> having insisted my allowance was myself.

Likewise, the old man at immigration 'desired me when I got home / to consider myself a representative / and to speak on their behalf in my own tongue'.

In the Republic of Conscience, 'You carried your own burden and... / your symptoms of creeping privilege disappeared'. But if this is a place where the salt has not lost its savour, it is also a place where everything has to be taken with a pinch of salt. For speaking in your own tongue means avoiding the folly of 'the fork-tongued natives' of 'Parable Island', who 'keep repeating / prophecies they pretend not to believe', and who, in some perpetually deferred future, are going to start mining for truth beneath the mountain where, it is said, 'all the names converge', and all the conflicting narratives are reconciled.

In the title sequence of *Station Island*, the ghost of Carleton laments being made by Ribbonmen and Orange bigots 'into the old fork-tongued turncoat / who mucked the byre of their politics'. In 'Whatever You Say Say Nothing' (*North*) it is difficult not to be 'fork-tongued on the border bit' in a world 'Where tongues lie coiled, as under flames lie wicks' and '"You know them by their eyes" and hold your tongue.' It is in the context of these locutions and locations that we must understand the title of *The Government of the Tongue*. It is a characteristically tricksy phrase, and its tricks lie in that multiple-choice preposition: government of the tongue, by the tongue, for the tongue? The book itself offers the first two possibilities:

> what I had in mind was this aspect of poetry as its own vindicating force. In this dispensation, the tongue (representing both a poet's personal gift of utterance and the common resources of language itself) has been granted the right to govern. The poetic art is credited with an authority of its own. As readers, we submit to the jurisdiction of achieved form, even though that form is achieved not by dint of the moral and ethical exercise of mind but by the self-validating operations of what we call inspiration. (p. 92)

However, such a jurisdiction may be that of a poetic Diplock Court, and a poet who has inscribed in a poem's title the homespun political wisdom of the Irishism 'Whatever You Say Say Nothing' (almost a performative injunction, self-exemplifying, nullifying itself in a paradox in which nothing is said, twice), knows that utterance is never quite so undemanding. I am not sure whether Heaney got his title from an existing political slogan, whether the Provisional IRA got it from Heaney, or whether both adapted a pre-existent popular saw. Whatever the case, the poetry accrues legitimacy to the political slogan, putting the poem in the same compromised place as those Yeats fretted over in 'The Man and the Echo', opening up a whole new area in the relations between poetry and politics. The poem refers to 'The famous // Northern reticence, the tight gag of place'. If, in *The Government of the Tongue* (p.166), Heaney claims that on the whole he has been 'inclined to give the tongue its freedom', the poem defines the constraints of a freedom which 'Still leaves us fork-tongued on the border bit'. The border may be the bit that is between the teeth, but the poem leaves us with the biter bit, and biting his own tongue. *The Government of the Tongue* likewise speaks with a forked tongue, immediately qualifying its grandiose reiteration of Romantic clichés with a word to the wise:

> All the same, as I warm to this theme, a voice from another part of me speaks in rebuke. 'Govern your tongue,' it says, compelling me to remember that my title can also imply a denial of the tongue's autonomy and permission. In this reading, 'the government of the tongue' is full of monastic and ascetic strictness. One remembers Hopkins's 'Habit of Perfection', with its command to the eyes to be 'shelled', the ears to attend to silence and the tongue to know its place. (p. 96)

Its place here is firmly in the cheek. It is noticeable that Heaney nominates an equally Romantic, inspirational source for this countervailing instruction: 'a voice from another part of me... compelling me'. Yet it is an impersonal 'one' who remembers, not from the poet's original place, but from a position where the voice assumes, not the vatic authority of the bard, but that of a well-placed member of the literary ascendancy, languidly calling up fellow members of the club. Just which place is it that Heaney is knowing about, here?

A moment in *The Haw Lantern* sneakily qualifies this authority, reminding us from what part of himself that voice may have spoken, as well as *what* he may know better, in the fourth sonnet of the elegiac sequence for his mother, 'Clearances':

> With more challenge than pride she'd tell me, 'You
> Know all them things.' So I governed my tongue
> In front of her, a genuinely well-

> Adjusted adequate betrayal
> Of what I knew better.

The maternal reproach arises from her own 'Fear of affectation', her mispro-
nunciation of words 'beyond her' expressing – possibly – fear of betraying
'The hampered and inadequate by too / Well-adjusted a vocabulary'. The
already readjusted poet, condescendingly relapsing into 'the wrong / Grammar
which kept us allied and at bay', only obliquely questions how this community's demotic is somehow ruled 'wrong' in the discourse of polite society.
Although the poet is instructed to govern his tongue, it seems that it is the
mother's tongue – the mother tongue – which is put in its place, and that
place is *in the wrong*. However, the poem's tongue is subtle and diverse here, as
I will argue later.

There is another moment in *The Haw Lantern* where the poet governs his
tongue, self-consciously submitting, not to the voice of inspiration, but to a
formal tradition of occasional verse which has 'English' written all over it. 'A
Peacock's Feather' is a poem written for the christening of an English niece
(as the text designates her), and it squirms with polite embarrassment at so
bridling its tongue as to utter something alien but in keeping with the pastoral
'mellowness' of a Gloucestershire landscape. Even here the poem still knows
where it comes from:

> I come from scraggy farm and moss,
> Old patchworks that the pitch and toss
> Of history have left dishevelled.

But it is not so sure of where it is going. Compelled by occasion, status, loyalty, to govern its tongue and provide a light celebratory poem, one thinks of
Yeats, that earlier voice which spoke with Ascendancy accents in a good cause,
recognising that, a guest at this green court, 'Self-consciously in gathering
dark. / I might as well be in Coole Park'. Slyly coiled in the 'in-law maze' of
the tongue, in the poem's absolving 'touch of love', the voices wait to speak
out through the mask: 'Couldn't you do the Yeats touch?' One thinks too, that
is, of Joyce, deflating Yeats's flattery of Lady Gregory: 'The most beautiful
book that has come out of our country in my time. One thinks of Homer.'[6]

The tone is very different from Yeats's. A 'billet-doux', a nursery rhyme,
quiet, casual, governed, wishing no harm, its blushful whimsy calls up the de
la Mare of *Peacock Pie*. But there is an altogether more strident resonance to
the bird, recalling that peacock which screamed among a rich man's flowering
lawns in Yeats's 'Ancestral Houses', betokening the end of a civilisation,
adding a deeper darkness to the gathering dark. If the future's not our own,
neither is the past. This levelled landscape requires a prayer for its future
precisely because of that past. The semi-archaic vocabulary of 'tilth and loam'

of the final stanza gestures fancifully to a time when Celt and Saxon fought over this now idyllically peaceful ground. But the sense that this soil is 'darkened' with their blood darkens the whole tone of the poem, as does the disturbing enjambment of 'blood / Breastfeed' in the penultimate couplet, in which, surreptitiously, the mother's milk might seem to run with blood. The slate of the opening may not, after all, be wiped clean, for all our pious hopes. The poem sounds out through the persona it assumes against the place to which it is quite sincerely addressed – a place identified in an essay in *Preoccupations* as 'In the Country of Convention: English Pastoral Verse'. Pastoral is a conventionally innocent realm, certainly; but England is a country governed by the false naiveties, the feigned ingenuousness, and the evasive conventions of pastoral.

Thinking In and Back Into Place

Kavanagh's landscapes, Heaney says, are 'hallowed by associations that come from growing up and thinking oneself in and back into the place' (*Preoccupations*, p.145). Heaney's own most Kavanaghish poem is probably 'The Old Team' in *The Haw Lantern*, but even here the real places 'Have, in your absence, grown historical', part of a history which is a repertoire of antagonistic stories. The title of *Field Work* had pointed the way to these later developments, poised equivocally between the local – the real fields and hedges of this sequence, from which the particular poetic talent emerged – and the larger field of meanings within which that life now finds itself, which, as indicated in a poem such as 'A Postcard from North Antrim', is always elsewhere. 'A Postcard from Iceland' in *The Haw Lantern* reads like an ironic postscript to Auden's and MacNeice's *Letters from Iceland*. Auden may have had his Northern Irish travelling companion in mind when he wrote, in the opening poem to that volume, 'North means to all: reject!' Certainly Heaney seemed to be recalling this when, in the title poem of his own *North*, he 'faced the unmagical / invitations of Iceland', foremost of which is the invitation to encompass by going beyond, rejecting his native culture, as Auden and MacNeice did in casting from Iceland a cold anthropologist's eye on Englishness and Irishness alike. Heaney's island parables (including 'Station Island' and 'Parable Island' itself), all test and transcend the limits of Irish insularity, the better to return to and interpret it – to rediscover, thinking in and back into the place, from this vantage point on the ultimate margin of Europe, 'How usual that waft and pressure felt / When the inner palm of water found my palm'.

It is from outside the field that the pattern of forces can best be understood, rather than simply suffered. That identity is best found in displacement, in both the literal and the psychoanalytic sense, is the point of the important lecture on

Place and Displacement Heaney delivered at Dove Cottage in 1984, seeing in the uprootedness of the returning native Wordsworth, a displaced person, *persona non grata* in his own country, a model for all subsequent poetic displacements:

> The good place where Wordsworth's nurture happened and to which his habit-ual feelings are most naturally attuned has become... the wrong place. He is dis-placed from his own affections by a vision of the good that is located elsewhere. His political, utopian aspirations deracinate him from the beloved actuality of his surroundings so that his instinctive being and his appetitive intelligence are knocked out of alignment. He feels like a traitor among those he knows and loves.[7]

Recent Northern Irish poetry, he says, reveals the same double displace-ment. The way to cope with 'the strain of being in two places at once, of needing to accommodate two opposing conditions of truthfulness simultane-ously' (p. 4) is not despair, however, but Jung's strategy of finding a 'displaced perspective' in which the suffering individual can outgrow particularised allegiance while managing to 'keep faith with... origins', 'stretched between politics and transcendence... displaced from a confidence in a single position by his disposition to be affected by all positions, negatively rather than posi-tively capable' (p. 8). The echo of Keats's 'negative capability' as an answer to Wordsworth's 'egotistical sublime' indicates the way out from the Northern Irish deadlock Heaney was to seek from *Field Work* onwards. It is in the 'lyric stance', in language as itself a site of displacement, 'the whispering gallery of absence', 'the voice from beyond' of which the Grasmere lecture speaks (pp. 7, 9, 10), that the writer can seek the hopeful imaginary resolution of real con-flicts.

Heaney's poetry has consistently pursued language as political metaphor and metonymy through to its source, a recognition of its function as both place of necessary exile and site of a perpetual return home. *Station Island* was the product of such a recognition, a volume full of departures and returns. Displacement there was seen not as exile but as freedom, and the faithful infidelity of the émigré who, like Wordsworth, is now just 'visiting' that which he's left behind, provided the central impulse of the volume. *The Haw Lantern* goes a step further, beyond the margins altogether, to deconstruct those blar-ney-laden tales of nativity, decentring and redefining a self-regarding Irishness. In the words of the title poem, it is not enough to bask in 'a small light for small people'. The modest wish to prevent 'the wick of self-respect from dying out, / not having to blind them with illumination' is too limited, too easy an ambition. Now it requires a Diogenes with his lantern, searching for a single just man, to be the true measure of this field, scrutinising with a gaze which makes one flinch, with a 'blood-prick that you wish would test and clear you'. The terror of being tested, assessed, and the anxious yearning for clearance, run through most of the poems in the volume. The gaze that here scans and then moves on brings to bear both a moral and a poetic measure. 'Parable Island' tells us that there are no authenticating origins, only a plethora of story-tellings which push the origin further back into an original emptiness, scrawled over with too much meaning. It is in this area of dense secondary signification, where script dissembles an original emptiness, that, for Heaney, Ireland 'begins'.

Drawing a Line Through

'Whatever You Say Say Nothing' (*North*) speaks of the ends of art:

> To lure the tribal shoals
> To epigram and order. I believe any of us
> Could draw the line through bigotry and sham
> Given the right line, *aere perennius*.

The word 'order' crosses its customary frontiers here, negotiating familiar trans-actions between political and literary structures, as is indicated by that multiple paronomasia on 'line' as boundary demarcation, poetic line and, possibly, ideological narrative. The further, suppressed meaning of 'line' (taking up 'gaff and bait') adds a rather more dubious resonance, for the fisher of men may lure the tribal shoals into those Joycean nets which ensnare the soul, though purification, in the echo of Mallarmé mediated by Eliot, is clearly the poet's aim. In 'The Sense of Place', Heaney wrote *en passant* of Synge, 'whom Yeats sent west to express the life of Aran, in the language of the tribe', thereby creating 'a new country of the mind' (*Preoccupations*, p.135). Although he here sees this as positive, in 'A Tale of Two Islands: Reflections on the Irish Literary Revival' he is rather more wary of Synge's enterprise, invoking in support not only Kavanagh but, most potently, Stephen Dedalus's intense and satiric rejection, at the end of *Portrait*, of the old man of the west, whose mountain cabin is 'hung with the nets of nationality, religion, family, the arresting abstractions'. But, Heaney adds, though Stephen fears, he will not destroy him:

> The old man is as much a victim as the writer. His illiterate fidelities are the object of Stephen's scepticism, the substance of what Stephen rejects; and yet they are a part of Stephen himself. Stephen is angry that all his culture can offer him for veneration is this peasant oracle, yet understanding the ruination that he and the old man share, he is not prepared to struggle to the death. [8]

There is a poetic course to be charted here between the demands of 'native' *orality* and 'universal' *writing*. But if the siren voices of an illiterate oracle are not to run the project aground on populist mudbanks it must take on board those instructions to 'purify the dialect of the tribe' from 'Little Gidding' which resonate in Heaney's own ghostly Dantescan sequence, 'Station Island'. Eliot, Dante and Jung rub shoulders in the last displacing moments of the essay. However, the fullest account of Dante as role-model in this later poetry is given in Heaney's 1985 article, 'Envies and Identifications: Dante and the Modern Poet':

> The way in which Dante could place himself in an historical world yet submit that world to scrutiny from a perspective beyond history, the way he could accommodate the political and the transcendent, this too encouraged my attempt at a sequence of poems which would explore the typical strains which the consciousness labours under in this country. The main tension is between two often contradictory commands: to be faithful to the collective historical experience and to be true to the recognitions of the emerging self.[9]

Heaney's use of the phrase 'the language of the tribe' is suggestive, for it reproduces the mis-citation of that Eliot Donald Davie deploys throughout his seminal 1952 study *Purity of Diction in English Verse*.[10] Davie speaks of 'Mr Eliot's phrase, "to purify the language of the tribe"' (p.31) and uses this formula for the title of his crucial chapter. Eliot's actual formulation, following Mallarmé, is 'the dialect of the tribe'. Davie's book, written while he was a lecturer in Dublin, also deploys Synge as an example of a suspect linguistic populism which exploits the 'bathetic' and 'brutal'; while in an important chapter he sets up Dante as an antithetical model of how poetry should relate to 'the vulgar tongue'. Davie's introduction raises questions of diction as political and moral touchstones in terms which are strikingly consonant with those Heaney later deploys:

> [T]he poet who uses a diction must be very sure of the audience which he addresses. He dare not be merely the spokesman of their sentiments and habits, for he must purify the one and correct the other. Yet he dare not be quite at odds with his age, but must share with his readers certain assumptions... At this point, discussion of diction becomes discussion of the poet's place in the national community, or, under modern conditions (where true community exists only in pockets), his place in the state. This aspect of the matter will become clearer when we ask how the poet, in his choice of language, should be governed, if at all, by principles of taste. And this is inseparable from the question of what Goldsmith and others understood by chastity and propriety in language. (p.17)

Dante's treatise *De Vulgari Eloquentia* is a key item in Davie's argument (pp. 82–90), and the terms in which Dante negotiates the relation between the vernacular ('The Vulgar Tongue') and 'Grammar' (Latin) are cast in a language suggestively similar to that which Heaney later deploys in *The Haw Lantern*. This is specifically a question of the relations between 'the language of the tribe' and its various dialects, and the distinction, in many ways corresponding to the Saussurean one between *langue* and *parole*, explains why both Davie and Heaney misquote Eliot's formula.

Davie observes: 'Dante remarks that no one of the dialects can be considered the most illustrious, since the best poets have always departed from their own dialect for the purposes of their poetry.' What Dante calls the '"Illustrious Vulgar Tongue"' is 'the perfection of a common language', 'intelligible to all … but peculiar to none'. And, in words which recall the figure of the lantern-bearing Diogenes in the title poem of *The Haw Lantern*, he quotes Dante's observations that '"our Illustrious Language wanders about like a wayfarer and is welcomed in humble shelters"' and '"shines forth illuminating and illuminated"'. It recognises no local princely court or court of justice, Dante claimed, because it is itself 'courtly' and 'curial', carrying within itself '"the justly balanced rule of things which have to be done"', itself the final court of linguistic appeal, '"though, as a body, it is scattered"' (pp.86–8).[11] This is, in fact, language as that 'frugal republic' with 'embassies… everywhere' of which the poet is required to be 'a representative / and to speak on their behalf in my own tongue', of 'From the Republic of Conscience'.

Dante's discourse on the 'Illustrious Language', and Davie's commentary on it, call up many of the preoccupations of *Station Island* and *The Haw Lantern*. In particular, they go some way to explaining that complex, multiply punning play on 'clear' and clearance' in the latter volume, linking the blood-prick of the haw lantern 'that you wish would test and clear you', and 'the squawk / of clearance' of 'From the Frontier', to the running motif of the elegiac sequence 'Clearances', where his mother's death effects a clarification of meanings and clears a space which is momentarily common:

> And we all knew one thing by being there.
> The space we stood around had been emptied
> Into us to keep, it penetrated
> Clearances that suddenly stood open.
> High cries were felled and a pure change happened.

The inconspicuous metaphor 'felled' then leads on to the final clearance of the sequence, and the poet's sense of his own mortality in the image of the chestnut tree, coeval with him, now long gone from the hedge where it was planted, no more than 'a space / Utterly empty, utterly a source', having 'lost its place', 'become a bright nowhere, / A soul ramifying and forever / Silent, beyond silence listened for'. The motif here is not finally personal life and death, but the sources of poetry, calling up both that line quoted in *The Government of the Tongue* as evidence of Philip Larkin's unlikely affinity with

Dante, 'Such attics cleared of me, such absences' (p. 22), and Auden's elegy for Yeats, who 'became his admirers', 'scattered among a hundred cities / And wholly given over to unfamiliar affections'.

Heaney's prose gloss of this anecdote, in 'The Placeless Heaven: Another Look at Kavanagh', makes it clear that it is a parable about the relation between the poet's actual and linguistic universes. As a child, he says, he identified with the tree. Now he identifies with the 'luminous emptiness' its absence creates:

> Except that this time it was not so much a matter of attaching oneself to a living symbol of being rooted in the native ground; it was more a matter of preparing to be unrooted, to be spirited away into some transparent, yet indigenous afterlife. The new place was all idea, if you like; it was generated out of my experience of the old place but it was not a topographical location. It was and remains an imagined realm, even if it can be located at an earthly spot, a placeless heaven rather than a heavenly place. (*Government*, pp. 3–4)

Dante offers an authority for effecting such a clearance of the linguistic ground, asking, of the 'Illustrious Vulgar Tongue' in a metaphor Heaney seems to pick up from Davie's citation, '"Does it not daily root out the thorny bushes from the Italian wood? Does it not daily insert cuttings or plant young trees? What else have its foresters to do but to bring in and take away as has been said?"', with the result that writing is '"brought to such a degree of excellence, clearness, completeness, and polish"'. A poem ends in a clarification of life, says *The Government of the Tongue*, echoing Robert Frost. Heaney, however, in a poem such as 'The Mud Vision', knows how easy it is to forfeit such clarification. The truly vulgar may overwhelm the possible 'new place', 'transparent, yet indigenous', of the illustrious language:

> Just like that, we forgot that the vision was ours,
> Our one chance to know the incomparable
> And dive to a future. What might have been origin
> We dissipated in news. The clarified place
> Had retrieved neither us nor itself.

For this project of clarifying and clearance Davie's polemic offers ample precedents. His exposition of Owen Barfield's analogy between 'metaphor: language: meaning :: legal fiction: law: civil life' (pp. 29 ff) runs parallel with Heaney's own recurrent analogy between poetic form and political jurisdiction:

> For just as law is consistent, inflexible and determinate, yet must, to keep pace with social changes, have recourse to fictions; so language is fixed and determi-

nate, to satisfy needs of logic, yet must, to keep pace with changes in thought and life, evolve new meanings by way of metaphor.

But of singular application to this volume is Davie's account of how diction can be purified when 'the dead metaphors of poetry are brought to life by the tang of common usage; and vice versa'. This revivification of dead metaphors has itself a social and political implication: 'For if the poet who coins new metaphors *enlarges* the language the poet who enlivens dead metaphors can be said to *purify* the language'. Heaney exposes the artifice of language throughout *The Haw Lantern* by showing both these processes at work. He foregrounds language, not by thickening it into the opacities of his earlier work, reinforcing that 'sensation of opaque fidelity' which is the history of 'a dispersed people' in 'From the Land of the Unspoken', but by insisting instead on a classical austerity and bareness of diction. The more transparent it is, 'a bare wire' after all that 'textured stuff',[12] the more, paradoxically, it manifests its status as language, a medium.

Heaney in fact does a remarkable thing in this volume. He inverts the traditional critical argument that language is inflected either towards its signifieds or to its signifiers, either self-effacingly presents its meanings or self-importantly calls attention to itself as a medium. In the empiricist ideology, language should ideally efface itself, act as a clear window through which meanings are immediately and unmediatedly visible. In the radical, Modernist assault on this, language is distrusted as a suborner of meanings, and has to be fractured, dislocated, foregrounded in order to expose its ideological predisposings. Baring the device alerts us to the fact that language is not innocent but complicit, distorting or transforming that which it communicates. Heaney in these later poems demonstrates the opposite. The clearer, the more transparent the language, the more we become aware of its artifice. For in this apparent bareness it becomes clear that *no* language is free of metaphor, every word may double its meaning, and all discourse can turn back on itself in coy or brazen self-consciousness. If the clogged, sedimented streams of his earlier poetry here run clear, free of mud visions, they are still (in the words of 'The Summer of Lost Rachel') 'thick-webbed currents', and, in an image from 'Grotus and Coventina' which recalls analogies in Mandelstam and Pasternak, this clear flowing can bring

> Jubilation at the tap's full force, the sheer
> Given fact of water, how you felt you'd never
> Waste one drop but know its worth better always.

Moving towards an eighteenth-century clarity of utterance, Heaney in such parables as 'From the Land of the Unspoken' and 'From the Canton of Expectation' is able to write of his condition in cool, generalising narratives which imply a view of relation and order in the universe, and in Davie's words, 'turn their back upon sense-experience and appeal beyond it, logically, to known truths deduced from it' (*Purity*, p. 48). Personified concepts like 'Conscience', Davie says, 'specify only to the extent that they place a thing in its appropriate class, or assign it its appropriate function' (p. 52), in a system of classification like that of Linnaeus. This verse, as Heaney says of Elizabeth Bishop in *The Government of the Tongue*, 'establishes reliable, unassertive relations with the world by steady attention to detail, by equable classification and level-toned enumeration' (p.102).

Of personification, Davie observes, 'an abstraction is personified to some extent as soon as it can govern an active verb'. Heaney turns this to good effect when, in 'Alphabets', he depicts language taking precedence over the subjects who utter and are uttered by it: 'Declensions sang on air like a *hosanna*', rising up like columns of cherubim and seraphim in the young boy. 'The Song of the Bullets' is even more explicitly classical in its personifications ('As justice stands aghast and stares') though it marries these with a Hardyesque bitter whimsy. Such techniques combine with periphrasis and circumlocution to make us see things in a new way, draw new lines through experience, in parables about the dangers of confusing storytelling with reality such as 'Parable Island' and 'From the Canton of Expectation', or fables about fable-making like 'A Daylight Art'.

Standing In and Standing For

The Haw Lantern shows a remarkable retreat from the linguistic density of metaphor which characterised Heaney's earlier volumes. Metaphor overrides all the differences between tenor and vehicle, concentrating them into some fused and compacted unity of meaning. Instead, these poems demonstrate language's incessantly metaphoric power by foregrounding it in the cooler, more explicit procedures of simile, where likeness is established between two items which nevertheless remain discrete, unfused. These poems abound in the quasi-prepositional connective 'like', from the very first analogical moment in 'Alphabets', where the child is initiated into the human world of comparisons, shadows and reflections that become substances, similes that overwhelm their referents, as the father's hands make on the wall a shadow 'like a rabbit's head'.

Throughout this poem, the child grows by learning to recognise and make analogies for himself, acquiring that simile-making process which maps a world of general categories, constructing more and more elaborate systems out of comparisons between the discrete phenomena of the world, learning to seek out 'the figure of the universe / And "not just single things"'. 'The Spoonbait' reveals the secret of this analogical habit at the heart of language. Inflected into archaism by its preposition ('unto'), the process takes on an odd and artificial character. We cannot slide unself-consciously from tenor to vehicle as if this were the most natural thing in the world:

> So a new similitude is given us
> And we say: the soul may be compared
> unto a spoonbait that a child discovers.

As the analogy is developed, metaphor crowds out the original similitude until the narrative generates its own new simile ('Like the single drop that Dives implored'). But the poem then disrupts this naturalising of simile into metaphor by offering two equally unexpected alternative endings, foregrounding the fact that we are dealing here with analogies, not literal acts. One is a fanciful metaphor achieved simply by omitting the 'like'; the other stresses its 'alternative' status, and insists once again on the gratuitousness of the simile, 'spooling out of nowhere' and 'snagging on nothing'.

By calling our attention to the process of analogy-making, these poems emphasise that meaning is a linguistic construct, subject to choice and capriciousness, and not a natural event. 'Parable Island' is the clearest exploration of such a process. Stressing in the idea of parable the gratuitous and deliberate drawing of analogies between one narrative and another, it offers a meta-narrative in the parable-making act itself. Even Heaney's own recurrent argument from etymology is here satirised, in deriving 'Island' from 'eye' and 'land', in a parable of visions and revisions. The dilemma of 'Parable Island' is that the competing narratives that dominate this terrain, so close and so far from 'Ire-land', do not know they are metaphoric, and so condemn themselves to beating their heads against stone.

As so often, Heaney's precedent here is Joyce. Not, this time, the much-quoted encounter between Dedalus and the old English Dean, but that earlier episode in which the infant Stephen naively tries to resolve the political and religious squabbles of the Christmas dinner by dissolving them into problems of metaphor and metonymy: 'Tower of Ivory', 'House of Gold'. Purifying the dialect of the tribe is then not just an act of linguistic reclamation. It also clarifies moral and political confusions generated by the opacities of language itself, melting down and reforging in the smithy of the soul those clanking narratives that 'From the Canton of Expectation' calls 'songs they had learned by rote in the old language'.

The poems in *The Haw Lantern* illustrate the ways in which the dead political and religious metaphors of everyday language can come alive in unexpected clarifications of meaning. There is 'The Wishing Tree', for example, 'lifted, root and branch, to heaven'. In the sequence 'Clearances', 'Cold comforts *set* between us' sees the ordinary past participle of place turn into a verb which sets (seals and solidifies) a covenant of comfort between mother and son. The dead metaphor of 'bring us to our senses' in the same poem is

135

renewed by being taken literally, just as the priest going 'hammer and tongs at the prayers for the dying' comes alive in the echo back to the coal hammer of the opening, the household implements of the previous poem and the soldering iron, bucket and 'fluent dipping knives' of this. Elsewhere in the sequence the simple chore of folding sheets 'hand to hand' and 'touch and go' opens up these dead metaphors by figuring them forth in real space as enacted moments in a complicated relation:

> So we'd stretch and fold and end up hand to hand
> For a split second...
> Beforehand, day by day, just touch and go,
> Coming close again by holding back.

An implied pun in 'Parable Island' says it all, speaking of archaeologists who variously interpret stone circles as 'pure symbol' or 'assembly spots or hut foundations':

> One school thinks a post-hole in an ancient floor
> stands first of all for a pupil in an iris.
> The other thinks a post-hole is a post-hole.

The exasperation of that last bald statement restores the dead metaphor of 'stands for' back to an original literalness, in which a post-hole *stands for* the post which stood in it. A change of preposition converts literal into metaphoric and back again. By insisting on such clarifications of experience in language the poet can, in the words of 'The Sense of Place', define 'where he stands and he can also watch himself taking his stand'.

It is perhaps in the Latinate pun that Heaney most clearly fulfils Davie's prescription for purity of diction. 'The clarified place' of 'The Mud Vision' refers to both a physical and an intellectual process. The soul 'ramifying' (branching out) in 'Clearances' extends the analogy with the chestnut tree. 'Clearances' is particularly rich in the device. Religious and everyday meanings of 'incensation' are brought out by juxtaposition with 'the psalmist's outcry taken up with pride'. A scarcely noticed series of these in the fourth sonnet plays on a range of etymologies to suggest the complex negotiations of mother and son. The mutual jostlings of 'affectation' and 'affect' (to put to, aspire to something beyond, put on), 'adequate' (made level with, equal to) and 'adjusted' (put next to) open up the central ambiguity of the clause 'whenever it came to / Pronouncing words "beyond her"'. The relation of the here and now ('came to') to a 'beyond' is in fact the subtext of the whole sequence, even at the level of its prepositions. 'Adjusted' (actually from *adjuxtare*) according to the Complete Oxford English Dictionary was early confused with the idea of an equalizing 'justice' (*ad justus*) which put things in their proper place, thus establishing a kind of punning relation with 'adequate'. The poet enacts this adequation by juxtaposing them in his own 'genuinely well- / adjusted ade-quate betrayal'. 'Pronouncing words "beyond her"' thus overlays the simple speech act with the pronouncement of an edict of expulsion by and from the tongue's seat of government. This in turn opens up the politic adjustments of 'manage': in 'affecting' incompetence (all she could manage) she adroitly manoeuvres the son to fall fittingly back into his place ('decently relapse').

The Latinate pun is most brilliantly affected, however, in the concluding lines: 'I'd *naw* and *aye* / And decently relapse into the wrong / Grammar which kept us allied and at bay.' 'Allied' (from *alligare*) can mean bound together either by kinship or treaty, and so keeps open the nature of the truce negoti-ated between them. 'At bay', however, pointedly recalling Dedalus's response to the old Dean's words, 'My voice holds them at bay', is a dead metaphor which ramifies into remarkable life when its etymology is considered. According to the Complete Oxford English Dictionary (p. 712):

> Two different words seem to be here inextricably confused. Originally the phrase *to hold at bay* seems ad. OF *tenir a bay* (Godefroy) It. *tenere a bada*, where *bay, bada*, means the state of suspense, expectation, or unfulfilled desire, indicated by the open mouth (late L. *badare* to open the mouth); but *to stand at bay, be brought to bay*, correspond to mod. Fr. *être aux abois*, meaning to be at close quarters with the barking dogs, and *bay* is here aphetically formed from ABAY, a. OF *abai* barking.

'Allied and at bay' is itself a state of suspension between decency and lapse, wrong grammar and right place, silence and speech. The poem's open-mouthed closure, a fork-tongued moment of unfulfilled desire in the govern-ment of the tongue, speaks from the central reticences of Heaney's verse. What 'Grammar' (Greek *gramma*, a written mark) and 'at bay' (open-mouthed) set up at either end of this line is the same antithesis uttered in the Latinate pun of the opening poem of the sequence, which speaks of a 'co-opted and obliterated echo' struck off the real world, which may 'teach me now to listen / To strike it rich behind the linear black' of a written text. 'Obliterated', literally, means *erased from writing*: in a Derridean sense, the voice's echo or trace erased and yet co-opted in the lines of writing. It is by making such clearings in the undergrowth of language that the bewildered self can find a place to stand, a place to make a stand.

The Distance Between

The relation between mother and son, 'allied and at bay', is also a relation between two moments of language – between writing and speech, and between *Langue*, 'Grammar', and *parole*, voice. It is a relation of kinship and treaty, not hostility. It reproduces, therefore, a more condign version of that stand-off Stephen Dedalus effects in relation to the 'illiterate fidelities' of a 'peasant oracle'. An alternative relation in *Portrait* is figured in a passage to which Heaney has adverted on several occasions, Stephen's encounter with the old English Dean. 'Stephen, in that famous passage,' Heaney says in the lecture *Among Schoolchildren*, 'feels inadequate when he hears the English Jesuit speaking English'. The differences between them, differences according to Heaney of 'cultural and geographic placing', are the oral register, 'on his lips and mine', of a *différance* within a shared 'language, so familiar and so foreign' ('allied and at bay'). Heaney first drew on this passage for the epigraph to 'The Wool Trade' (in *Wintering Out*),[13] where the words are finally left to 'hang / Fading, in the gallery of the tongue'. In the lecture, however, he moves on, calling our attention to Stephen's less frequently remarked comeback, in which, brooding on his linguistic displacement, he looks up the word 'tundish' in the dictionary only to 'find it English and good old blunt English too'. Heaney's comment is significant:

> What had seemed disabling and provincial is suddenly found to be corroborating and fundamental and potentially universal. To belong to Ireland, to speak its dialect, is not necessarily to be cut off from the world's banquet because that banquet is eaten at the table of one's own life, savoured by the tongue one speaks. Stephen now trusts what he calls 'our own language' and in that trust he will go to encounter what he calls 'the reality of experience'. But it will be his own specific Dublin experience, with all its religious and historical freight, so different from the English experience to which he had heretofore stood in a subservient relationship.[14]

In his encounter with the ghost of Joyce at the end of 'Station Island', the poet returns to this episode, referring to it jokily as 'The Feast of the Holy Tundish', canonizing it among his stars as Stephen had turned it into a governing myth in his diary. (It takes place, coincidentally, on the poet's birthday, which Heaney reads as an omen.)

I take these three writing events to be crucial for Heaney. Stephen recuperates the event by writing it up, and he turns to the higher authority of the dictionary, to find the true lineage of the word restored in the authentic history on the printed page, rather than in the unreliable local narratives of the oral order. He thus delivers the rationale for Heaney's own compulsive resort to etymology, not as a search for lost origins, but so as to restore language to a living, changing history, to underwrite (I use the metaphor deliberately) the written synchronic *Langue* and the diachronic spoken *parole* with the print that establishes authentic relation between them. Joyce refuses to be displaced by linguistic nationalism, English or Irish, because, as Heaney notes in a Latinate pun, he 'is against all such alibis'. In refusing to claim he was somewhere else (the etymological meaning of '*alibi*'), 'he is also intent on deconstructing the prescriptive myth of Irishness which was burgeoning in his youth and which survives in various sympathetic and unsympathetic forms to this day'.

Rewriting this episode in 'Station Island', Heaney attempts a similar deconstruction, putting words into the mouth of a dead man which, as I pointed out in an earlier chapter, turn in the mouth itself into a highly material image of *writing*:

> his voice eddying with the vowels of all rivers
> came back to me, though he did not speak yet,
> a voice like a prosecutor's or a singer's,
>
> cunning, narcotic, mimic, definite
> as a steel nib's downstroke, quick and clean.

Joyce's peroration likewise homes in on writing as a physical, bodily act:

> '...The main thing is to write
> for the joy of it. Cultivate a work-lust
> that imagines its haven like your hands at night
> dreaming the sun in the sunspot of a breast'.

A final ironic transformation of the wireless imagery turns the broadcast voice into a metaphor of that writing which most intimately defines the unique, autonomous self, urging him to '"swim / out on your own and fill the element / with signatures on your own frequency."' Heaney here gives a subtle, original twist to the cliché of the poet finding his own voice. It is no accident, then, that the poem which follows this and opens the next sequence, 'The First Gloss', should instruct the poet to hold his pen like a spade ('Take hold of the shaft of the pen'), in an intensely physical act of writing which recalls the resolution in the first poem of his first collection:

> Between my finger and my thumb
> The squat pen rests.
> I'll dig with it.

'Subscription', in 'The First Gloss', means paying one's dues, accepting a lineage and an authority, even as one takes the first step into the margin. 'Alphabets', the opening poem of *The Haw Lantern*, spells out this subscription in the most literal of terms, exploring the child's conscription to his culture through the succession of writing styles he acquires. Writing here is a manual labour, acquired with difficulty: 'there is a right / Way to hold the pen and a wrong way'. We are reminded that words themselves, no matter how seamlessly interwoven in utterance, are really made up of more primary units, represented by written signs (*gramma*) which arbitrarily and artificially stand in for consonants and vowels. The poem plays games with its own origin, starting with the alphabetic Greek of the Harvard 'Phi Beta Kappa' poem, to reconstruct a whole series of other signs the child has lived through, from his father's shadow-drawing, through modes of writing pictographically only a step away from this – the letter 'Y' seen as a forked stick, '2' as a swan's neck and back, 'A' as 'Two rafters and a cross-tie on the slate', 'O' a schoolroom globe, the teacher's tick 'a little leaning hoe' – through the joined-up writing of 'new calligraphy that felt like home', the Ogham whose 'alphabet were trees', 'The lines of script like briars', the bare Merovingian style, the Latin capitals of the sky-writing 'IN HOC SIGNO' which converted Constantine, until it returns abstract signs to material reality in the balers dropping bales 'like printouts where stooked sheaves / Made lambdas', the potato pit with a 'delta face', and omega as the shape of a horseshoe over the door.

Such analogies between arbitrary signs and the referents they invoke are not just accidental but, as this aetiology of writing suggests, grow out of an incorrigible tendency to see correspondences in the world itself, to draw similitudes, deploying that little word 'like' which runs through the poem to construct 'the figure of the universe / And "not just single things"'. The astronaut is the first human whose 'O' is not a figurative representation of the world but the great globe itself, seen unprecedentedly not as an emblem but as

> all he has sprung from,
> The risen, aqueous, singular, lucent O
> Like a magnified and buoyant ovum.

Going back to the origins, this poem proposes, means rediscovering in one's own prehistory (before writing) the origin of the species as a sign-making, tool-making animal; means recovering a state where writing is seen to be as material as that 'buoyant ovum', and as manual a labour as plastering a wall:

> Or like my own wide pre-reflective stare
> All agog at the plasterer on his ladder
> Skimming our gable and writing our name there
> With his trowel point, letter by strange letter.

This estrangement is simultaneously a homecoming – not a return to origins but to a new '*sensing* of place' in a landscape 'instinct with signs'. In an interview, Heaney explained the origin of the poem as a commission:

> I had a real problem: Write a poem for the Phi Beta Kappa at Harvard that had to
> be spoken aloud, and be concerned with learning. And that poem is precisely

about the distance that intervenes between the person standing up in Sanders' Theatre, being the donnish orator, and the child, pre-reflective and in its pre-writing odd state.[15]

That this 'pre-writing odd state' is not in any sense innocent, prior to discourse, the poem makes clear, since the child is already ensnared in the nets of language, and the whole poem explores the succession of discourses, as of alphabets, through which he learns to construct, not just a writing, but a self. And it is in some Popean 'middle state' that both poem and speaker find themselves, in that intercalated 'distance... between' of which Heaney speaks in the interview: 'there is a bemused, abstracted distance intervening between the sweetening energy of the original place and the consciousness that's getting back to it, looking for sweetness'.

Contemplating a prehistoric 'dried-up source' in the last poem of *Station Island*, Heaney speaks of keeping a stone-faced vigil 'For my book of changes',

> until the long dumbfounded
> spirit broke cover to raise a dust
> in the font of exhaustion.

Neil Corcoran sees this as a holy water font, and so it is.[16] But it is also the font of print itself, which is where all new texts find their origins. Here, in the punning metaphoric overlaying of particular life and printed page, Heaney figures forth that relation between place and displacement which is the very ground of his writing.

NOTES

1. Seamus Heaney, *The Government of the Tongue* (London: Faber and Faber, 1988), p.132; hereafter page references are indicated in the text.
2. Seamus Heaney, 'Feeling into Words', reprinted in *Preoccupations: Selected Prose 1968-1978* (London: Faber and Faber, 1980); hereafter page references are indicated in the text.
3. Reprinted in *Preoccupations*, pp. 131–49; this quotation p. 132.
4. Seamus Heaney, *The Haw Lantern* (London: Faber and Faber, 1987); except where otherwise indicated, the Heaney poems discussed in this chapter are all from this volume.
5. Sylvia Path, *Ariel* (London: Faber and Faber, 1963).
6. James Joyce, *Ulysses* (London: The Bodley Head, 1937), pp. 204–5.
7. Seamus Heaney, *Place and Displacement* (Grasmere: Trustees of Dove Cottage, 1984), p.3; hereafter page references are indicated in the text.
8. Seamus Heaney, 'A Tale of Two Islands: Reflections on the Irish Literary Revival', in P. J. Drudy (ed.) *Irish Studies* (Cambridge: Cambridge University Press, 1980), pp. 1–20.
9. Seamus Heaney, 'Envies and Identifications: Dante and the Modern Poet', *Irish University Review*, (Spring 1985), pp. 5–19.
10. Donald Davie, *Purity of Diction in English Verse* (London: Chatto, 1952); hereafter page references are indicated in the text. Heaney is likely to have encountered this book as an undergraduate. It was (rightly) regarded in the academy during this period as essential reading for anyone interested in

the workings of poetic language, and, while Davie was not a Leavisite, it would have had a strong appeal to anyone reared, like Heaney under the tutelage of Philip Hobsbaum at Queens, Belfast, in the tradition of 'practical criticism'.

11. There is a useful translation of Dante's *De Vulgari Eloquentia* by Sally Purcell, *Literature in the Vernacular* (Manchester: Carcanet, 1981).
12. On this, see Neil Corcoran, *Seamus Heaney* (London: Faber and Faber, 1986), p. 153.
13. See above, Chapter VII.
14. Seamus Heaney, *Among Schoolchildren* (Belfast: John Malone Memorial Committee, 1983), pp. 10–11.
15. Seamus Heaney, 'Interview' with Rand Brandes, *Salmagundi* (Fall, 1988), pp. 4–21.
16. Corcoran, *Seamus Heaney*, p. 179.

IX

Mind Changes:
Poets of the Postmodern

The Snake in the Scare Quotes

Explaining that the essays in his collection *Mistaken Identities* (1997) 'have as their subject the relation between poetry and notions of "identity" in Northern Ireland', Peter McDonald adds that

> my failure to provide inverted commas around the term [the Troubles] reflects, not any lack of awareness of its inadequacy, but a reluctance to litter the text with marks whose warning function would soon become tedious and unnecessary. I have tried to keep such marks away from the term 'identity' as far as possible, and for similar reasons.[1]

Not entirely successfully. If it is, in McDonald's words, 'one distinguishing feature of the post-modern intellectual that she or he knows which concepts to enclose in quotation-marks', *Mistaken Identities* is not immune from what he calls the 'trickiness' which signals 'the author's anxiety to be seen as intelligently self-conscious' (pp.41-2). McDonald's interesting and tetchy study of some of the leading Northern Irish poets of the last half century itself suffers from a kind of identity crisis, due in part, no doubt, to the diverse provenance of its essays, but also, as the scare-quotes which flicker on and off throughout the text suggest, because it shares in the confusions it addresses, foundering in the final incoherence, or insufficient thinking-through, of its ambitious ideological search-and-destroy mission.

The 'stony stability of "identity", as the word is commonly understood in Irish politics and cultural discussion' (p.56), McDonald argues, is founded in paradox. While the word ostensibly refers to 'the sheer individuality of experience, its unrepeatable particularity', in practice it is 'employed almost always to emphasise the *common* nature of experiences, and to provide those experiences with a significance and meaning already mapped out in cultural or historical terms' (p.7). This pre-mapping carries with it a 'prescriptive element' (p.3), identified in the opening chapter, using Heaney's description of poetry as 'Northern Ireland's "sixth sense"' (p.19), as a 'rhetoric of "identity"' (p.26) which fosters the cuckoo of a republican politico-cultural agenda. Heaney's own phrase is turned against the poet, to accuse him in, for example, *The Redress of Poetry* of orchestrating a 'fanciful' incorporation of Northern unionists into a spurious Irish communality (p.16), and, in 'The Toome Road', of a 'navel-gazing' which, in its 'validation of rootedness and origin', assimilates to 'vaguely nationalist cultural agendas' (p.52ff).

McDonald finds the same agenda writ large in the liberal embarrassments of the Opsahl Commission (pp.1–4 passim), which reported 'a conflict, even a confusion, of identity' in Northern Ireland, even as it found itself apologetically 'still forced to use the language of stereotypes for analysis', though 'the stereotypes no longer apply' because of the 'fragmentation of the old identities'. The central paradox, he says, is that '"Identities" seem to be the cause of the problem... and yet the problem continues to be discussed as one resolvable through identity'. The 'dangerous centrality of identity-thinking' is the unifying thesis of McDonald's study. But only just below the surface is a smouldering resentment that 'the vagueness of cultural identity-talk', the 'identity-prescriptions of one kind or another', conceal an international conspiracy to shoe-horn Northern Protestants, in the words of the Commission, into 'recognizing Protestant culture as part of an Irish identity'. His central premise is stronger than this, however, though circumspectly phrased:

> [T]he flirtation with identity-politics in which some of the literary intelligentsia (most commonly, academics and commentators from outside Northern Ireland itself) are able to indulge themselves is not entirely without its legitimating influence on those modes of discourse which have provided, especially in the USA, one kind of Irish identity with its lethal interpretative force. (p.7)

.'Lethal' is not used metaphorically here. 'Flirtation', in McDonald's perception, as for the 1930s poets around Auden (p.27), usually ends up in the arms of 'the men of violence'. This last conscripting soundbite, in discussing Seamus Deane's description of it as 'a propaganda phrase', McDonald seems keen to exempt from his general strictures on tendentious language. 'Is not Deane's "a propaganda phrase" itself already something of a propaganda phrase?', he asks, with the ring of *touché* in his voice (pp.78–9). To which one might well respond: 'Is not McDonald's putting this phrase in scare quotes not itself somewhat of a strategy in a propagandistic rhetoric?' We are here tottering on the brink of that vertiginous *mise en abyme* of narrative into which Beckett's dead dog plunges, its endless recessive embeddings mocking the follies of a self-absorbed historiography.

One of the more reprehensible poetic flirtations McDonald identifies is the *trahison des clercs* of such Protestant 'regionalists' as John Hewitt and W. R.

Rodgers, for whom 'To discover and define an "identity" for the self [was] also to flirt with ultimately determinist conceptions of character'. Flirting is not an innocent activity for McDonald, and 'determinism' always 'encodes a purpose, forcing discussion and thought in a predetermined direction'. To accept even the idea of 'a Northern Irish Protestant "identity"' means 'aligning the perspective in vital ways with certain determinist assumptions fundamental to nationalism' (p.39). Tom Paulin, in a hostile but percipient critique, is seen, similarly, as a stool pigeon, informing on his Protestant background to 'an English consensus' with 'media-friendly excursions into stereotypes of the Northern Irish Protestant identity', his 'fake... demotic' 'holding it up to an outside audience for easy ridicule', 'too quick to identify and embrace what looks to him like historical certainty' (pp.101–7 passim). In McDonald's reading, Paulin's 'telling the English what they want to hear' is a mirror-image of the Catholic Heaney's 'spectacular example' of a familiar Irish phenomenon: having it both ways, forging an 'Irish literary career' by playing up to 'English attempts to settle an identity on Ireland' (p.196). By contrast, 'the lonely extremities' (p.88) of Derek Mahon's verse 'win a freedom for the poetic voice not through a command of historical perspective but by a rejection of it' (p.85), in emulation of MacNeice's – as McDonald sees it – widely and wilfully marginalized achievement in resisting the agendas of identity politics.

McDonald is adamant that 'the primary business of his book is with poetry and not with political identity', seeking 'a critical language... not itself compromised by the insistent crises and demands of its cultural and political context', able to do justice to 'poetry's distinctiveness as a mode of discourse' (pp.18–19). 'Poets write poems', rather than seeking 'to provide cultural identity' (p.50). An authentic ('true', 'real') poetry offers 'resistance' to partisan 'rhetoric', which demands 'resonant and easily packaged versions of a certain kind of identity which will be recognizable, exportable, and politically applicable' (p.187). It espouses, not 'the totalizing narrative of violence'(p.69) justified by the 'grand narratives' of republican, marxist or postcolonial critical posturings associated *inter alia* with Field Day and its cis- and trans-Atlantic groupies, but 'the alternative discipline of the quotidian itself, with its right to apparent triviality' (p.154). This McDonald finds exemplified in Michael Longley's 'pastoral serenity' (p.119) and in Paul Muldoon's 'developing engagements with the demands of form in poetry', which, he avers, *pace* Edna Longley, do not necessarily lead to 'a mandarin remoteness, some vaguely decadent disavowal of "life" in favour of "art"', but simply refuse to have their content defined by those who have 'their own, rather precise ideas about what that "content" has to be' (p.187). Like 'determinism', 'content' for McDonald always comes wearing the green, expressing, as he says elsewhere, that 'demand for "content" in poetry that comes from the Troubles' (p.148).

There is a certain touching innocence to all this, the complement of the book's often jaundiced schoolmasterly sarcasm. But for all the naivety of that

Yeatsian antithesis of 'poetry' and 'rhetoric', McDonald is not quite the wide-eyed critical innocent he makes himself out. To insist on 'the alternative discipline of the quotidian' is itself to make a truth-claim based on a certain kind of content, with its own determinisms. The language of 'resistance' is both rhetorical and politically compromised. 'Ulster Resistance', after all, was the name of a once-powerful Loyalist paramilitary group. To speak of 'a language already infected by rhetoric' (p.63) is to deploy a rhetorical trope. McDonald justifies his own 'metaphor of sabotage' and his description of poetry as 'a subversive force' by an evasive manoeuvre that lays the responsibility elsewhere, since 'no critical analysis is likely, in present conditions, to be immune from the vocabulary of violence' (p.73). It is, he says, 'customary to repeat' in respectable critical circles that 'no literary discourse is transparent or innocently self-sufficient' (p.41), and he too, he concedes, 'could be accused of a strategic aestheticism which conceals its own political agenda' (p.73). But he has launched his pre-emptive strike already, in a modest third person impersonality that teeters between putting himself in his place and pulling rank over the critical interlopers who dare tread his native ground: 'the author of *Mistaken Identities* is no more free than any other writer from the pressures of identity discourses, and his own origins (as a Belfast-born Presbyterian) are visible plainly enough in the book's style and in certain emphases of its polemic' (p.18). However, as he observes elsewhere of others, 'merely acknowledging' a fault does not 'amend' it (p.146).

Muldoon may be commended for 'repeatedly manag[ing] to escape' from 'the language of politics and culture' (p.16), but when McDonald deploys him against the 'various distortions and political presumptions of the cultural intelligentsia' (p.153), those 'whole schools of not-thinking about literature' which have 'solid institutional presences' (p.5), he is a bit of a recruiting sergeant himself. The campaign ultimately, though, seems more concerned with status-jostling within 'a literary or academic culture open to the industry of "theory"' (p.42) than with the state of Northern Ireland. McDonald rightly argues that the rhetoric of an 'academically profitable' (p.5) and 'indiscriminate radicalism' (p.10), and 'the forensic tone of much theoretical discourse' (p.47), diminish 'the facts of murder', redefining individual lives and deaths

> within patterns of interpretation [which] take priority over the act itself, so that a man who murders (for example) can be defined and understood as a political offender – in this sense, he *is* his interpretation, and lives within a defining public identity... [T]he meaning of the victim and the meaning of the killer coexist within the same realm of discourse. One death cannot disrupt or divert the discourse by which it is interpreted. It is only one death, after all. (p.7)

But there's a sense in which the critic himself trivialises the deaths he invokes, simply to score a debating point, underlined by the formulaic repetition here, either sloppily or for rhetorical effect, of the claim a page earlier that in rhetoric 'the agenda is set outside the poem, and the poem has to conform to what the agenda requires. It is only a poem, after all' (p.6). If, 'for many of Northern Ireland's dead, the difference between being interpreted in the light of "a clear pro-republican stance" or of a "bourgeois nationalism" is indeed, in the narrowest sense, an academic one' (p.10), McDonald will not be the last academic to make the point.

Adapting Seamus Deane's observation that 'Identity is here and now, not elsewhere and at another time', McDonald affirms that

> [P]oems are to be distinguished from their interpretations, and constitute the complex 'here and now' of literary attention... more important and valuable than the assorted elsewheres of theoretical categories, just as literature is more important than the critical enterprise which may surround it. (p.8)

But, as McDonald's long, loving explication of Muldoon reveals, to read the poet as one who resists and toys with interpretation is still to offer an interpretation, and, moreover, one which enhances the critic's professional standing by demonstrating his hermeneutic ingenuity at the very moment that he fondly proclaims the poem's resistance to it. McDonald scoffs at the notion of a 'Marxist poetics' or a 'Marxist poetry', which, he says, is 'rather like cultivating Marxist flower-arranging or golf' (p.28). But the category confusion is obvious enough if we contemplate a golf or flower-arranging that, like Muldoon's poetry, 'works most powerfully, persuasively and entertainingly against grand narratives in relation to violence' (p.66). We do not speak of Christian, or Horatian, or, for that matter, revisionist golf, either, though we can and do apply all these adjectives to poetry and poetics.

For all this emphasis on the variousness of poetry's resistance to the 'totalising narrative of violence', and the 'distrust of the tendencies towards coherence which narrative generates' (p.64), there is a disturbing sameness in the chapter on 'Poetry, Narrative, and Violence' to the poems called in evidence, all of which seem to be fixated on that 'conjunction of violent death with a kind of particularity and precision' (p.65) in which an individual, 'quotidian' life is extinguished by terrorist atrocity: Longley's 'The Ice-Cream Man' and 'Wounds', Ciaran Carson's 'Campaign' and 'All Souls' with its surreal intertext of 'plastic explosive' tearing off the firemen's faces, Muldoon's 'A Trifle' and 'The More a Man Has'. It is as if McDonald had actually customised a new sub-genre of Northern Irish poetry: the snuff poem. Even Paulin receives a pat on the head when he writes of how 'Pulped bodies happen / In a charred street' (p.109). The one exception to this general amnesty is Montague's 'Foreign Field', taken to task for its 'callousness' towards a dying British soldier, 'looking away from the broken human body', McDonald alleges, to construct a 'quasi-historical' republican apologia for 'the violence that has just taken place', in a 'moment of imported analysis [that] is an infected rhetoric' (pp.51–2). Such self-righteousness hardly becomes one who a few pages later celebrates Muldoon's 'The More a Man Has' with its author's smarty-pants adolescent joke about 'an explosive end for a local politician' (p.67).

'Infection' by and 'importation' of extraneous meanings, in a furtive cross-border trade, constantly threaten McDonald's ethically-cleansed poetry. But since poetry, unlike golf, is made up of words, and words carry meanings, those supposedly illicit items of exchange are always already there, sweating away like Semtex in the false bottom of the linguistic suitcase. The claim that poetry's 'integrity' lies in 'insisting upon the privileges and proprieties of its own exist-ence'(p.17) sounds grand, especially in that Heaneyesque cadence, but is at once vatic and jejune, since 'its own existence' is so clearly a matter of those stained and compromised discourses without which it would not even make sense. W. R. Rodgers, taken to task for announcing 'I am Ulster', we are informed, has 'fallen into mere "identity" from that riskier, more precarious openness in which words are the agents of freedom rather than fixity' (pp.33–4). But without some kind of semantic fixity, no word could take a liberty, though the book's enthusiasm for the asyntactic lists in Carson, Longley and Muldoon may indicate a yearning towards some such airy post-modern free-fall.

McDonald may, like the post-modernists he allegedly disdains, prioritise a poetry 'uncoupled from the agendas of identity' (p.115) and celebrate the 'reso-nances of the inconclusive and the ambiguous' he admires in MacNeice (p.30), seeking that 'fluidity into which "character" in all good writing necessarily dis-solves' (p.40). Certainly McDonald's study, though it fans an important debate about the politics of 'identity', finds its major strengths in the little decentred details of style and cultural nuance which its author, an always astute and at his best a supersensitive reader of poetry, succeeds in teasing out. Often, to remain true to the opening manifesto, the pipe and drum band of its rhetoric has to make a detour down the *Via Negativa* of interpretation. Thus, a fine freestanding appraisal of 'Incantata' closes with the wrongheadedly negative claim that it establishes Muldoon as 'the Northern Irish poet whose work matters most in the continuation of the debate on poetry and identity in Northern Ireland', appar-ently simply by putting that 'dreary and familiar... debate' in question (pp.182–6). Similarly, the essay on Longley tacks on discussions of a concept which, in the previously published version, was hardly even considered. Even here it is resolutely resisted by the admission that 'Longley's work almost never addresses this problem of the supposed crisis of identity of the Protestant writer in Northern Ireland' (p.121), and by the concluding affirmation that 'The achieved poetic voice, therefore, has no real need to look for an identity, or offer it for mass consumption, since its business is somewhere else entirely' (pp.143–4). All of which recalls William Morris's joke in *News from Nowhere* about the chapter on 'Snakes in Iceland', which comprised one sentence: 'There are no snakes in Iceland.'

Brushing aside Field Day's toothless snakes in the grass, what this distinctly Po-Mo Peter McDonald admires most, in Muldoon, is 'The elusiveness of an authorial identity' (p.149) and 'the dissolution of identity in language' (p.70), and, in Longley, the picture of 'a self absorbed in, and maybe also in process of being absorbed by, its surroundings' (p.119), asking unanswerable 'Questions like "Who / Am I?" and "Where am I?"' (p.144). Indeed, he seems to have taken a little too seriously, almost as a touchstone, Muldoon's callow brush-off in an interview: 'I don't know if "I" exist.' To which, I suppose, the response of the sceptical reader has to be, 'Then you won't be needing that pint, then?'

Going Against the Grain: Medbh McGuckian

McDonald's predispositions are most apparent if one considers those poets he does not address, foremost among whom is Medbh McGuckian. 'Traditionally an oracle speaks in riddles', says Heaney in 'Feeling into Words', 'yielding its truths in disguise, offering its insights cunningly. And in the practice of poetry, there is a corresponding occasion of disguise, a protean, chameleon moment when the lump in the throat takes protective colouring in the new element of thought' (*Preoccupations*, p. 49). McGuckian's poetry adopts the riddling oracular tone in order to trick the language into recognitions which are not possible within the prevailing, hegemonic rhetoric, pursuing that Joycean tangent. Her second volume, *Venus and the Rain* (1984), I take to be a key moment in the struggle against the hegemony of a Yeatsian rhetoric and the kind of identity poetics McDonald abhors.[2]

McGuckian recognises that Irish impulse to name and fix, but she is also wary of the formulaic phrases in which a real meaning is occluded by the pat response. The ellipses of her writing, the elusive shimmer of a meaning that has to be tickled like a trout, refuses to come leaping into the hand, are deliberate strategies of resistance to the Yeatsian grand manner. In 'Isba Song' she speaks of the need to exorcise the insistent rhetorics and their 'almost too much meaning', to begin again in a language that recovers 'The sound the first-timeness of things we remember / Must make inside'. As with 'Venus and the Sun', the language of her poems is bent and refracted in the way the sun bends the light of the other stars. Yet the planet Venus shines only with reflected light, is 'thrown' by the gravitation and solar wind of the star she circles, which tells her how to move. The delicate relation between particular meaning and the tradition of significations in whose ambit she moves is caught in the complex quantum astrophysics of these poems. Freedom and necessity are balanced when, 'the sun's toy', held in its gravitational field, she goes 'against / The grain', and precisely because of this feels 'the brush of my authority'. Authority derives from resistance, the centrifugal urge: the power of gravity is registered at the moment of strain, and momentum itself is the product of an unequal balance of complex gravitational pulls. The play on 'holds good' in the last stanza links morality and facticity in a metaphor which makes the holding-on to meanings as much a physical process as the life-cycle of the sun. In its changing lifetime a sun will contract to a neutron star's dense vanishing-point before collapsing into a black hole from which no signals escape, though it still exerts a gravitational drag on meanings. The stars, the poem ends, remain at large, fly apart

> to a more soulful beginning;
> And the sun holds good till it makes a point
> Of telling itself to whiten to a traplight –
> This emptiness was left from the start; with any choice
> I'd double-back to the dullest blue of Mars.

That drag has a specifically Yeatsian gravity here in its echo of the claim in 'The Second Coming' that 'Things fall apart, the centre cannot hold'. But McGuckian's verbal talent is centrifugal, flying off at a tangent in an expanding universe where divergence generates further beginnings. The Yeatsian tradition holds good till it contracts to that point at which no light escapes from it, indeed all light is sucked over the threshold of its voracious event horizon. A cultural 'traplight', the binary discourse of a 'subject people' is simultaneously full, matter condensed to an enormous density, overstuffed with meaning, and empty, a devouring void. But in the language of this poem, the tangential escape is made by a deliberate displacement of metaphor. The planetary analogies translate elusively into mythological ones; Venus and Mars, from being planets, become the celestial lovers caught in a golden net in a story in the *Odyssey*. Even 'blue' here takes on an equivocal hue, from being the light of a star becoming the faintest hint of a 'blue' movie. The point about McGuckian's language is that it will not stay still; it refuses fixity, and in that process perpetually evades ideological recuperation. Protean, transformative, sliding elusively down the chain of signifiers, it defies appropriation, reminding us that language is a slippery and treacherous medium, which can only be fixed in place at our peril.

Occlusion is a keynote to this volume, as in the title poem, with its star, 'White on white', which 'can never be viewed / Against a heavy sky'. Venus here is not just the planet but the goddess of evolutionary procreative life on earth, as in Auden's 'Venus will now say a few words', her voice passing from leaf to leaf in the dripping rain, 'retelling the story / Of its provocative fractures' in a language of drifting continents and millennial erosions, rivers sawing the landscape into shape. But if meanings in this poem are quietly sewn together, they are also unstitched, as the final lines indicate, speaking of 'a waterfall / Unstitching itself down the front stairs'. The casual, unexplained domestication of this image strikes a characteristic note. The larger pattern of the verse is self-reflexive, considering its own relation, as language, to the immense gravitational pull of the dominant star, that Yeatsian centre in which all difference may be burnt out in a flare of incandescent 'Irishness'.

For McGuckian, such essentialist categories obscure and deflect meaning, as the opening poem of *On Ballycastle Beach* (1988) indicates, questioning significance in its very title: 'What does "Early" Mean?' It is a question it does not proceed to answer, ending only with more questions, 'puzzling / Over the meaning of six o'clock or seven' (do the two hours have different meanings?), or the oddity of the 'moist-day sort of name' (not given) over the house across the road.[3] Such puzzlement is the characteristic state of mind of the poems in this volume, as in the unanswerable questions which conclude 'To a Cuckoo at Coolanlough' ('And I wonder, after the three-minute / News, if you remember / The bits of road that I do?') or, in 'Frost in Beaconsfield', that enigmatic 'asking where does the day begin, / At the puritan dawn of the bosom?', the equally cryptic turning back of a question with a reiterative question in 'The Time before You' ('You ask the difference / Between a green shadow / And a brown one?') and with 'a green answer' which is no answer at all ('I can only say...'). In a manner which recalls the obliquities of Robert Creeley or some of the 'Constructivist' poems of the early Pasternak, Mandelstam and Akhmatova, or more recently, the ellipses and elisions of John Ashbery, it is the world itself which takes this interrogative stance towards human meanings. In 'On Not Being Listened To', while the 'you' addressed (whether self or another) is said to 'hold to words / Because they have been said', 'One / Quarter of the staircase asks to know / What you have written' on an envelope's 'closed throat'. The poem never makes clear why the staircase is so precisely quartered, or the rain is so keen to give examples to the window, or the sun 'imagines' the 'early / Farness' of nine o'clock in the morning. These poems do not anthropomorphise the material world. Rather they make it strange by attributing to its otherness a peculiarly attenuated form of awareness, an 'awareness' which is no more than a human interpretation of its mute questioning of human motives. This is 'The Dream-Language of Fergus', in which 'Conversation is as necessary / Among these familiar trees / As the apartness of torches'. The poem does not clarify whether the conversation is that of the people moving among the trees, or of the trees themselves, for in fact it is in 'the mistaken meaning of each' that some provisional significance is generated.

On Ballycastle Beach closes with the admission, in its title poem, that words are simultaneously 'meaningless and full of meaning', 'Sheltering just beyond my reach / In a city that has vanished to regain / Its language'. In a remote echo of *Portrait*'s 'nets' of language, the poem (and it is the poem rather than the poet) acknowledges that 'My words are traps / Through which you pick your way', that 'the water's speech', in an equally remote recollection of MacNeice's 'Sunlight on the Garden' is 'faithless to the end', that the world is everything which is the case, and ultimately beyond language. Yet, at the same time, it can only be experienced in language, as 'Turning the Moon into a Verb' in *Marconi's Cottage* (1991) reminds us, with playful seriousness, observing, of 'A secret year, a secret time' that 'Its flight is a written image / Of its cry', without explaining the relation between oral and written signs, or between them and the implied referent, itself opaque in its secrecy, secreted away from consciousness. The poem invites one to speculate that the moon here has something to do with menstruation and, possibly, with pregnancy, for it goes on to speak of how the sky becomes a womb, and of 'a vision of rivers' that, 'slanting / Across the doubly opened page / Of the moon turns her into a verb'. But the meaning is elusive, as the poem (again, it is the text itself which appears to assume first person status) turns back on the reader to emphasise its inescapable textuality, insisting that this is 'An image I have consciously / Broken...'. [4]

With the same skittish contrariness, a poem called 'The Book Room' in the same volume describes a room and an implied but enigmatic relationship of 'I' and 'he' somehow implicated in the room, without making any reference to the books which give both poem and room their names. Other poems in the same volume reinforce this sense of some disputatious irresolvable tug-of-war between language and reality: 'To Call Paula Paul', 'The Most Emily of All', 'The Unplayed Rosalind', 'East of Mozart', 'Oval of a Girl'. What McGuckian's poetry aspires to is summed up, perhaps, by the title of one poem here: 'A Different Same'. Identity is created only by the play of difference. Allegedly concrete particulars exist only within the abstractions of discourse, and such abstractions are not mere nebulous supplements to the real but integral to it, in a world 'Pierced by a sea as abstract and tough / As the infant around the next corner'. The title poem of *Marconi's Cottage* never explains why it is so called. But Marconi's invention made possible the transmission of messages, if not necessarily the transfer of meaning, over vast, abstract distances, ultimately spreading a net of communications and mis-communications around the globe, levelling the big abstractions and the minute particulars of discourse to the same semiotic plane, a kind of 'Here Comes Everybody' of the neural networks. In McGuckian's endlessly self-displacing, postmodern perspectives the 'big words' of ideological renunciation and revolt ('Non serviam') of a cosmopolitan modernist such as Dedalus become as meaningless, or as meaningful, as the settled 'identity' of that old man of the west whose cabin is 'hung with the nets of nationality, religion, family, the arresting abstractions'.

Imaginary Futures: Matthew Sweeney

Medbh McGuckian's sense of language as a 'traplight' issues in a deliberate complicating and obfuscating of speech in a way that uses difficulty to liberate us from the oppression of too obvious and given meanings. Other poets of this generation have found different strategies for deconstructing a hegemonic discourse fossilised into rhetoric. Matthew Sweeney, for example, born in Donegal, living in London, subverts the compromising hyperboles of the Yeatsian tradition by means of a deliberate flatness, the levelled, drained quality of a language which refuses the high drama of antithesis and confrontation, even if at times it goes too far down the road of indifference. Sweeney's world is one which often seems prematurely post mortem as well as post-mortification. Indeed 'After Closing Time', the final poem in *Cacti* (1992),[5] takes as its epigraph the notice in an office of Derry's city mortuary: '"Those who don't believe in life after death should be here after closing time."' The poem takes this graveyard humour literally, imagining a cemetery inhabited not by chuck-outs from the pubs, too drunk to go home, but by ghouls risen from their graves, bent on a can and a fag, for 'the dead are too many / to fit in the ground, too lively / to lie in a box'. The dead are often livelier than the living in Sweeney's poetry. After closing time is where most of the poems hang out, in a kind of washed-out post-apocalyptic end time of exhaustion, depletion, futility like that of Beckett's bleaker canvases. The tone is set by 'The Obituarist' in *The Lame Waltzer* (1985)[6], with 'His file of unfinished works' which includes Heinrich Böll, Ronald Reagan, Frank Sinatra and the Pope. The obituary is a genre in which all the narrative discriminations of the living are collapsed into a levelling retrospect. But here, since these were at the time of writing obituaries in advance of their subjects' deaths, there is a peculiar double displacement of the idea of 'a life' examined and evaluated in advance. Sweeney presents himself as an obituarist of the present, a re-hearser, one might say, of those rehearsals, apparently not the real thing, which actually constitute a life. His characters are like his 'Kipper', doubly mortified, not only 'caught alive and used for finance', but 'split, smoked and dyed this war-dance / red' simply for show, as 'evidence of much they'll never know'.

In poems such as 'The Applicants' and 'Watches', Sweeney is content to watch, and to watch other people watching and being watched, and he writes in a peculiar estranging way of behaviour rather than feelings, leaving these to be inferred from the predictable oddity of people's acts. As one poem says, 'there's little a man can do but look', sometimes with trained binoculars like a peeping tom, but without, it seems, the reckless distraction of real prurience. It is all terminal in Sweeney's universe, as with the 'Lame Waltzer' himself, pointlessly growing cacti by the tideline. 'Ends' seems to sum up the kind of emotional diet which Sweeney imposes on his subjects, speaking of the albino mouse he kept as a child, 'And when I holidayed once, he starved'. Yet here, as in *A Round House* (1983)[7], one feels that Sweeney is deliberately holding back a verbal energy which has a profoundly subversive power.

In the title poem of the latter volume he writes of his intention, in emulation perhaps of Stephen Dedalus with his Martello tower, 'to move there, like the birds in winter'. But, though he is already planning the minutiae of his move, unloading his trunk, applying a quick bucket of whitewash, he seems even less serious about his projected home than Yeats about the Lake Isle of Innisfree, for his opening line has pleaded, with some bathos, 'Will somebody build me a roundhouse / low on a headland'. Such self-subversion, calling up here the fatuous imaginary ambitions of Pinter's plays (one thinks, for example, of Davies and Aston in *The Caretaker*), makes a serious point. This verbal universe requires as its originating premise a world of work conducted by others. Its language is always second-hand and secondary, a parasite on these other activities.

Many of his taciturn narratives, made up of short, flat, unmetaphoric statements, assume in their very banality a kind of Pinteresque menace. Even narrative has been evacuated from a poem such as 'The Statues', in *Blue Shoes* (1989),[8] which opens with its speaker staring through a window, as so often in the poems, at nothing in particular, in this case 'a fly sunning itself', a magnolia, a rhododendron, and so on, in a listing of things which just happen to be there, the *blason* of a quotidian universe which has run down to an eventless stasis. Halfway through the poem, having exhausted what's seen, the speaker goes on to imagine all thirty doors in the house, its rooms and corridors, all empty and unused, with, 'everywhere, statues / watching over nobody / in those rooms, those corridors'. 'Everywhere': 'nobody': the two words constitute a binary demarcating the conceptual boundaries of this universe, in which, as in 'North' in the same volume, the road outside the window goes a half-mile north or three hundred miles south, apparently without a sign of life, and, out at sea, 'nothing crawls across the horizon'. Sometimes, however, as in the same volume's 'Hitchhiking', the world can suddenly spawn an intimidating and unwelcome plethora of people and places, discontinuous, serially linked only by the disjunctive scenario of hitchhiking itself.

The visionary dreariness of all this is reflected in the analogy in *A Round House*, between his own trek to bed and that of 'The Domestic Slugs', a poem which seems to offer a self-reflexive commentary on Sweeney's minimalist narratives. The slugs, whimsically seen as engaged on some 'final mapping of their planet', are known only by the tracks they leave behind, a 'complex, crystalline structure / spun out, a pattern, on the dead carpet', their gossamer tones reflecting back the light to 'net my eyes in this bathroom / where water's cold, ceiling paper droops.' Whether that netting of his eyes is lineally descended from Stephen Dedalus's 'arresting abstractions' is perhaps neither here nor there. It signals the same kind of state of arrest, of dead-end stasis, that Joyce's protagonist feared.

Absence is as tangible as presence in such a world. In *Cacti* the poem called, characteristically, 'The Aunt I Never Met' attributes a richness of activity and event to the absent person often denied those observed directly in other poems. 'Banknotes' opens in 'A room empty except for banknotes / scattered on floorboards', into which comes a woman identified, repeatedly, only as 'she', who, having received the key and the address, had for four weeks deferred trudging to the place, 'begrudging the fare'. Collecting as much of the money as she can, she departs, locking the door and keeping the key. There is no attempt to provide an explanatory narrative, or even to speculate about what this all means, only the bare recording of the events. Similarly, in 'A Peculiar Suicide', a man disappears, leaving a note which says '"You'll never find me"', and the whole poem then becomes an investigation aimed at refuting this, at finding the missing person, who is finally delivered dead to the reader, 'just him', without explanations, in the final stanza. 'Here', in the same volume, moves from the scene here and now, where the poet sits once again staring out of a window, 'happy to let seconds evaporate' until days or a month are passed, to a recollection, largely in negatives, of what is precisely *not* here. Wanting to take a grip on itself, the poem insists on the reality of the here and now, only to slip away at once to an imaginary lost fullness and self-presence, placing the present *sous rature* for a second time by evoking a future which will be the same, 'so completely am I here, / but so fully was I there, too, / that I will be again'.

This is a post-structuralist poetry which has unravelled all the familiar 'nets' of narrative. It doesn't always work, but at its best it has the fascinating aimless stare of Sweeney's slugs themselves, the residual consciousness of a terminal world. It may be that this deliberate minimalism is what 'The Window', in *A Round House*, calls 'camouflage. No one must be seen', simple 'survival tactics'. Another poem in the same volume, 'Lost Mail', offers an image of a displaced, misplaced language which seems the figure of a larger crisis, 'letters diverted, parcels returned... Spies... infiltrating newspapers... wrong numbers... and the dull hum of the bug'. This is a world in which 'secrets were monochrome', setting up a discrepancy between the larger, fantasy narratives of interpretation and the occasions they discover. At times, the evacuated narrative has a pulse of real horror, as in 'The Vanished', which offers 'many alphabets for the names of others', the absence at its centre that of those *desparacedos* euphemistically 'disappeared', made to vanish, by murderous Latin American dictatorships. In 'Lili Marlene' or 'Imagined Arrival' the encounter of mundane and extraordinary assumes real power. The latter's gawky parable of a parachute landing in a 'world long dead' moves from being 'unhindered by involvement' to, in the final lines, the need to explain to onlookers. The narrative sums up the precise menace of Sweeney's dead-pan world, something transfixed, too, in the last poem of *A Round House*, 'An Imaginary Future', which, having ditched like Beckett all the excitements of an expected narrative, concludes, ominously: 'But even in this imaginary future / storm will not wait for ever.'

Something Misplaced: Gerald Dawe

Gerald Dawe, born into a middle-class Protestant background in Belfast, choosing to define himself in secular, republican and socialist terms south of the border, in Galway and then Dublin, broke with the rhetorical absolutes of a Yeatsian poetic in order to enter a more difficult place. The title of one of his essay collections sums up the quest, positing, with Heaneyesque double-entendre, *A Real Life Elsewhere* (1993).[9] For him, as for Heaney, that step across a justified line is the flight, tangential, oblique, which 'deconstructs the pre-scriptive myths of Irishness', seeking a place where insight may grow. As Heaney's Sweeney admits, such a strategy 'in the end ... opened my path to a kingdom / of such scope and neuter allegiance / my emptiness reigns at its whim'. Such an emptiness, displacing the stuffed fullness of an overblown inheritance, becomes for Dawe the necessary condition of grace. The title poem of his first volume, *Sheltering Places*,[10] had already realised that the first dilemma of the modern Irish poet is the self-consciousness at being precisely that, thrust into a pattern of expectations where it is difficult for him or her to find a voice without confronting a fabricated Irishness donated by Yeats and his heirs and apostles. Such a confrontation cannot any longer be deferred, for

> The storm is reaching
> home territory, stretching
> over the hills down
> into our sheltering places.

'Names' moves inexorably from the country that shaped him to that naming of the self by which the country lays hands on one even as one abandons it. Its opening line ('They call this "Black North"') hints at the school playground bigotries of 'calling names' which, for Dawe, is where all the snakes and ladders start. Dawe exploits paradox in order to deconstruct it, speaking iron-ically here of the 'faithful journey /'of turning your back', in which rejection becomes ratification, seeing even in emigration, literal or symbolic, the figure of a predetermined and typecast destiny. But if, in the first version of the poem in *Sheltering Places* in 1978, he invites, or instructs, his archetypal IRISH POET to 'Line up and through the turn- / stile, click the ticket / and wait till you're / clear of it', from the revised version published in *Sheltering Places & Company* in 1993,[11] he significantly omits the crude but forceful formula which sees the capitalised vocation 'glued' in his passport, identifying his destina-tion as 'America or / Early Grave'. A passport, of course, confers identity, personal and national, but it is only required when one moves beyond a margin, and in Ireland, at least before the Troubles, was not needed to cross the border between North and South. But those lurking puns on 'line' and 'style', foregrounded by the turn-stile enjambment of 'turn-stile', lingering on the brink of 'turncoat', recall a hyphenation which remains linguistic as well as political.

Being 'blood-drunk with destinations', Dawe says in 'The temptation', because he 'had no place for real to go', he had fabricated a landscape half day-dream, half nightmare – almost, it might seem, a cross between Yeats's and Joyce's universes. For Dawe, Irishness is not 'native' in any simple sense, but emerges from a complex web of artifice mediated through collective imaginings. 'Supreme fiction', recalling a significantly recurrent reference point for Irish poets in this lineage, Wallace Stevens, sees the landscape of Galway not as a barren natural scene but as a remaindered human one, making marginality the key to an understanding of the so-called centre. 'Bloody Foreland' advises that

> You cannot turn
> and walk and talk
> of our past
>   as something
> natural.

The line breaks here, as in Carlos Williams's poetry, force the reader to pause and ponder each word, though the revised version, besides dropping its dedication and adjusting punctuation and paragraph breaks, dispenses with the dramatically effective isolation of 'as something', which calls attention to the nebulous indeterminacy of 'our past'.

'Bard's contention' takes issue with Stevens in a clipped stanza form that recalls not only Carlos Williams and Robert Creeley, but also the staccato utterances of John Montague, seeing Stevens's 'rage for order' rebuffed by the wind from off the sea, 'folding you in / silence, numb'.[12] This is a very different conceptualisation of that wind from Yeats's 'haystack- and roof-levelling wind / Bred on the Atlantic', in 'A Prayer for My Daughter',[13] which, despite the 'great gloom' it precipitates, impels the poet to ten stanzas of impassioned exposition of his ideas, disguised as a prayer for his daughter's future well-being which pre-emptively endows the child, in imagination at least, with all those qualities Yeats most admires in a woman. 'Bard's contention' is dropped from the revised volume, perhaps because the poet felt the ironic use of the Romantic epithet was not sufficiently distancing, or because in retrospect the poem seemed too derivative in its ventriloquial format. 'Empty Raft', similarly omitted, picks up on and turns back the rhetoric of Yeats's imagined will in 'The Tower', conferring a new contractual relation, and denouncing current Irish identity as a forged 'contract', constructed from the 'half-truths' of '"A People" / who marched to the call / of imagination'. Perhaps, again, the Yeatsian rhetoric the poem was rejecting was felt to have infected, by association, the act of rejection itself. Such all-encompassing discourses, it might seem, can only be deconstructed from the margins inwards. But if, for Yeats, things fell apart in the failure of the centre to hold, Dawe's poetry is founded on the invigorating conviction that the way forward lies in a collapsing of the centre in upon itself. Vitality can be found in that centrifugal release of energies that follows, in McGuckian's image, the star's inward collapse.

Wary of sentimentalising the Irish situation, in 'Pauper and Poet', retained almost unchanged in the later volume, Dawe rounds on a poetry closer to parasitism than to pity. The precedent attacked in this critique of 'The ways out... the facts of going' is not the literal émigré, Joyce, but a fantasy exile such as Yeats, setting sail in an imagination 'desperate for revenge' for an illusory Byzantium, while still in fact sitting 'in civilised houses', writing till famous. The emigration of such poets, unlike the pauper's, was a profitable and privileged one, their 'plight' feeding on 'images of the dead', though 'They weren't among the dying'. Dawe recognises the appeal of such Irish motifs, but his key, displacing strategy is that enacted in the peculiar, unsettling non-rhyme, just failing to be rime riche, 'place' / 'displaced', which rounds a stanza in 'Exchange':

> that is your place,
> going back as if something,
> an heirloom, memory had
> been lost or misplaced.

In such a landscape rain is an alibi which silences the past, and the wind an excuse offered in exchange for commitment. Whatever this dealer in barren landscapes came to seek, no longer remains. What these strangely understated lines achieve is a foregrounding of the human, and compromised, transactions involved in any attempt to touch the real, developing with a sudden shock the commercial metaphor of the opening line into a whole sense of trading on and trading off associations: 'alibi' leading on to the final tainted trade-off, 'offered as exchange'.

In his early poetry Dawe can affect the vatic only to achieve the obvious, but at his best an elliptical syntax which draws on a non-Irish strand of Modernism can secrete strange felicities of perception. In such poems as 'Scene', 'Candlelight', 'Dream Council' a noun-packed syntax insists on the relations between things uncovered and confirmed by the enquiring eye, and language works not just to record but to *produce* a perception. 'At Inishowen' ends 'We know our place', the deployment of the familiar formula preceding Heaney's use of it in 'Station Island' by several years, but the admission ironically displaces, registering the falsity of being placed by others. 'Seanchai' instead speaks of one with tales of 'the great cities / shining in his mind', in whose eyes nevertheless 'I saw / drawn out / an inarticulate / mythology that / had no place / to celebrate'. 'Memory' shows the poet aware both of the intractable nature of physical things and incensed, too, by the stubbornness of illusions. At home only in a 'man-forsaken' place such as this, which refuses easy assimilation and 'must / carry like the trees a silent / immaculate history', Dawe offers, in his final lines, a fusion of the material and the mental in a single image which could also characterise his own particular talent: 'Nearby the tide closes in / master of the forgotten thing.'

Gerald Dawe is himself a master of the forgotten thing, asking in 'The Journals' of some mundane early morning scene, 'Who will ever remember that this was so?', recognising his own untrustworthiness in the matter. 'Heart of Hearts', the title poem of the volume in which this appears,[14] opens with a deliberately distanced syntax recalling Christopher Middleton's early and mysterious poem 'Pointed Boots' ('There is always a man on the platform / Who is waiting'), before homing in on the implications of those two articles ('*a* man', '*the* platform'), to imagine the man standing apart, muttering to himself 'At some distance from directions', as a figure of the bemused postmodern subject, 'look[ing] intently / at each passer-by because he never knows'. For Dawe, the contemporary subject, with its self-image as the 'subject supposed to know', knows in reality only the bewilderment of its ignorance. 'One of These Days' in *Heart of Hearts* opens with a similar, impersonal syntax ('There are gates to the caretaker's house'), but in elaborating its description of the external quotidian scene finally comes back to an overwhelming question: 'But where am I?' Not far below the surface of a poem whose title suggests the possibility of leaving ('One of these days, you're gonna miss me, honey') is that even more disturbing question, 'Who am I?' 'Brio' in the same volume opens with the vignette of a normally stiff man letting his 'secret self' momentarily go in playing the piano. But its second stanza reveals the poem's speaker enviously unable to emulate him: 'I wanted to shout at the top / of my voice, but didn't know what. Hadn't a clue.' Dawe's poetry explores, centrally, a terrain mapped out by the post-ideological admissions of a subject who no longer aspires to a hegemonic, world-mastering discourse, a master only of the forgotten – which is possibly the truly distinguished – thing.

Changing Minds: Paul Durcan

Such bemused and bewildered subjects are a long way from the histrionic self-assertions of a Yeats who, even confronting death and supersession in 'The Tower', can draw up an agenda for the future of Ireland: 'It is time that I wrote my will; / I choose upstanding men....' But in the work of such Northern poets as Dawe, McGuckian and Sweeney the forgotten, marginalised things of a rather different Ireland, the flotsam stranded on Yeats's abandoned and storm-levelled shore, find their authentic and authenticating voice. Such poetry had effectively dissolved the border long before the Anglo-Irish

Agreement on power-sharing and the creation of a joint British and Irish authority. The title of the Dublin-born Paul Durcan's 1985 volume, *The Berlin Wall Café*,[15] for example, called up as if in analogy a world riven by the brutal antinomies of the Cold War, only at once to subvert such dehumanising absolutes by the comically inappropriate intrusion of the very different assumptions of café culture. Durcan's poetry adopts an absurdist narrative structure which draws on Dada and Surrealism, but preserves a surface logic both as syntax and diegesis, so that its explosions of rational discourse appear all the more alarming. The verbal universes his poetry constructs reduce to absurdity the authoritarian discourses of an ossified political and social order. The hegemonic ideologies and apocalyptic images of the Cold War, as of conflicts and divisions nearer home, appear to function only as grandiose and passing analogies for the domestic crises of marriage and divorce. The disproportion of such analogies is part of Durcan's strategy of unsettlement.

'Our Father', The final poem of Durcan's 1990 collection, *Daddy, Daddy*,[16] dedicated to his recently dead father (the two titles shifting between earthly and heavenly patriarchs) remarks, of a sudden and capricious change of buses on the way to visit his widowed mother: 'I do not know why I changed my mind', though he then goes on to speculate that it has something rather Oedipal to do with his father's expectations of him. Much of the rest of the poem follows the roundabout, digressive itinerary of the bus journey, recounting the bus conductor's libidinously charged chat-up, which opens with admiration for the bunch of irises he's taking to his mother. But it returns, at the end, to the purpose of his visit, which is also the pretext, and pre-text, of the poem. 'Our Father' adds a queer, paradoxically anachronistic and self-referential postscript to the book in which it appears, since it describes his mother's response to a text, *Daddy, Daddy* itself, which contains as its closing poem this account of her response to it:

> She says that she does not understand my new book of poems
> Which are poems I have composed for my dead father.
> 'But' – she smiles knowingly – 'I like your irises.'

That knowing smile is one of both complicity and evasion, like the clinching reference to the irises, which displaces once again the ostensible purpose of the visit, and re-centres the apparently irrelevant exchanges with the bus conductor, leaving poem and poet smiling unknowingly. The mundane idiom, 'changing one's mind', takes on a deeper significance in Durcan's poetry. For Durcan, the mind is in a state of perpetual flux, the experiencing subject has no fixity, but repeatedly wanders off into the kind of digressions and eccentric associations represented in a narrative such as 'Our Father'. Such a self is shut out from self-comprehension, lives in perpetual belatedness in relation to its own acts and decisions, the passive vehicle and recipient, rather than agent and owner, of its own experience. The speaker of these poems, like the personae of McGuckian's, Dawe's and Sweeney's poetry, is another 'subject supposed to know' who is damned if he does (and damned if he doesn't). The surreal moving of an obsessive subject in and out of history, as if Kafka were adrift in the fantasy world of Joyce's Nighttown, is a feature of Durcan's poems, evident in its more comic aspects in such poems as 'The Man who Thought he was Miss Havisham' and 'Archbishop of Kerry to Have Abortion'. The irreverent absurdity of that last title indicates how far, by the mid 1980s, the ground had been prepared for the deconstruction of the old antithetical absolutes of Irish identity and allegiance, creating the conditions for a new and fertile displacement.

Many of Durcan's poems are about the mortifications of marriage, the bewilderments and revelations it affords, and particularly those belated discoveries that one is not the person one believed oneself to be which accompany its break-up, cast into narrative modes which are on the surface inappropriate vehicles for the material. 'The Day My Wife Purchased Herself a Handgun', invoking the melodrama of the *fleuve noir*, is one of these, quirkily compounding the usual husbandly complaints with a little extra exasperation at 'her laid-back habit at bedtime / Of leaving her handgun strewn about on top of her underwear'. Though it is not until his wife takes to scattering a pair of hand grenades 'desultorily around the sacred bedroom / With the pins out' that he goes off the deep end. It can take Durcan a long time to get the point, but the best poems in *The Berlin Wall Café* are precisely about that final humiliation for a self-absorbed man who discovers that his narrative assumptions no longer fit experience. 'The Pieta's Over', in which the woman herself renounces her role as *mater dolorosa*, makes the point forcibly: 'It is time for you to get down off my knees / And learn to walk on your own two feet.' These poems get their tartness from the (mutual) bitterness of such a recognition, and from the further embarrassment for the poet at having to reassess all his past behaviour in the long shadows cast by a sinking marriage.

As the Talmudic epigraph of the volume ('The world is a wedding') makes clear, however, Durcan is writing about more than a failed personal relationship. 'The Jewish Bride' may be 'After Rembrandt', but it has shades too of Anne Frank; and the Nazi-Jew motif becomes a repeated one for the unequal and destructive relations between the sexes, a world divided by the barbed-wire and Berlin Wall of gender. 'Death Camp' deploys the persona of a man in Birkenau, contemplating the smile of a wife who was 'turned into lampshades six months ago / On my say-so', when he was Camp Commandant at a Treblinka simultaneously literal and symbolic, himself locked 'into a tiny white world of pure evil.' The wife's face is described three times as 'smiling'; his own shame, by contrast, is described as 'slime', an anagram and antithesis of that repressed 'smile'.

'Slime' is an important concept in Durcan's moral universe. His 1993 collection, *A Snail in My Prime*,[17] bringing together a selection from his earlier volumes with the new poems of the final, eponymous section, revisits the lowly viewpoint of Sweeney's slugs with an epigraph from Francis Bacon: 'I would like my pictures to look as if a human being had passed between them, like a snail, leaving a trail of the human presence and memory trace of past events as the snail leaves its slime.' Presence is registered only in its absence. This secretion which is the mere trace of an origin refers as much to the human being as to the work of art which testifies to its passage through the world. Durcan's title poem attempts to project itself into the rudimentary consciousness of a '*Slug love: / Older than the pyramids*'. It imagines the strange, post-mortem experience of the neolithic chieftain buried in the Newgrange passage grave 'mud millennia' ago, dreaming his own embalming, in which a daughter daubs slime on his face and inserts it into every crevice of his body. Discerning correspondences between the whorls of a snail's shell and the stone-carved spiral designs at Newgrange,[18] the poem gradually interweaves and then reduces into a single, overlaid and interpenetrating narrative the postmodern consciousness of the dreamer, the sense impressions of his pre-historic predecessor, and the primordial sensorium of a 'snail-soul' whose whole life is slime.

This a rich and complex poem, one of Durcan's best to date. The poem explicitly subverts Yeats's grandiose Modernist rhetoric of self-fashioning by presenting this as merely the boast of the snail which, in secreting its spiral shell, 'comes full circle / Into the completion of his partial self', as 'Round and round I trundle my bundle of ego'. Like many of Yeats's poems, 'A Snail in My Prime' is about coming to terms with supersession, inheriting from his 'extend-ed family' of snails 'a bequeathal of slime' to be passed on to daughters who will eat and cremate him, after which 'there will be from me no more poems'. The poem, like the snail's shell, is the carapace into which a life transforms and exteriorises itself, creating a momentary stay against confusion which then outlasts its ephemeral subjective source, which is no more than a 'smudge of froth'. Such a metaphor addresses much more than poetic cre-ation. It speaks of the way human history itself is bequeathed as the ground upon which subsequent generations come into existence. The poem ends with a vision of copulating molluscs ('My tail in your tail, my slime in your slime') which recasts the self-aggrandisement of 'a snail in my prime' – the last words of the poem and the whole collection – as a form of megalomania that salts its own tail / tale in the very process of mouthing it. The dream sce-narios and landscapes which invest this poem are not those of Stephen Dedalus's nightmare of history, but of Earwicker's millennial dreaming, in a night as old as time, where individual mind dissolves and disperses in the delirium of the collective unconscious.

All Durcan's poems are uneasily aware of this primordial substratum of being from which the 'bundle of ego' of the completed but always partial self emerges. 'A Goose in the Frost', which closes the 1996 volume *Christmas Day*,[19] is dedicated to Seamus Heaney, receiving the Nobel Prize in Stockholm in 1995. The poem oscillates between tribute and satire, with, in its own phrase, 'gauche élan', converting Heaney's themes, and many of the motifs of Irish literature in the preceding century, into ludicrous conceits, so that it is never quite clear just how serious is any particular formulation. At its centre is another question about identity, asking 'what?' not 'who?', putting the subject in its place in a world of objects and processes. But though the speed with which the question is answered seems to offer some assurance, this is then dislocated, displaced, by the paratactic elaborations which follow, with their drunken recollections of Ingmar Bergman's *Dance of Death* and of that whole world of associations between hegemonic discourse and testosterone, from which even Joyce's exemplary advice in 'Station Island' to 'swim / out on your own and fill the element / with signatures on your own frequency' is not entirely free:

> What are we? Vehicles of memory,
> Long memory, capacious with curiosity;
> Queue-maestros in file swaying along skylines;
> Males oozing at our orifices with hegemony;
> Airbuses zigzagging across ocean floors.

To be a vehicle of memory, those oozing orifices remind us, is finally to be the passive transmitter of some ulterior process that lies beyond and underlies all partial human discourse, at the very moment that one supposedly finds one's 'own frequency' (the image is that of tuning a wireless to the right station). Durcan's catechism, then, catches how much, or how little, may be involved in changing one's mind.

NOTES

1. Peter McDonald, *Mistaken Identities: Poetry and Northern Ireland* (Oxford: The Clarendon Press, 1997), p.vii; hereafter page numbers are indicated in the text.
2. Medbh McGuckian, *Venus and the Rain* (Oxford: Oxford University Press, 1984).
3. Medbh McGuckian, *On Ballycastle Beach* (Oxford: Oxford University Press, 1988).
4. Medbh McGuckian, *Marconi's Cottage* (Newcastle upon Tyne: Bloodaxe Books, 1992).
5. Matthew Sweeney, *Cacti* (London: Secker and Warburg, 1992).
6. Matthew Sweeney, *The Lame Waltzer* (London: Alison & Busby, 1985).
7. Matthew Sweeney, *A Round House* (London: Alison & Busby, 1983).
8. Matthew Sweeney, *Blue Shoes* (London: Secker and Warburg, 1989).
9. Gerald Dawe, *A Real Life Elsewhere* (Belfast: Lagan Press, 1993). The title derives from one of the essays in the collection, on Thomas Murphy's drama, originally published in *Linen Hall Review*, Summer, 1987.
10. Gerald Dawe, *Sheltering Places* (Belfast: Blackstaff Press, 1978).
11. Gerald Dawe, *Sheltering Places & Company* (Biddulph Moor: The Rudyard Press, 1993).
12. On the peculiar significance of Stevens's phrase for Northern Irish writing, see the discussion of Derek Mahon's 'Rage for Order' in the next chapter.

13. W. B. Yeats, *Michael Robartes and the Dancer* (Dundrum: Cuala Press, 1921).
14. Gerald Dawe, *Heart of Hearts* (Oldcastle: Gallery Press, 1995).
15. Paul Durcan, *The Berlin Wall Café* (Belfast: Blackstaff Press, 1985).
16. Paul Durcan, *Daddy, Daddy* (Belfast: Blackstaff Press, 1990).
17. Paul Durcan, *A Snail in My Prime: New and Selected Poems* (London: Harvill Press, 1993).
18. The designs are illustrated in Michael J. O'Kelly, *Early Ireland: An Introduction to Irish Prehistory* (Cambridge: Cambridge University Press, 1993), pp. 112–13.
19. Paul Durcan, *Christmas Day* (London: The Harvill Press, 1996).

X

The Twilight of the Cities: Derek Mahon's Dark Cinema

Dark Origins

The commonest word in Derek Mahon's *Poems 1962–1978* is 'light'. It occurs sixty times, together with four 'lights', twelve 'sunlight', and one 'dawnlight'. After an intervenient 'sea' or 'seas' (singular and plural together, sixty-one instances), 'light' is followed by 'dark', with forty-five occurrences, plus ten 'darkness', two 'darker', one 'darken', and one 'darkening'. Thereafter, the most frequent word is 'night/s', with thirty-nine singular and ten plural instances, one 'nightfall', eight 'midnight', and, more dubiously relevant, six 'tonight', two 'nightly', and two 'nightmare/s'. 'Day' is almost as frequent, with thirty-four singular and seventeen plural instances, two 'daylight', and one 'daylong'. Even if based only on the three volumes, *Night-Crossing* (1968), *Lives* (1972), and *The Snow Party* (1975), that went to make up this selection from Mahon's early writings, this is a striking assemblage of frequencies. A non-electronic scan of the expanded *Selected Poems* (1991) tends to confirm the impression. Leaving aside the perambulations of *The Hudson Letter* (1995), with its very different ethos and themes, the play of light and dark seems to be at the heart of Mahon's poetic project.[1]

One might infer from this that Mahon's is a chiaroscuro vision, operating through strong contrasts, and proceed to generalise about the poetry's reflection of a rigidly antithetical Northern Irish culture, what the poem 'Ecclesiastes' calls Ulster's 'bleak / afflatus', to which, it suggests, his own bosom returns a ready echo, as a 'God-fearing, God- / chosen purist little puritan', capable himself of standing on 'a corner stiff / with rhetoric, promising nothing under the sun'. The black and white statistics of a concordance can, however, deceive. Setting aside that small number of instances where 'light' refers to weight rather than illumination, a high proportion of the contexts in which 'light' is used in the main sense indicate a much more equivocal picture, one hinted at by that cluster of variants on 'dawn', and by the comparative stress of 'darker', 'darken' and 'darkening'.

Equivocation, indeed, is the very element in which light and dark meet in Mahon's poetry. Their characteristic encounter is not in the sharp contrasts of bright sunlight and shade, but in the play of shadow and half light, the gradations of dawn and dusk. As the little poem 'Spring' suggests, it is in a 'Dawnlight pearling the branches' that Mahon finds an apter insight into the human condition. Besides that single 'dawnlight', 'dawn' itself occurs twenty-two times in *Poems 1962–1978*, and 'dawns' once, always either as nouns or, twice, epithet nouns. 'Twilight' occurs five times in the volume, and in two further instances is generalised, in the plural, into a recurrent state of things, while 'shadow/s' (eleven single, five plural) and two instances of 'shadowy', reinforce the suggestions of a more ambiguous and rather different agenda. That fine elegy at the grave of his Northern 'Protestant' mentor, Louis MacNeice, 'In Carrowdore Churchyard', insists that the 'play of shadow' offers a 'humane perspective', which (addressing both himself and the dead poet in a playful paronomasia) 'Suits you down to the ground', its 'ironical' incongruities offering, in 'Each fragile, solving ambiguity', an image of 'how we ought to live'.

It is in what 'The Studio' calls 'the play / Of light and shadow (shadow mostly)' that Mahon's mental universe is constituted. In his poetry, as in Beckett's bleaker cosmos, 'we are running out of light / And love', as 'Girls in their Seasons' puts it. But this itself is a not unambiguous condition, for, repeatedly, Mahon's poetic evinces what his 'Epitaph for Robert Flaherty' speaks of as relief at being in a northern latitude again, where, in the long winter, 'Only a little light / Gets through'. 'The Spring Vacation' deploys a similar imagery to describe how one makes one's accommodations in a divided Ulster, addressing a Michael Longley equally in the know, likewise able to 'keep sullen silence in light and shade, / Rehearsing our astute salvations under / The cold gaze of a sanctimonious God'. To walk among one's own, 'In a tide of sunlight between shower and shower', is to resume an old conspiracy with the givens of a fallen world. Mahon's poems inhabit that 'quivering silence' where, 'The Studio' says, the play of light and shadow 'Repeats itself, though never exactly'. Such repetition without exactitude is as much a feature of Mahon's as of Beckett's universe, taking on a metaphysical significance intimately linked, as here, to the play of half-lights. Confronting a world that lives only in repetition, 'The Studio' yearns for the destruction of the present and actual scene, 'Remembering its dark origins', in a way which links the primal chaos with more recent states of political anarchy and disintegrative violence. The apocalyptic vision of this imagined disintegration recalls the weirdly beautiful slo-mo explosion of a hotel at the climax of Antonioni's 1970 film *Zabriskie Point*. But, the poem adds sardonically, it 'Never happens like that'. In Mahon's universe, stubbornly persisting in its own inertia and facticity, such apocalyptic prospects remain unrealised. Instead, the apocalyptic dwindles, as in Beckett, into the endless repetitive attrition of things in which the world wears down, for ever.

The Beckett comparison is one that Mahon not only invites but openly acknowledges, writing, in 'An Image from Beckett', for example, of being 'haunted' by a northern landscape of houses huddled by a shore, a place of 'hard boards / And darkness once again', interrupted for an instant by a flash of 'sweetness and light', in which one spends one's time imagining not only 'grave / Cities' (another pun), but also the emergence of new civilizations from the humus they deposit. Life may be a 'Biblical span', 'good while it lasted', which ends in a Beckettian 'drop six feet / Through a glitter of wintry light', but the poem closes with the speaker imagining those who come after him, 'To whom, in my will, / I have left my will', in the hope that they have enough time and light, to read it. In a parodic repetition of Yeats's performative utterance in 'The Tower' ('It is time that I wrote my will'), the poem itself becomes both the will and the thing willed, accompanied by the equally wilful hope with which both conclude, in a tenebrous echo of the self-inscribing double-takes of *Molloy* and *Malone Dies*. In eschewing the metaphysical in the name of the material, Mahon resumes, reinvents a metaphysics, repeating, in a residual poetry of life's residues, what 'Beyond Howth Head' identifies as 'Beckett's bleak *reductio*'. It is characteristic of Mahon's lightly-worn intertextuality that his profound imaginative debt to that paradoxical nihilist should be acknowledged in a poem which purports to be no more than a gloss on and reiteration of 'An Image from Beckett'.

The fourth and final section of 'Breton Walks', renamed 'Four Walks in the Country Near Saint-Brieuc' in *Selected Poems*, is called 'Exit Molloy', in a self-consciously stagey stage-direction which situates its eponymous speaker, 'Now at the end' of things, 'wintering' in a 'dark ditch', Yeats's drunken beggar transformed into Beckett's lugubrious derelict, smelling spring, while only a mile away the little town nestles 'Happy and fatuous in the light of day'. This multiply interstitial location (between winter and spring, dark and light, earth and air, rural and urban, Yeats and Beckett) is existentially double also, since the speaker observes that 'I am not important and I have to die', only immediately to concede that 'Strictly speaking I am already dead'. The second section of the sequence had spoken of birds watching, as they have always done, 'The shadowy ingress of mankind', while the third, 'After Midnight', had evoked a 'self-made man', surrounded in the dark by hostile creatures of the field, 'Their slit-eyes glittering everywhere'. But it is the first, 'Early Morning', which most centrally evokes Beckett, amidst rumours of Yeats's mad old women, while evoking a scene which is quintessentially Mahon.

The poem opens with the typology of the creation myth from *Genesis*. This, however, is no big bang but rather a process of gradual emergence which is as much the slow reverse rewind of an endless attrition, so that the renewing light of each dawn seems more like a running down of darkness, a vision of creation in which:

> First there is darkness, then somehow light;
> We call this day and the other night,
> And watch in vain for the second of sunrise.

This separation is not the categorical demarcation of light and dark of the original creation. No divine fiat marks out this universe into antithetical principles. Indeed, the observer is baffled by his inability to spot what seems more like a trick of prestidigitation than act of creation, as that helpless 'somehow' suggests. Such watching in vain implies a general *vanitas vanitatum* in the rising and going down of suns. *Ecclesiastes*, after all, provides title and imagery for that fierce denunciation of Northern Protestantism, 'Ecclesiastes', referred to earlier. That poem combines self-denunciation, casting love of the liminal world of January rain darkening already dark doorsteps as a compromising, complicitous vulnerability, with a *contemptus mundi* for a worldly rhetoric which promises 'nothing under the sun' – a dry echo of the Preacher's reflections on the tedium of earthly repetition, 'There is nothing new under the sun'.

In 'Early Morning', boundaries and divisions are arbitrary human impositions on the indeterminacies of a cosmos bored by repetition. The old woman suddenly apprehended in the click of her wooden shoe may be a Beckettian creature, but she also appears out of the 'primeval shapes' of dawn as a figure of the *Unheimlich* like the witches in *Macbeth*. The image, however, resists Yeatsian romanticisation. This is no Crazy Jane. Instead, she is seen at once, in another, dignifying Shakespearian idiom, as 'Abroad in the field of light', a this-worldly figure, capable of human discriminations (between, for example, good days and bad days), and casts her eyes down politely after greeting. Indeed, the old woman stands as an antidote to all myth-making *in extremis* of the Yeatsian variety, even as location and idiom recall the mythic scenarios of Ted Hughes's 'Pibroch'. She may have seen ten thousand similar dawns, but she is not impressed. The fantasy of origins envisaged in the poem's opening is replaced in its close by one of stale recurrence, the same of which a disabused Macbeth, victim of the witches' equivocations, came to speak, lamenting a 'Tomorrow and tomorrow and tomorrow' that 'Creeps in this petty pace from day to day, / To the last syllable of recorded time'. But there are other, more unlikely intertexts at work here.

What the poem explores, in this apparently primal scene, is precisely those 'Ghostlier demarcations, keener / Sounds' Wallace Stevens wrote of in 'The Idea of Order at Key West'. Mahon quotes Stevens's phrase, relocating the line break, in the *Poems 1963–1978* text of his verse epistle to Desmond O'Grady, 'The Sea in Winter', though the passage is dropped from subsequent versions. Mahon's poem actually called 'Rage for Order', a phrase from the same poem by Stevens, is also dropped from the later volume. As we have seen, 'The Idea of Order at Key West' is a frequent intertext of Northern Irish poetry, to the extent that, in 1992, taking his cue from Mahon's poem, the

Northern poet Frank Ormsby, editor for twenty years of the influential poetry magazine *The Honest Ulsterman*, produced an anthology of a hundred contemporary Northern poems with the title *A Rage for Order: Poetry of the Northern Ireland Troubles*,[2] which in his introduction explicitly developed Stevens's phrase as a model for the relation between poetry and political violence in the North.

Mahon's 'The Sea in Winter' opens with a contrast between the 'blue nights' of O'Grady's Greek island and the thinner, colder air of Mahon's Portstewart, where, recalling Matthew Arnold's contrast of Sophocles' Aegean and his own 'distant northern sea', Mahon gestures towards the burden of 'Dover Beach': that the Sea of Faith has ebbed, leaving the human subject stranded on the shore in postmodern disenchantment. In the poem renamed 'A Portrait of the Artist' in *Selected Poems*, Mahon had van Gogh speak of himself as moving like a glow-worm among the caged Belgian miners, the lamp on his helmet 'the dying light of faith', in which, he says, 'God gutters down to metaphor'. But this secular nihilism (for Arnold partially redeemed by the ersatz transcendences of art) 'The Sea in Winter', in a recursive embedding of allusions, presents as nothing new. Centuries before Mahon, Arnold or, even, Sophocles, the poet of *Ecclesiastes* had reached the same conclusion: 'Meanwhile the given life goes on; / There is nothing new under the sun.'

'It all happened before', says the blasé speaker of 'One of These Nights', while another poem that nods in Stevens's direction, 'Another Sunday Morning', speaks wearily of 'so many empires come and gone', all essentially the same, so as to put the speaker in his generic place as a cultural item, suffering 'the strife / And strain of the late bourgeois life'. Mahon's verse epistle is prefaced by an epigraph from Rimbaud: *'Nous ne sommes pas au monde; / la vraie vie est absente'* ('We are not in the world; the true life is absent'). Sometimes, the epistle says, 'rounding the cliff top / at dusk' – the enjambment suggesting its own little drama of thresholds crossed – and finding the town lit up as if for a festival, 'I pretend not to be here at all'. The given life is not the real life, but a shadow existence, always alluding to but never disclosing the authentic being whose shadow it is, pretending to be itself, but with pretensions elsewhere, remembering its dark origins.

False Dawns

The allusion to Stevens's 'Idea of Order at Key West' in the earlier version of 'The Sea in Winter' is complexly ambivalent. Mahon describes himself here as returned, like the prodigal son in Ibsen's *Ghosts*, to 'the grim, arthritic coasts / of the cold north', finding himself 'unnerved, his talents on the shelf', 'while light dies in the choral hills', or again, like Theseus, knowing the fear of 'chthonic echoes'. This self-subverting stance can be explained in part by reference to the account of the archetypal poet in the poem 'Rage for Order', irresponsibly 'indulging / his wretched rage for order' while Rome – or Ulster – burns. The poet here is framed in 'the fitful glare of his high window', which, in a deliberate disjunction of third and first persons, is contrasted with 'our scattered glass' down in the historical and chaotic street. His 'dying art' is no more than 'an eddy of semantic scruples / in an unstructurable sea', giving the lie to Stevens's eloquent vision of a redemptive poetic making on the linguistic thresholds of mind and world:

> The maker's rage to order words of the sea,
> Words of the fragrant portals, dimly-starred,
> And of ourselves and of our origins,
> In ghostlier demarcations, keener sounds.[3]

In Mahon's poem the artistic posture is not 'blessed' but 'grandiloquent and deprecating', and 'his talk of justice and his mother / the rhetorical device / of an etiolated emperor' – closer, that is, to Stevens's 'Emperor of Ice Cream', a poem in which the death of the mother evacuates the universe of significance, so that 'be', mere facticity, becomes the 'finale of seem'.[4] But Mahon's poem then turns the tables on this contempt for the poetic maker, as its reproachful speaker is revealed not as the poet at all but as some self-styled maker of history, a politico contemptuous of poets, but admitting at last that his 'desperate love', which claims to tear down in order to build up, will before long have need of the poet's 'desperate ironies'.

The play between the history-maker's singular and 'desperate love' and the poet's plurally 'desperate ironies' is a key one in Mahon's perception of the relation of art to politics. Ovid in exile, the subject of a whole poem, 'Ovid in Tomis', in *Selected Poems*, is the figure behind the poet of 'The Sea in Winter', a poem important enough for Mahon to place it last in *Poems 1962–1978*. But in the latter, exile to the margins of significance is not contingent, a chance expulsion, but essential: it comes with the territory. What the poem calls the poet's 'curious sense / Of working on the circumference', is something shared by both the letter writer and his addressee. For while the writer envies his addressees' white island in the south, with all its sensual charms, each is alike in exile, moping in the linguistic margins of the real, 'trapped... / In [his] own idiom' as much as those whose shouts, as of 'souls in torment round the town', can be heard from the street outside. Seeking the 'Elusive dawn epiphany, / Faith that the trivia doodled here / Will bear their fruit sometime, somewhere', each knows in his own way that those indeterminate sometimes and somewheres are the true location of the real, which words can never access.

In the order of discourse, as in the material world, 'morning scatters down the strand / Relics of last night's gale-force wind', while 'Far out', the Atlantic of the real 'faintly breaks'. The world of consciousness, constructed in language, is always necessarily at a remove, and the poet's self-reproach, 'Why am I always staring out / Of windows, preferably from a height?', is not just an indictment of patronising liberal abstentionism, but defines, rather, an ontological condition. Such voyeurism is not a twentieth century invention but, the poem suggests, the perennial condition of the human subject, forever deluded by its desire to enter into some unmediated rapport with the real, but always frustrated, cast out of an Edenic Imaginary of real presence which can be envisaged only through the language of lack, abjection, exile. For that fullness of self-presence, the complete union with the world's body, the delusory ambition of Romantic cults of the Sublime, was seen in the very origins of western philosophy, long before Christianity, as the fantasy of a soul cast out from the divine harmony of the Forms. Mahon's anguish at the alienation of the subject from its object world may be couched in the phenomenology of Wordsworth or Coleridge, or in the politics of twentieth-century social-democracy, but its ancient lineage is indicated in the recognition that the 'elusive dawn epiphany' he desires is of necessity a second-hand construct, shaped by consciousness out of 'relics' of a reality which is always, by definition, elsewhere: the true life is absent.

All art shares in the peculiar mix of fraudulence and authenticity represented by van Meegeren, the brilliant forger of Old Masters, in 'The Forger', a man who sold fake Vermeers to Goering. At the end of the war, van Meegeren was arraigned as a collaborator by the Allies, though is legally unclear how defrauding the Nazis of their money could be interpreted as giving aid and comfort to the enemy. The political ambiguity is matched by one in aesthetics. Van Meegeren sees himself as heroically 'working beyond criticism / And better than the best' because, as long as his forgeries remained undiscovered, it would be the alleged original artists who would be the object of any criticism, but also because his fakes surpassed critical analysis. The only way to judge them properly would be to evaluate them as genuine works of forgery. In not spotting his fakes, and in uttering self-justifying 'claptrap' after they were disclosed, it was the art critics who were the real frauds, he argues. There is a sense in which the forger is better than, not only the critics, but also the painters whose work he simulates. Van Meegeren is confident that his 'genius will live on... even at one remove', because 'The thing I meant was love'. From his 'obscurity and derision', his deceits cast on reality 'A light to transform the world'. In a universe where the multiplication of traces, echoes, reflections is the truth of things, the authentic fake may be the truly original.

'At one remove' is a resonant phrase in Mahon's poetry. It recurs in, for example, 'Preface to a Love Poem', in a similar context of disenchantment about the meretriciousness of art. The immediate ancestor of Mahon's poem is W. H. Auden's '*Dichtung und Wahrheit*' ('Poetry and Truth'), a prose meditation pointedly subtitled 'An Unwritten Poem', which argues that 'love poetry' is an oxymoron, since a true lover does not expend his spirit on artful words, and all poems which do are merely deceitful feignings, literary artifices whose real intention is the production of a work of literature. Elsewhere, Auden said roughly the same about literature that addressed the atrocities of modern history: in so far as the intention was to produce a lasting work of art, the work simply exploited, parasitically, the atrocities it lamented or protested. In a similar vein, Mahon's lines are merely a *preface* to poetry, an apology for not writing the 'true' love poem which by definition cannot be written.

This poem, then, as its first line tells us, is merely a provisional approximation, a fallen simulacrum of the *echt* poem he wants to write, circling itself and the loved one alike:

> A form of words, compact and compromise,
> Prepared in the false dawn of the half-true
> Beyond which the shapes of truth materialize.

A blind through which sunlight filters with reduced intensity, the insufficient text is multiply displaced, shut out from its true identity like the desiring lover himself, a mere 'ghostly echo' from the dead which includes that Shakespeare who, the poem reminds us without naming, famously promised to write a love poem outlasting stone and bronze. The poem, then, like all its predecessors (which themselves become prefaces to this latest variant of the genre) is necessarily 'at one remove, a substitute / For final answers'. The wise man may know to hold firm to the 'living absolute / beyond paraphrase', but this poem can offer only inadequate paraphrase of its own inexpressible desire, its words, recalling Keats, 'aching' in pursuit of themselves. It is again the image of the sea, as deployed by Stevens and by Auden in *The Sea and the Mirror* and *The Enchafèd Flood* as metaphor for the inexpressible historical world, which Mahon deploys here, in the subjunctive, to define that realm of the *really real* which art can only dissimulate, 'Drifting inconsequently among islands.' In the end, this apology for a poem is left simply airing its distraught love of the beloved's silence. As for Auden, it is as 'the soul of silence' that the loved one embodies the desired but unachievable authenticity of self-presence, totally consonant with itself. As Auden wrote in his critical study *Secondary Worlds*, deploying the Platonic simile, 'One might say that for Truth the word *silence* is the least inadequate metaphor, and that words can only bear witness to silence as shadows bear witness to light'.[5]

Behind such an attitude lies that ancient philosophical lineage originating in Plato. But neoplatonism has always had two main inflexions. The positive inflexion concedes that the things of this fallen world are mere copies of eternal, ideal Forms, but takes consolation from the existence of those Forms: somewhere, they really exist, sustaining, casting their shadows onto, the fallen world of mortality. The extreme version of such optimism is Sir Philip Sidney's assertion, in *An Apologie for Poetrie*, that art in general and poetry in particular offer truer versions of the ideal forms than our transient time-bound histories permit, offering, in his memorable phrase, 'a golden world for nature's world of brass'. The pessimistic strand of neoplatonism, however, represented in our own time by Jacques Derrida, insists with melancholy frequency that the world we know is unreal, a phantasma, or, in the idiom he shares with Baudrillard (as I shall discuss in the next chapter), a mere 'simulacrum' of a true reality we can never apprehend directly, leaving us permanently exiled among *disjecta membra* which are the relics, in the empirical world, of those ideal and inapprehensible Forms. Mahon's forger as image of the poetic maker then wittily and ironically works the changes on both lineages of neoplatonism, while remaining at one remove from the struggle, just as 'Preface to a Love Poem' epitomises poetry's notorious ability to have it both ways, for, as Auden put it in the title of a poem which retreaded Shakespeare, '"The Truest Poetry is the Most Feigning, The"'. In Mahon's poetry, however, it is the material world itself which, in a Kantian variation on the neoplatonic motif, constitutes the unknowable reality of which consciousness produces fake and factitious copies, and it is among these and with these that we must make our peace, find our accommodation, amidst the false dawns of the half-true.

Traces

Whereas for Auden it is the creations of art that are 'secondary worlds', for the epistemologically sceptical Mahon it is consciousness itself which is condemned to secondariness and dependency. 'Preface to a Love Poem' situates the subject as prefatory to experience. Mahon's poetry repeatedly seems to be remembering the future, as if what is yet-to-be is already past-and-gone. Anticipation is converted into a peculiar kind of dispossession and nostalgia for an always-already absconded reality. 'Afterlives', for example, opens with the speaker waking in a dark flat, to find in the morning light a premonition of that future in which, lit by a 'bright / Reason', the 'long-term solutions' will have put an end to the orators' yap and the sound of gunfire, 'And the dark places [will] be / Ablaze with love and poetry'. But the poem shifts at once to self-indictment, contrasting 'our privileged ideals' with our actual 'dim / Forms', kneeling in abjection. Its second part then, in a familiar pattern of return to origins, imagines 'I am going home by sea' to a dawn-lit world of memories and regrets. Enjambment here may allow both 'Reason' and 'Forms' to be ambiguously capitalised, but the poem closes (on the repeated word 'home'), with a sense of loss and exclusion, in a fallen world felt to be unreal, a repetition of memoried places and faces, in the dim light of a Belfast which is already historical, living in its own and the poet's past.

Mahon's poems are haunted by the idea that the lives we have are already

– a repeated motif – 'afterlives': second-hand, ghostly imitations and repetitions of some lost original. 'Leaves', recalling a passage in *Godot*, speculates that 'Somewhere there is an afterlife / Of dead leaves', a stadium filled with an infinite rustling and sighing, and goes on to distinguish the supposedly 'real' lives we might have lived, 'Somewhere in the heaven / Of lost futures', from the lives we have actually led, the future becoming a peculiar past-future subjunctive. 'Beyond Howth Head' writes of offering one's life as a 'forfeiture' to 'a phantom future', 'Our afterlives a coming true / Of perfect worlds we never knew'.

The first of Mahon's poems to be called 'Going Home', addressed to Douglas Dunn, observes, in the Hull estuary's daylong mist, that 'ours is the afterlife / Of the unjudgeable', and speaks of the self in the past tense, as if already posthumous:

> Extraordinary people
> We were in our time,
> How we lived in our time
>
> As if blindfold
> Or not wholly serious
> Inventing names for things
>
> To propitiate silence.

'Going home', of course, is a proverbial euphemism for things which have outworn their use, and for dying. The poem sees those shift workers crossing on the river ferry, associating Humber and Acheron, as figures of us all, who will likewise vanish for ever under the same cindery sky that broke, millennia ago, the hearts of Roman legionaries. Each life is a repetition of other lives, and we are all transient spirits under that same waning 'pale light' that guides them, and us, home

> To the blank Elysium
> Predicated on our
> Eschewal of metaphysics.

A rotting barge in the mud then becomes an omen, set there to discredit 'A residual poetry of / Leavetaking and homecoming', for the last homecoming is precisely to this universal dereliction.

Those who report on the transitoriness of human cultures, whether poets, as here, or 'The Early Anthropologists' in the poem of that name, are themselves part of the story they tell, shiftwork signifiers circulating what is finally not signification but insignificance, signifying nothing. In a characteristic bracketing, Mahon casts the anthropologists as themselves the stuff of anthropology, who have 'Left traces of their / Lives everywhere', in 'Gibbering tapes / Nobody can decipher,' in photographs assumed erroneously, now, to be snaps of their ancestors from the family album, shaking their spears at the camera.

Such 'traces' are ambiguous or downright misleading in their very nature, either indecipherable or misinterpreted. Only fancifully could the photographs of Trobriand Islanders or Inuits be seen as pictures of the anthropologists' ancestors: fancifully, because, it could be argued, without those 'primitive' peoples to provide its raw material, the discipline could not have come into existence in the first place. Now the anthropologists have been appropriated by the objects of their study, misinterpreted by posterity as the progeny of the alien people whose lives they recorded. But that posterity will in turn be misinterpreted by those who succeed them, in an endlessly embedded recursion which recalls Vladimir's song of the dog at the start of Act II of *Waiting for Godot*. Once anthropology studied man, the poem notes, an inconsequential series of dots allowing the reader to supply the first element in the interminable sequence: 'Now it studies the study of man, / Soon it will study...', like a baking-soda tin inside another baking-soda tin inside another baking-soda tin.

With every recension, the dark origins recede further and further into framing discourses, traces of traces of traces. But the shadows are also cast forward, as the tanka-like poem 'Rory' suggests, speaking of how he is led into 'a grainy twilight / of old photographs'. This 'grainy twilight' is, in fact, the true address of the human, where we all live. As a shared dedicatee of both verse selections, Rory, one infers, is Mahon's son, which allows a punning play on the 'sun' of which the poet has become the shadow. But both son and father are here united in the shadow cast by the originary sun of remote ancestors, those ideal forms who lurk in the twilight of family photograph albums. For, as Hardy put it in 'The Family Face', the individual perishes, but the family face – what we might nowadays punningly call the genetic profile – lives on, a ghostly paradigm investing the real.

In 'Glengormley', the world has been made safe from monsters and giants: 'Only words can hurt us now'. But this means also that a postulated holy and heroic age of authentic being has been replaced by the simulacra of a time where life resides in a second-hand textuality, so that the heirs are dispossessed of their rightful inheritance. Now neither saint nor hero 'brings dangerous tokens to the new era – / Their sad names linger in the histories'. If, as the poet says, he would 'rather praise / A worldly time under this worldly sky', because, 'By / Necessity, if not choice', he lives here too, that conditional is all-important, for it is the sense of loss, rather than achievement, which gives the poem a mellow melancholy not totally disguised by its surface jolliness. The worldliness of this world retreats into wordiness the more it is examined. The present we inhabit is a fallen age, a mere simulacrum of the 'real time' that preceded us. 'Kinsale' laments that even 'The kind of rain we knew is a thing of the past'. As 'Girls on the Bridge' says, 'We live / These days as on a different planet', dreaming of some lost originary moment which was really real, some

> Lost evening when
> Our grandmothers, if grand
> Mothers we had, stood at the edge
> Of womanhood on a country bridge
> And gazed at a still pond
> And knew no pain.

Even the reality of those grandmothers may be in dispute, that 'if' suggests, in what is a characteristic grammatico-rhetorical strategy. For, as 'His Song' confesses, self-consciously deploying the neoplatonic topos:

> I shall never know them again
> but still your bright shadow
> puts out its shadow, daylight, on
> the shadows I lie with now.

The little poem 'Rocks', itself 'after' the Breton poet Guillevic, calls up a world where the real has everywhere been turned into traces of itself. The rocks, the poem says, would not recognize the image of themselves entertained by the lovers lying in their shadows, in what for them are 'the last traces of time'. The rocks, for the lovers, are themselves these last traces. But the reality of 'the thing itself', the Kantian *Ding-an-sich*, defers to the consciousness which reads it out from its traces. The lovers who 'entertain' these rocks in consciousness may be transitory, just passing through, but since they are – for the present at least – the present, they also constitute the 'last traces of time'. Similarly 'The Banished Gods', in hiding in the margins of existence, 'Lost in a reverie of their own natures', depend for their survival on those who come after, who read their traces in the half light. Only the itinerant tourist's 'flash-bulb firing squad', in the words of 'A Disused Shed in Co. Wexford', restores the 'feverish forms' of the actual, 'Grown beyond nature now', to a human world in which they have meaning. The concept of the ghost, an afterlife which is simply the trace of some original presence, is pervasive in Mahon's poetry, and this *unheimlich*, fake 'presence' is repeatedly associated with a textuality which reruns the always absent original event. The 'restless ghost' of 'The Poet in Residence' ('*after* Corbière'), for example, 'dreamed his life, his dream the tide that flows / Rattling among the stones, the tide that ebbs', perhaps listening, 'Up there on the exposed / Roof of himself', for 'his own lost / Contumacious spirit'. Similarly, Captain Oates in 'Antarctica', 'Goading his ghost into the howling snow', becomes in his numb self-sacrifice a figure of ludic heroism in the midst of 'the earthly pantomime', disclosing 'At the heart of the ridiculous, the sublime'. Again, the 'curious ghost' of 'Father-in-Law' stares from the photograph on the mantelpiece, a sea-captain who 'lost [his] balance like Li Po', leaving 'unfinished poems in [his] sea-chest', speaking, thus, to the 'lyric lunacy' of his son-in-law.

Mahon's seas are frequently haunted – by the ghosts of the real and of literature alike. In 'Beyond Howth Head', for example, the Irish Sea is 'the troubled / Channel between us and North Wales / Where Lycid's ghost for ever sails', where the Miltonic ghost, mediated by Dedalus's classroom reflections, clearly has much to do with the historic 'troubles' of Britain and Ireland. This is a poem full of intertextual hauntings, linking, *inter alia*, Yeats's Celtic Twilight with Spengler's Germanic one, a wind out of 'A Prayer for my Daughter' banging in from the Atlantic to hammer on 'Dark doors of the declining west', seeing TV aerials moved about to catch BBC signals as 'Our heliotropic Birnam Wood', and imagining that Spenserian world of armadas and massacres when '"Lewde libertie"['s] midnight work / Disturbed the peace of Co Cork'. Summoning up ghosts from the vasty deep, like Milton or Shakespeare's Glendower, Mahon's late-night epistle invites that spirit to 'Come back and be with us again!', but in a more congenial form, flashing 'an *aisling*, through the dawn / Where Yeats's hill-men still break stone'. But this last echo of Yeats's disenchantment with Irish independence, in his epigrammatic two-liner 'Parnell', suggests that such ghostly repetitions are just that – mere compulsion-repetitions of a paradigmatic act which never finds outcome or egress, perpetually fixed in the unreality of its endless replay. In the same way, in 'Antarctica', the recycled lines of the villanelle form mock that original act in which Oates sought to break the closed circle of event. In 'After the Titanic', likewise, the captain who escaped from his sinking ship goes down every night in his dreams 'with all those dim / Lost faces'. In a world perpetually reinscribed under the rubric of recurrence, as 'Lives' admits, 'It all seems / A little unreal to me now', for 'I know too much / To be anything any more'. Nevertheless, as its paired poem 'Deaths' responds, we must 'Fight now for our / Fourth lives with an / informed, articulate / Fury'.

Earthed

'The Golden Bough', its title playfully alluding to Sir James Frazer's study in anthropological relativism, fluctuates between the diurnal and the apocalyptic, to imagine 'The twilight of cities' and an atavistic return to origins among 'the soft / Vegetables where our / Politics were conceived'. But Mahon is clear that, though history is repetition, you can't go home again, either politically or personally, in a world inscribed under the banner of mutability. 'Heraclitus on Rivers' nominates one philosophical source of this sceptical vision, which may hold terror or reassurance according to the inclination of the observer. Certainly, the poem says, nobody steps into the same river twice, and 'your changing metabolism / Means that you are no longer you'. But if the cells die, and the 'precise / Configuration' of the heavens when a loved one said she loved you won't come again in this lifetime, what abides, at least for the moment, is the memory that this happened. Monuments of bronze will disappear too, for even bronze is perishable; but, taking on Shakespeare's famous sonnet about poetic immortality, words too will also disappear, finally; 'All these things will pass away in time', not only your best poem, but the language in which it is written, and even the idea of language itself.

In 'The Return', renamed 'Going Home' in *Selected Poems*, Mahon fancifully imagines being rooted in one place by turning into a tree, 'Like somebody in Ovid'. But the tree with which he really identifies is one twisted by the sea-wind, which has 'nothing to recommend it / But its harsh tenacity', significant only in its liminal situation between windows and sea, 'On the edge of everything', like, he says, 'a burnt-out angel / Raising petitionary hands'. An 'almost tragic figure' of anguish and despair at twilight, it merges into night's 'Cloud-continent', in the last words of the poem, 'As if it belongs there'. 'Cloud-continent' is beautifully apposite, implying both the durability of continents but also the recognition that, like clouds, they too are subject to drift, but on a vastly slower time-scale. Even a tree's rootedness is merely provisional. He too, now moving on, had behaved here 'As if I owned the place'. This delusion of ownership may be a necessary human conceit, but it is revealed as pure fabrication in the act of transit, which compels him to recognise the hubris in acting 'As if the trees responded / To my ignorant admiration / Before dawn when the branches / Glitter at first light'. The only home this poem acknowledges is the provisional one of half-light and marginality. Yet the peripatetic self yearns towards a lost *Heimlichkeit*, a rootedness in which it might be earthed for ever.

'The Studio', discussed above, projects the speaker's frustration in a finely imagined empathy with the ceiling light bulb, world wearied by the perpetual failure

> ...by only a few tenths
> Of an inch but completely and for ever
> Of the ends of a carefully drawn equator
> To meet, sing and be one.

The bulb's filament, in a series of amplificatory analogies with Blakean vividness, is seen as inadequate, a worm of pain, a hair of heat, a light snowflake in a dark river, because its glowing arc never reaches the completeness of a circle (unlike the earth's equator). But this is of course deliberately to misunderstand the nature of electricity. If the filament were a resistanceless completed circle (that traditional Platonic image of perfection) it could not give light. The light cast is a product of the filament's imperfection, its failure to be united with itself in a self-enclosing closed circuit: electricity has to flow in and flow out, its origins and destination simultaneously elsewhere and everywhere. Such frustrated yearning for completeness, 'completely and for ever', ought to compel the bulb to 'Roar into the floor', as the poet himself is tempted to do. But it doesn't happen like that. On the contrary, the very precondition of singing is the failure to make ends meet.

Mahon's elaborate metaphysical conceit here recalls a similarly complex playing with fire and electricity in 'In the Aran Islands' (later, 'Aran'), where the folksinger in the pub, 'Singing the darkness into the light', seems to be united with, 'earthed' to his culture, his art, his girlfriend, in a way the poet envies but cannot emulate. Suffering jealousy, 'scorched' with admiration, the poet, his own rural origins fifty years behind him, dreams himself into that tradition,

> ...the reverberation
> Down light-years of the imagination...
> The long glow leaps from the dark soil, however –
> No marsh-light holds a candle to this.

The conceit doggedly chews the bone of the poet's dilemma, wanting himself to sing the darkness of origins into the light of the mind. Unable to return unequivocally to his own dark origins, racked by all that implied distrust of any *nostalgie de la boue*, the metaphor mutates through that of domestic national economy (electrification of the countryside was a recent event in rural Ireland when the poem was written) to a cosmic vision, speaking of the 'light-years of the imagination' in which time becomes space, before returning, to close, with that homely yet also *unheimlich* image of the marsh gas bubbling up from dark soil, with all its Gothic associations of death, ghosts and vampirism. Drawn to the dark origins of his art, the poet finds only reflections and repetitions, the ghostly echoes of other, played-out stories and folk-tales. That strange adjective 'scorched', used to describe how admiration affects the speaker, suggests a scorched earth policy in which any such return is bound to be scotched, in which the prolonging of echoes is also a loss of substance, presence, in a welter of vibrations and reverberations, second-hand hand-holdings, a burning bush of delusory fantasies, offering only a will-o'-the-wisp enlightenment. If Mahon's folk-singer imagines himself 'earthed' to the chthonic powers of his native Ireland, we are all truly earthed in a rather different sense, one more keenly apprehended by the archaeologist who prises the *disjecta membra* of human remains from their 'organic relation' to the earth in which they are buried.

Terminal Lights

It is in what 'North Sea' calls 'The terminal light of beaches', with 'old tins at the tide-line', that Mahon's poetry feels most at home, treading the margins among the residual bric-à-brac of the real. And it is among such bric-à-brac that it posits a kind of survival. 'The Apotheosis of Tins' situates Mahon's nostalgia for the present in terms which merge the 'retarded pathos' of origins with the sophistication of an idiom that puts them in their place. The discarded tins, consoled by a 'moon-glow' half light, welcome their abjection:

> Deprived of use, we are safe now
> from the historical nightmare
> and may give our attention at last
> to things of the spirit.

This is the 'terminal democracy' of flotsam, the pointless ebb and flow of rubbish in a perpetual rush-hour. If they have learnt anything from their desertion, the tins say,

> it is the value of self-definition.
> No one, not even the poet
> whose shadow halts above us after
> dawn and before dark,
> will have our trust.

Resisting the patronage of the poet in his reflective leisure, such flotsam is everything that history casts aside as of little value, the mere spindrift of Stephen Dedalus's 'historical nightmare'. Yet the tins have immortal longings, too. They imagine themselves not only eternal in their returns on the tide, but also as somehow elevated above their present lowly status as mass-produced rejects, promoted in the science museums of a remote future into unique artefacts which will witness, as 'Imperishable by-products of the perishable will', to a time when there was an 'organic relation / of art to life', spurious lessons with which future generations will reproach themselves, deludely, for their own loss of authenticity.

The folk-singer of 'Aran' represents one version of art as something organically 'earthed' in its community, though Mahon even there hints at the factitious, secondary quality of that relation, as a form of cultural revivalism, which means that the singer is not simply the 'authentic' antithesis of the 'inauthentic' forger van Meegeren. Furthermore, the latter, like any 'genuine' Romantic artist, has suffered obscurity and derision, sheltering in his heart of hearts 'A light to transform the world'. Both figures raise the question of authenticity, in conflict with the neoplatonic idea of art as a copy of a copy, only ever a shadow of the real thing on the walls of the human cave. These cans, in their hubris, however, represent another possibility. Having lost their function as objects of use, they imagine themselves apotheosised, in the museums of the future, into self-sufficient works of art, just as so many, possibly mass-produced artefacts from ancient or alien cultures are transfigured in the museums of the present.

The title poem of *The Hunt by Night* (1982),[6] reflecting on Uccello's famous painting in the Ashmolean Museum, Oxford, addressed several times in Mahon's poetry, uses the Platonic myth of the cave explicitly to focus on the changing function of art, its historical transformation from utility to entertainment. Resituating Uccello's sophisticated artwork and the Platonic myth itself amidst the Stone Age origins of image-making, and then linking them all to the still-active terrors of the modern nursery, the poem itself enacts the transformation of the primal cave's 'Flickering shades' and 'ancient fears' into 'pleasant mysteries', 'Tamed and framed to courtly uses', neolithic bush becoming, ultimately, 'The midnight woods / Of nursery walls', terror 'mutated / To play'. It is as if, the poem suggests, the human hunt in the long night of history,

> In what dark cave begun
> And not yet done, were not the great
> Adventure we suppose but some elaborate
> Spectacle put on for fun.

Art now, in its self-contained aesthetic autonomy, is representation, re-presentation, not the thing itself, unlike those images painted on the walls of the Magdalenian caves as direct, practical interventions in the magico-economic strategies of the hunt. Far from elevating art, this descent could be seen as a degeneration, a falling away from an 'original' authenticity, creating simulacra which are mere copies of copies. But Mahon is not here espousing a fashionable primitivism. The poem suggests, rather, that this hunt by night, so tense, so long pursued, is something that continues, not only in our dreams, but in the originating dark cave of the unconscious. The twilight of the cities is always with us, and we have never, in truth, escaped from 'the soft / Vegetables where our / Politics were conceived' into an existential rootlessness.

'Death and the Sun', Mahon's elegiac memoir of Albert Camus, placed last in the *Selected Poems* and later renamed 'Camus in Ulster', self-consciously invites the reader to

> Imagine Plato's neolithic troglodyte
> Released from his dark cinema, released even
> From the fire proper, so that he stands at last,
> Absurd and anxious, out in the open air

> And gazes, shading his eyes, at the world there –
> Tangible fact ablaze in a clear light
> That casts no shadow, where the vast
> Sun gongs its lenity from a brazen heaven
> Listening in silence to his rich despair.

That oxymoron, with which the book closes, plunges the human back into the dark cinema from which it would like to think it had escaped. The men in the Belfast dole queues still, in a different, punning sense, 'roll their own', remote descendants of Sisyphus, briefly contented with their next hand-rolled cigarette. In *The Myth of Sisyphus*, Camus, writing in post-war disillusion with the utopian aspirations of Stalinist Communism, had argued that human history was no more than an endless Sisyphean struggle to roll an intransigent real to the top of the hill, only to have it roll down the other side, compelling us, like Beckett's Vladimir and Estragon, in another text of absurdity and postwar disenchantment, to 'resume the struggle'. Reading Camus as a teenage existentialist, Mahon confides, he numbered himself among the 'Wee shadows fighting in a smoky cave / Who would be one day brought to light', and found a role-model in the artist who rejected suicide as the answer to absurdity. 'We too knew the familiar foe', he says, in allusion to the small animosities of Irish history, but, in the cold Ulster night, 'never imagined the plague to come, / So long had it crouched there in the dark'.

In 'The Globe in North Carolina', Mahon had observed that, here as elsewhere, he recognizes 'A wood invisible for its trees, / Where everything must change except / The fact of change', and our trite scepticism and irony must fall silent 'Before the new thing that must come', even though that new thing turns out to be simply the old thing in a new guise. Mahon's poetry repeatedly returns to those commonplaces of the neoplatonic tradition, seeing the generic paradigms that underlie, and presume to render unreal, all passing and particular human experience. But his obvious strength as a poet lies in his ability to see each tree in turn in all its particularity, without forgetting the wood. 'A Garage in Co. Cork' lovingly anatomises this marginal place he thinks he may have passed through once before, in his nomadic youth. At first it seems unreal, ephemeral, and, 'Like a frontier store-front in an old western / It might have nothing behind it but thin air'. The poem speculates on all the disappearances and departures which have left the garage in its semi-abandoned state. But, in the end, what impresses him is its quiet confidence in its own abidingness, its rootedness in itself: 'We might be anywhere, but are in one place only'. This is 'One of the milestones of earth-residence / Unique in each particular', even as it embodies a generic pattern, living, not in the hope of any resplendent future, but in a serene present tense, with 'a sure sense of its intrinsic nature'. Such a scene is a paradigmatic one in Mahon's poetry, its unique particularity itself polemically and paradoxically constituting its representativeness.

By contrast, the unremitting, pitiless sunlight of a desert without shadow evoked at the end of 'Death and the Sun' is no place for the human being: 'One cannot look for long at death or the sun.' Confronting the wide glare of the absolutist's heaven, that clear and brazen light which casts no shadow, the oxymoron with which *Selected Poems* closes, 'rich despair', ushers the human back into the dark cinema from which it had thought, foolishly, to escape.

NOTES

1. Except where otherwise indicated, the poems considered in this chapter are to be found in Derek Mahon, *Poems 1962-1978* (London: Oxford University Press, 1979) and *Selected Poems* (Oldcastle: Gallery Press, 1991). For a fuller transcript of Mahon's various volumes, see the Select Bibliography. The word counts provided here exclude, as is customary, those high-frequency function words (prepositions, pronouns, auxiliaries, and similar locators) normally omitted from concordances. The concordance of *Poems 1962–1978* was made using the program devised by R. J. C. Watt of the Auden Concordance programme, Dundee University. A concordance of all Mahon's volumes, together with their variant readings, while ideal, is beyond the scope of the present chapter, which does not substantially address work published after *Selected Poems* (1991). Such a concordance might throw some light on, *inter alia*, the reasons for the substantial changes, not all for obviously stylistic reasons, to such poems as the verse epistle 'The Sea in Winter' between the two volumes, and the possible structural relations between the poem called 'Going Home, for Douglas Dunn', in the earlier book, and that called 'Going Home', dedicated to John Hewitt, in the later one, entitled 'The Return' in *Poems 1962-1978*. It might also clarify the reasons for changing the exclamatory disgust of 'Afterlives', 'What middle-class cunts we are', in the earlier volume into the mild self-irritation of 'middle-class twits' in *Selected Poems*. Far from improving the poem, this diminishes the vigour of its outrage at 'our privileged ideals' amidst the real violence and squalor of the external world.
2. Frank Ormsby (ed.), *A Rage for Order: Poetry of the Northern Ireland Troubles* (Belfast: Blackstaff Press, 1992).
3. Wallace Stevens, *The Collected Poems* (London: Faber and Faber, 1959).
4. Ibid, p. 64.
5. W. H. Auden, *Secondary Worlds* (London: Faber and Faber, 1968), p. 136.
6. Derek Mahon, *The Hunt by Night* (Oxford: Oxford University Press, 1982).

XI

Paul Muldoon's Leavings

Leaving No Clues

There is an obvious sense in which every Irish poet's work has to be a *poésie de départs* before it can address the problematics of residence: the reality of emigration underlies every conscious choice to remain. The grand narrative of exile may have been rewritten as the short story of the lecture tour or the tall tales of a steady job, but it still underwrites the corporate identity of 'Irish Poetry Inc.' Nowhere is this more apparent than in the work of Paul Muldoon, one in a long line of those Irish writers who have chosen elsewhere as their homeland. The motif is explicit from his earliest volumes. In his first volume, *New Weather* (1973),[1] for example, 'February', in a characteristically oblique manner, juxtaposes the reality of departure with the near impossible thought of remaining:

> What was he watching and waiting for...?
> For one intending to leave at the end of the year,
> Who would break the laws of time and stay.

But that which stays, which from another point of view is that which is left behind, suffers the fate of that cold fish bought as a gift for his lover in 'Thinking of the Goldfish', which looked in its plastic bag like 'a change of heart', but was, in fact, far too cold, so that all he could do was leave it to die alone at the top of an old house apparently in the process of being abandoned. The minimalist tone and 'moral' of the story here provide precedents for Matthew Sweeney's early work, foreshadowing, for example, that pathetic pet mouse left to die in 'Ends'. But the play on 'change of heart', overwhelming the dead metaphor so that the simile, ghoulishly, becomes an almost literal image, is already distinctively Muldoon. Abandoned, the goldfish becomes a figure of all that the self leaves behind in following its destiny, in seeking to 'Own the light above my head, / If simply borrow from my side', in a complex play of indebtedness and supposed self-possession in which only your own breath and light can be taken with you when you go. 'Identities', a poem that plays, *avant la lettre*, with identity politics, or at least with the politics of 'identity', prefigures in many ways Heaney's preoccupations with the frontier of writing in *The Haw Lantern*. The protagonist of this poem, fleeing, falls in with another, a woman from the interior whose family had 'figured' (the word has resonance) in a previous regime, now out of favour. Arriving at the coast, she proposes they obtain false papers and so escape. The conclusion is enigmatic, in a way which foreshadows the options of much of Muldoon's subsequent poetry:

> I have been wandering since, back up the streams
> That had once flowed simply one into the other,
> One taking the other's name.

The poem doesn't make it absolutely clear whether these wanderings follow a successful escape, or an attempted return to origins, but origins now forever lost in the confusion of waters and names. The poem speaks, enigmatically, of the coast as 'determined', but does not indicate whether this imputes decisiveness and choice to the speaker, or his woman companion, or, contrariwise, refers to the geographic and cultural boundaries which determine and restrict, predispose, their identities. If, in assuming the false papers of another identity, he has lost himself, it is really just another instance of that Heraclitean flux of identity, or rather identities, which was to become a theme of Muldoon's subsequent work. For in one sense, all 'identity' is a series of leavings, of departures from origins which were themselves only points of transit, provisional locations of the subject. In 'Good Friday, 1971. Driving Westward' the poet drives not only through named places on the road to the border, to cross 'the last great frontier at Lifford'; he also drives through the literary locations of, among others, Donne and Wordsworth, to end, having 'just dropped in from nowhere for lunch' at a place where they are in turn walked out on, left behind by those lunching parents and children embarrassed by his companion's loud, drunken announcement (on Good Friday of all days), 'that she and I were to blame / For something killed along the way we came'. It would be a mistake, however, to read this poem as just another parable about leaving the Northern Irish statelet to enter the true Republic of Letters. Such a reading is what the poem invites us to, only to leave *us* stranded in archaic definitions of identity and allegiance. It is a poem, in part, about refusing the traditional grand narratives of Irish identity.

The options in *New Weather* are polarised between on the one hand that postscript on experience in 'Leaving an Island' – 'This is just to say / We have left no clues', the real happily reduced to imaginings of 'The sea in shells' – and, on the other, that hope in 'Seanchas' that 'if we play back the tape / He may take up where he left off', with its disillusioned conclusion: 'Nothing.

And no heroes people this landscape / Through which he sees us off.' These poems perpetually see us off, as readers, leaving us, in Eliot's phrase, really in the dark. As in the poem called simply 'Elizabeth', where migratory birds 'will stay long / Enough to underline how soon they will be gone', it is as much the sense of being abandoned as of moving on which implicates the reader in this early poetry. The 'Grass Widow' soliloquizes of her departed husband, in terms which might seem to relate to Muldoon's own Transatlantic translations:

> And of course I cried
> As I watched him go away.
> Europe must have cried
> For Europe had no more to say
> When America left her.

But this is not what Muldoon means at all, at all. The clue is in that throwaway phrase 'no more to say', and its problematic relation to leaving.

Which brings me to the ambiguity of my chapter title. I have no wish to cover, once again, the much-trodden ground of expatriation and deracination in Irish poetry. My intention, rather, is to move us along to that postmodern space which is Muldoon's peculiar territory. The poem which provides the title to *New Weather*, 'Wind and Tree', suggests where this might be. 'In the way', it begins, 'that the most of the wind / Happens where there are trees, / Most of the world is centred / About ourselves'. But it moves to a different conclusion. If, often, he thinks he ought to emulate the single tree with nowhere to go, his broken bones nevertheless manage to predict new weather. Leaving also involves an 'unleaving' of the self, in the double sense of that punning neologism coined in Hopkins's 'Spring and Fall': 'Márgarét, áre you grieving / Over Goldengrove unleaving?'

A Mystery Even Now

Muldoon's celebrated 1980 collection, *Why Brownlee Left*,[2] foregrounds, in its title poem, an unavoidable leaving. But for all its invitations to place the poem, and the volume, within a specific tradition of national lamentations about emigration, it functions in a quite different, indeed duplicitous way. Brownlee the man, whose identity we can only infer from the traces he leaves behind, seems to need no further introduction. But both poem and volume title appear to promise an explanation of his problematic departure which is then refused in the turn of the enjambment into the poem's second line: 'Why Brownlee left, and where he went, / Is a mystery even now.' This 'mystery' is a 'leaving' in a second and quite different sense. Just as, in 'Making the Move', the Ulysses who left for the war also 'left his bow with Penelope', Brownlee leaves a mystery behind him, as he also leaves those very tangible presences which the poem proceeds to enumerate, the acres of barley and potatoes, the bullocks and the milch cow, the slated farmhouse, the lurking pun on 'slated' suggesting that he didn't think it was necessarily all it was cracked up to be. He leaves, however, not only a mystery, or these properties, but a reputation, fame, for by noon, after years, it is implied, of being disregarded, Brownlee has become famous.

It is worth reflecting on the etymology of this word, from the Latin 'fama', a report, as the *OED* defines it: 'That which people say; public report, common talk, a rumour... Reputation... The condition of being much talked about. Chiefly in good sense. Celebrity, honour, renown.' But also, with a citation from 1592: 'Evil repute'. And there is a particularly apposite citation from that early, ill-famed and ill-fated poet, Henry Howard, Earl of Surrey: 'A mischefe Fame... that mouing growes, and flitting gathers force'. 'Famous' has the same doubleness, inscribed as both 'celebrated' and 'notorious'. To put it succinctly, fame is what you leave behind which also goes before you: it gives and it takes away, fills and empties, and is itself, as Falstaff observes, mere air. For if Brownlee's absence is one of many Irish leavings, those things he leaves behind him, including his fame, are the leavings of a life, the presences from which an identity may be retrospectively imagined.

We can open up this double, contradictory sense of 'leavings', as both absence and presence, by referring to Derrida's development, from Plato, of the idea of the *pharmakon*, a word with contradictory or incompatible associations, positive and negative valencies. *Pharmakon*, Derrida proposes, can in the Greek mean both a cure and a poison (as the English equivalent 'drug' has a similar double signification).[3] Brownlee is himself the locus of such a paradoxical, contrary discourse, celebrated only in his absence, a signifier over a void, like the crew of the *Marie Celeste* leaving his leavings behind him. For if these are 'abandoned', by inference his life must also have been in some sense an 'abandoned' one, about which no one really knows, an emptiness within all the reportings. The two enjambments in the poem's sestet which end on prepositions carry the repute and report over into that future which lies forever beyond the poem's closure, 'foot to' inadequately rhyming with 'future' as the enjambment itself enacts that pause in the air between foot and foot. The repeated 'foot' reminds of that traditional observation about poetry, reiterated most recently by Seamus Heaney,[4] that the word 'verse' is derived from the Latin *versus*, the turning of the plough backwards and forwards across a field, textual lines reproducing material ones, that a metrical foot is also the rhythmic stamping of a foot, and that one talks of shifting the 'weight' of a syllable in a metric foot. Muldoon's reference to Brownlee's unbroken last rig itself involves a kind of *pharmakon*, for besides being a dialect version of 'ridge' (plough ridge), signifying work, the present product of past labour, it is also, according to the OED, slang for 'Sport, banter, ridicule. Chiefly in phr. *to run* (one's) *rig(s) upon* (another), to make sport or game of... A trick, scheme, or dodge... A method of cheating or swindling... A frolic or prank; an act of a mischievous or wanton kind; a "game".' And there's something particularly galling and mischievous, a kind of unfulfilled punchline, in the fact that Brownlee neither finished the job, breaking off before breaking the last rig, nor decamped before starting it at all – as if the decision to leave was a totally unpremeditated spur-of-the-moment impulse, without rhyme or reason.

Brownlee's leaving certainly has the effect of a practical joke on those left behind, generating speculation and smoke, but little light. That offhand analogy of the horses being like man and wife hints likewise either at the actual emptiness within that life in which he should have been content, recalling Kavanagh's Patrick Maguire in *The Great Hunger*, or, alternatively, implies the full and fulfilling motive for departure – a woman. Just as the transit between the March morning, bright and early, when he was seen going out, and the noontide fame when he is already gone, crosses the empty space between octet and sestet, so the sonnet in its conclusion looks out into futurity with a blank, uncomprehending gaze like that of the horses.

The octet's only real pause at the line-ending, observing of Brownlee that if anyone 'should have been content / It was him', reinforced by the caesura at the semi-colon which follows it, is posited on that difference between expectation and actuality, as it poises between subjunctive and indicative, 'should have been' and 'was'. It recalls, playfully, Edward Thomas's 'As the Team's Headbrass' (a poem more recently echoed in *Hay*'s 'Third Epistle for Timothy'), which also hinges on the conditional temporalities around that 'if', in a poem about ploughmen leaving or staying in their place in a time of war and uprooting. Muldoon himself, here as elsewhere, runs a rig on the reader in the sense Brownlee does on his 'readers', that is, the interpreters of his mystery, as the *OED* defines the idiom: 'to hoax, play tricks on, befool... to manage or manipulate in some underhand way', as a joke, a game. In 'Plato's Pharmacy', Derrida makes play with the idea of play as a serious activity, living in the conditional dimension of the 'if', and I'd suggest that Muldoon is himself, here, as in so many of his poems, engaged in an unbroken (that is unexplained, undeciphered) rig:

> As soon as it comes into being and into language play *erases itself as such*. Just as writing must erase itself as such before truth, etc. The point is that there *is* no *as such* where writing or play are concerned. Having no essence, introducing difference as the condition for the presence of essence, opening up the possibility of the double, the copy, the imitation, the simulacrum – the game and the *graphē* are constantly disappearing as they go along. They cannot, in classical affirmation, be affirmed without being negated.[5]

Like Brownlee, then, the poem called 'Why Brownlee Left' performs its own disappearance as writing, and the perpetual deferral of meaning. It is always leaving. That is why it came.[6]

One might infer that Muldoon may have read Derrida's essay, since in the ironically titled 'Long Finish', in *Hay*, he himself reflects, in terms which recall Derrida's idea of the *pharmakon*, on 'the double meaning of "pine"', which

> is much the same in Japanese as English, coming across
> both in the sense of 'tree' and the sense we assign
> between 'longing' and 'loss'.

Signifying both the solid presence of the tree from which books are made, and the absences of which those books speak and on which they are posited, 'pine' then hovers, in this second sense, between a further presence and absence, for loss involves that which has always already left, an absent presence, as longing is that which it leaves behind, a present emptiness that craves to be filled. And, the poem suggests, both are the same: 'Let's not distinguish between longing and loss, but rouse / ourselves each dawn.' 'Long Finish' is actually about never finishing, perpetual deferral of closure, in marriage as in writing. If textuality, like sexuality, is always moving between longing and loss, its true element is not absence but plenitude, that overflowing of meaning, that precious supplement, spoken of in the recurring addendum and refrain with which the poem closes by refusing closure: 'and then some'.[7]

The volume *Why Brownlee Left* is everywhere concerned with this inscription and de-inscription of meaning, defining the archetypal postmodern relation of self and history. 'October 1950', a poem, it transpires, about its author's own conception, quests earnestly, like some latter-day Grail Knight, after that authentic, originary moment, beyond legend, where the subject is inserted into a reality which is at once generic, a product of genre, and genetic. Literally genetic, in this poem, which leads elliptically from the half comprehensions of the opening lines, 'Whatever it is, it all comes down to this', to the brutal abruptness which spells out what 'this' is: 'My father's cock / Between my mother's thighs'. An apparent digression about winding up the clock recalls the most famous conception scene in literature, at the start of *Tristram Shandy*, a novel much concerned with the treacherous liaisons between the flow of history and the tergiversations of narrative. The middle section of Muldoon's irregular sonnet then picks apparently random moments from the life set going like a wound-up clock, fancifully imagining various possible narratives of conception, before bringing us, at the close, to the unresolved repetition of its opening uncertainty: 'Whatever it is, it leaves me in the dark.' He's left in the dark because, like everyone else, he can't ever really know how he came to be conceived, though he knows roughly when: October 1950. But he is also metaphysically in the dark, absent from his own origin, as we all are, since what is literally the seminal event of our lives is something which, by definition, leaves us out as it counts us in. In the crudest physical sense, the self we are is simply a leftover or supplement, a residue from some earlier and self-sufficient act, the leavings of an unimaginable intercourse between mother and father.

The very condition of 'being', in its ontological sense, is of necessity always 'in the dark', transfixed in mystery. 'The Geography Lesson' recalls a fellow pupil at school called Mungo Park, who'd 'made his mark'. That is, though he couldn't read, he could write his name. To labour the point: he was able to inscribe but not decipher himself. Like an old explorer christening a river, Mungo had no idea, when they were studying the map of Africa, that he derived his name from one of its great eighteenth-century explorers, who had discovered the source of the Niger. Though another pupil, Lefty Lynch, idiomatically 'knew it all' – a dismissive remark, this – the poem ends with 'unremembering darkness, an unsteady hold'. This is the dark unsteady hold of the ship in which bananas (and slaves) were transported from Africa, but it is also the 'unsteady hold' we all have on reality, on history and geography, an exiling from the known to an inner darkness poignantly figured in the class photograph:

> You should have seen them, small and wild
> Against a map of the known world
>
> The back row of the class of '61.
> Internal exiles at thirteen or fourteen.

At its most extreme, Muldoon's poetry seems to speak with the rueful melancholy of Jean Baudrillard's essay, 'Simulacra and Simulations', of a postmodern world locked in 'the generation by models of a real without origin or reality: the hyperreal', constituted in the endless play of referentless signifiers. 'The Geography Lesson' could be read in one way as a commentary on Baudrillard's assertion that today: 'The territory no longer precedes the map, nor survives it. Henceforth, it is the map that precedes the territory... it is the map that engenders the territory... It is the real, and not the map, whose vestiges subsist here and there, in the deserts which are... our own. *The desert of the real itself.*'[8] And certainly Muldoon can often be seen, in his narratorial insistence, to be resisting those 'false prophets proclaiming the return of the referent' against whom Baudrillard warns, that 'proliferation of myths of origin and signs of reality; of second-hand truth, objectivity and authenticity' which is in reality a snare and a delusion, that 'escalation of the true, of the lived experience; a resurrection of the figurative where the object and substance have disappeared' which issues in 'a panic-stricken production of the real and

the referential'. Nevertheless, there is also in Muldoon's poetry a most traditional nostalgia for the fullness of self-presence, for that always-already lost
unity of being where the sign and the referent are one, like lovers, figured in
the idea of weight in 'Palm Sunday':

> I was wondering if you'd bring me through
> To a world where everything stands
> For itself, and carries
> Just as much weight as me on you...

His many poems of bereavement express the same longing for some imputed lost object, for a wholeness and fixity of signification, in a kind of retrospect
by a Faust who has missed his chance to say to the moment: 'Be still'. The
strength of the poetry lies in the tension between this impulse and that other
recognition, in, say, 'Something of a Departure', that such unity has always-
already absconded, the words themselves having run away, making the subjunctive and conditional the very grounds of an indicative longing: 'Had words
not escaped us both / I would have liked to hear you sing.' What he imagines
the woman singing, however, is precisely a celebration of departures, 'Farewell
to Tarwathie' or 'Ramble Away'. Language can ramble away on the spot; but a
person has to move on. The 'departure' of which the poem speaks here, then,
is both a literal leave-taking, and, as the idiomatic title suggests, a discursive
one, 'something of a departure' from the normal. The sting in the tale of this
'departure' finds its rhetorical consummation, though the lewd physical congress it proposes remains unconsummated, textually at least, in the double
entendre of the final line, contemplating the departing lover's buttocks and
asking her to 'take it like a man'.

'Cuba', in *Brownlee*, is one of the most subtle explorations of Muldoon's
characteristic ambivalences, since it is posited, in the end, on two non-
events, one of global significance, the other personal and trivial, both of them
inhabiting a common history which we can confirm actually happened, but
which now exists only in that second-order realm of written or oral 'history'.
This is a collective history lived in its personal vestiges, those 'spots of time'
which are its residuary presence in the unfolding of our lives, here summed
up by the one word which is left behind in the memories of all those who
lived through (that is, survived) that sequence of world-threatening events:
'Cuba'. The poem is a short story, mainly in reported speech, as if allowing
its characters to speak for themselves. But in fact it is the reader who has to
read between the lines, deduce the non-events which are its narrative point
from the vestiges it offers. In the first two stanzas the words are, allegedly,
those of Muldoon's father, ticking off his teenage daughter for arriving home
the morning after a dance. In this domestic cameo, the potential global
catastrophe implied by the one-word title becomes simply an item in the

father's reproachful rhetoric, rich in the conditional and subjunctive: "'As though we hadn't enough bother / With the world at war, if not at an end.'" The father's mind is clearly on other things then, so that his unwitting self-deprecation is not so much an unconscious Irishism as testimony to his global anxiety: "'Those Yankees were touch and go as it was... / But this Kennedy's nearly an Irishman / So he's not much better than ourselves.'"

Kennedy's real difference lies in his access to the master narratives of destruction. He has only 'to say the word' to blow them all up. Words can make something happen, make everything cease to happen. For this little domestic squabble can be precisely dated from the history books to the weekend of the Cuban Missile Crisis, in the last week of October, 1962. Kennedy, however, doesn't (say the word, end the world). The last stanza comprises a different kind of dialogue, between the poet's sister May, gone 'to make her peace with God' at what could be the world's end, and her *spiritual* Father, the priest in the confessional. The brother overhears how totally innocent was her brush with sin. The boy's touch, echoing her father's 'touch and go', becomes an analogy with the world's own brush with death, the Great Powers brushing against each other very gently, then stepping back. For the poem, after all, is called 'Cuba', not 'My Sister', its own light personal touch tactfully reminding us that we all live in history, and can be touched at the core of our lives by its master narratives of power and violence.

Muldoon's uncollected poem 'The Ancestor' contains an image which gives exact formulation to this idea of human existence in history, speaking of 'all those heirlooms / to which we are now the heirs'. For the point about such heirlooms is that (a) they are only ours because we adopt them – otherwise they have no connection with us – and (b) the heirloom as a residue carries with it, as an imputed presence, all that has not survived, its originating, substantiating context, including those absent subjects who once believed they possessed it. The poem in *Why Brownlee Left* called 'History' turns out to be an entirely private affair, opening with the quizzical attempt to recall the time and place of a first sexual encounter, but ending at an intersection with literary anecdote, and with possibly *imaginary* histories, asking whether this was in 'the room where MacNeice wrote "Snow", / Or the room where they say he wrote "Snow"'. That final qualification, dispensing with the sentence's longing for a question mark, illustrates the way all Muldoon's poetry relates to the interplay of history and story. For public events may be as speculative and unverifiable, as much a matter of contradictory and possibly imaginary recollections (what I and you say as much as what 'they say'), as the irrecoverable private event, a mere lacuna, with which the poem opened.

Something about an Identity Parade

This is a specifically postmodern scepticism, founded in the suspicion that all alleged events may be merely stories told after the event, the leavings of discourse, leaving that 'real' event forever unknowable. This is the point, I suspect, of Muldoon's *interleavings*, his intertextual allusiveness. At times, in *Madoc: A Mystery* (1990)[9] for example, such interleavings may seem little more than the leftovers of various leafings through literature. Yet set against this epistemological scepticism is that yearning for a lost, impossible authenticity like that which concludes the last poem of *New Weather*.

'The Year of the Sloes, for Ishi', prays for a saving remnant that in its survival might preserve some traces of an originary authenticity, the hope that 'Then perhaps something of this original / Beauty would be retained'. The actual context is a deadly and a deathly one, a massacre of native Americans by white men, and the wish enunciated here denies itself as it is uttered. For to retain 'something of this original' is, by definition, to forfeit the whole thing, making do with the leavings of that original wholeness. A remnant by its very nature is a mere leftover, and Muldoon is too sophisticated a reader of cultural history to make the same mistake as his intellectual predecessors, for whom the American Indian became a figuration of their own desire, the Noble Savage a trope for that which the European Enlightenment and Romantic poets found lacking in their own culture. And yet what's expressed here is a noble and a generous ambition, speaking out, like Walter Benjamin, for the defeated of history, seeking to recover, re-member, those effaced and erased generations in the name of a wider humanity.

By contrast, *Madoc's* poetics of interleavings, fabricated from the dribs and drabs of many factual or fanciful narratives, subordinates the unhappy history of the sometimes genocidal relations between European settlers and native Americans to the ludic contortions of a specifically postmodern discourse. The sequence's succession of titles using the bracketed names of western thinkers – not just philosophers, but epistemologists, teleologists, theorising scientists, anthropologists and social commentators – implies a whole history of thought reduced, now, to the leftovers of many leafings through history's leavings. Many of these allusions, however, sound like the half-knowledge culled from casual reading in, *inter alia*, the Sunday supplements, as, for example, in the one-liner called '[Camus]', which speaks of Mandan villages ravaged by smallpox (one is surprised he doesn't say 'pestered'); or even, in '[Archimedes]', from a *1066-and-All-That*-style schoolboy history, in which 'Coleridge leaps out the tub. Imagine that'. (Should we cry 'Eureka!', and conclude that Coleridge, like Archimedes, had a loose screw?) *Madoc* squanders its noble impulse to recovery in a display of postmodern cleverness which seems to testify, ultimately, only to the facility (and omnipresence) of the allegedly self-effacing author.

'The Key', the opening prose-poem to the volume, dangles before us what it implies to be the key to all its mysteries, only then to pull it away on a string, converting itself into an anecdote about the role of a dropped key in an identity parade in a film, focusing on the difficulty of 'matching sound to picture on this last effect' at 'a critical moment' in the film. This is a 'critical moment' for us as readers, for the critical moment of reading is as much an effect of the text as anything else, as the idea of synchronising disparate discursive events is teasingly revived in the closing, self-regarding observations of the passage.   Here, repeating that 'post-production on a remake', rerunning and in the process misquoting himself – an impossible act, because the misquotation, when from the same author, becomes an original source in its own right[10] – Muldoon finds that he has 'sometimes run a little ahead of myself, but mostly I lag behind, my footfalls already pre-empted by their echoes'.

The poem's reflections on the dinner jackets worn unnecessarily by old-time radio announcers, like Foley's ultramarine tuxedo while he edits the film, invite the reader to reflect on the redundancy of information in a text all dressed up with nowhere to go, even if that nowhere is as far away in space as Oregon or, in time, as Anaximander. But it is the postmodern self-reflexiveness which is the real theme of this book, not its alternative histories and mysteries, as is indicated by that putative remake, sometime in the late 1980s, of a real 1961 film, *The Hoodlum Priest*, described in *Halliwell's Film Guide* (1977) as follows: 'A Jesuit teacher tries to help young criminals, especially a condemned murderer. Moderately well-done, very depressing and downbeat chunk of social conscience based on the life of Charles Dismas Clark.'

Before rushing off to investigate that life, one should note how gratuitous is this piece of contemporary cultural pseudo-reference. It could have been some quite different film, and only our obsessive hermeneutic impulse drives us, as it drives the poet (if it is he who is speaking here), to attribute such merely personal importance to a film in which his cousin Marina was, allegedly, 'an extra in the first version'. This family association is, however, offered to us, the readers, but not to his interlocutor Foley, for it figures only as an unfulfilled subjunctive in this recollection of an alleged encounter: 'I wanted to say something about Marina, something about an "identity parade" in which I once took part, something about the etymology of "tuxedo", but I found myself savouring the play between "booth" and "bath", 'quits' and "mesquite", and began to "misquote"myself…'

Just as *Madoc* does serially and *passim*, this account records an event which didn't happen. The text shifts, as in Beckett's Trilogy, from the event (supposedly) narrated to the event of narration itself, now, in this foreword and teasingly alleged 'Key' to the whole. Just as Foley, never subsequently identified or referred to, is allegedly engaged 'half-way through post-production on a remake', so Muldoon here is working at a double distance. According to Muldoon, 'Foley artist' is the name given in film production to a dubbing specialist. Thus, here, he is not a real individual with a personal name, but a generic and emblematic figure, as insubstantial, perhaps, as that 'cousin, Marina McCall', whose filmic simulacrum probably got excised (and then something) on the cutting-room floor. Like the poet fruitlessly looking for his cousin, we too, it might seem, are expected to sit through several showings of the poem, and possibly the obscure film, looking for the key.

The 'dubbing suite' is indeed a kind of key, since the whole text of *Madoc* is about the dubbing of alien soundtracks on to depicted events. Seneca the Roman Stoic, for example, is punningly dubbed onto the creation myth of the Seneca Indians. But in this opening, probably imaginary 'event', Muldoon is stopped from speaking to Foley by a series of internal association on the words he is *only now* using to *narrate* the event. The run-on to 'misquote myself' is more relevant, since the passage then proceeds to speak of what he is best about, the idea of language, with its contrast of Indo-European and !Kung clicks, as alternative discursive modes. 'You seemed content to ventriloquize the surf', he observes, ventriloquizing and addressing himself simultaneously; but what's alluded to here is not so much the sea-surf as a surfing of meaning, history, language itself. '[T]hat same old patch of turf' of which Foley speaks could be the peasant Ireland of calves, boreens, donkeys and dung, the stage effects of Muldoon's early poetry, deriving via Heaney from a dominant literary tradition; but it is also the textual turf of Muldoon's writings, the rhetorical domain he now controls like any San Francisco street-gang hoodlum. If '"hoodlum" is back-slang' for the leader of such a gang, then, almost invited to perform a similar reversal, and coming up with 'muldooh', I am tempted to note that *Madoc*, backwards, becomes, near enough, 'Code 'em', or, even, possibly, 'cod 'em'. For we are indeed being codded by this coded text, in our 'critical moment' made to consider the momentously crisis-ridden nature of the critical act. Foley has here become the poet's internal critic, and the exchange between the two, 'our only exchange', is indeed 'remarkable for its banality'. But banality, including what Hannah Arendt, writing of another history of genocide, called the banality of evil, is precisely what *Madoc* is about.

The succeeding poem, 'Tea', speaks in and of another key – that Key West now forever associated with (yet again!) Wallace Stevens's reflections on the maker's rage to order words of the sea. In the process it announces the thematics of the whole volume. All he has in the house, he says, is 'some left-over / squid cooked in its own ink' and a cup of tea described, enigmatically, as 'unfortunate', which the reader is invited to take and drink. For all the echo of Robert Frost's 'Drink and be whole again beyond confusion' (words which can be read as speaking autoreferentially of the poem they conclude), the text of *Madoc* is here presented as a squid cooked in its own ink, dishing up the left-overs of many earlier texts, some real and some imagined, including, perhaps, as is suggested by the mysteriously drifting tea-chests with which it opens, that American foundation myth, the story of the Boston Tea Party. This prefatory sequence ends with a poem about 'The Briefcase', a briefcase which at one point allegedly contained 'the first / inkling of this poem'. The play on 'inkling', with its pun on ink and its sense of enigmatic metonymies, homes in on the central paradox of all self-reflexive narratives, that they contain themselves, and thus are, like Dr Who's Tardis, bigger on the inside than on the outside. The leftovers, mere traces of a meaning that has departed from us, become the thing itself.

There is one passage in James Wilson's impassioned study, *The Earth Shall Weep: A History of Native America*, just before his account of the smallpox epidemic among the Iroquois of 1634, which is singularly appropriate to *Madoc*. Wilson describes the native American ontology to be found among the Iroquoian-speaking League of Five (later Six) Nations, which made such an impact on Enlightenment and then Romantic Europe. In the beliefs of 'the Iroquois and other native peoples', he says, 'the Great Law was not founded on the kind of abstract concept of individual human rights developed in Europe during the Enlightenment... indeed the very *idea* of an individual as an unchanging entity with inalienable rights would have been largely meaningless in a society in which, through ritual, a captive could be given the identity of someone who had died'.[11]

We can see here some kind of rationale for those metempsychoses of identity, name, signifier in *Madoc* by which the Roman Seneca can punningly be resurrected in the title of a poem which repeats the creation myth of the League, of whom the Seneca were one tribe; or the process by which the mere coincidence of a name, that of a far-west people, the Modocs, can lead to the overlaying of histories of the Iroquoian League with the quite distinct narrative of Lewis and Clarke's search for an overland route to the Pacific, simply because, perhaps, the nineteenth-century American historian Francis Parkman, who wrote a history of *The Conspiracy of Pontiac*, also in the 1840s shadowed much of their route, and wrote about it in *The Oregon Trail*. Such fantasised semiotic transmigrations may be justified by the whole premise of a book founded in two prior flights of fancy: the pantisocratic fantasies of Southey, Coleridge and Wordsworth, and the legend of a medieval Welsh colonisation of North America, revived by that John Evans referred to in '[Hakluyt]' as searching for 'the tell-tale / blue eyes and fair skins / of the scions / of the prince of Wales' beyond the villages of the Mandan, the latter having failed as candidates for honorary Welshness. Hakluyt played a major part in reviving the medieval legend, as part of his campaign, as an ideologist of Tudor expansionism (the Tudors were a Welsh dynasty), in support of the quest for a North West Passage to the Pacific.

In the title poem of *Meeting the British* (1987)[12] the unexpected evocation of a little-known incident in early American history brilliantly deconstructs reader expectations. For had we not all assumed, on first seeing the volume's title, that this was another meditation on British-Irish relations? The 1763 incident which forms the basis of the poem is recounted in Wilson.[13] During what was erroneously called 'Pontiac's War', the British commander of Fort Pitt treacherously distributed smallpox-laden blankets to the Delaware Indians he had invited to a peace parley. There is of course a larger syntax to the relations between imperial powers and subaltern peoples which makes the structural correspondence between Delaware and Irish histories a possible and, indeed, an inevitable one. It is an analogy to which the poem teasingly invites us, even as it scrupulously resists all attempts to recruit the one to the other, insisting instead on the particularity of this betrayal, its irreducible quiddity. Much of the poem's effect is achieved by the indirection and downbeat triviality of its ending: 'They gave us six fishhooks / and two blankets embroidered with smallpox', the treacherous domesticity of that 'embroidered' resonating after the poem's close. This is the kind of little significant detail, leavings which metonymically stand in for whole histories of cultural exchange, in which Muldoon excels.

'Something Else' in *Meeting the British* comes clean about Muldoon's allusive and elusive tic or trick of style. In it, a lobster lifted out a restaurant tank leads him to think 'of woad, / of madders, of fugitive, indigo inks', of Gérard de Nerval's probably apocryphal lobster-walking, and of the latter's suicide from a lamp-post, 'which made me think / of something else, then something else again'. It doesn't matter what these 'something elses' are. Or, for that matter, whether this is a lobster shared at some dinner with the Seamus Heaney of 'Away from It All' in *Station Island* in 1984. Their function is simply to *be* something else, to hurry along, using – the clue is there in the opening stanza – more 'fugitive' ink in their inscribing. The lobster turns red only when it's boiled for our delectation. Muldoon's most moving negotiations of native American history preserve a respect for the 'redskins' he calls (or sometimes cooks) up. *Madoc* remains 'A Mystery' because, half uttering pseudo-histories founded in paranoid speculations and whimsical fantasias, unlike Thomas Pynchon's *V*, which it brokenbackedly emulates, it has no urgent inner narrative to offer, but only an artful self-display. The poet is here caught forever in that 'identity parade' referred to in 'The Key', the parading of identity, in which his primary objective is *not to be identified as the culprit*, not to be identified at all. The poem becomes, like pantisocracy itself, another Romantic folly.

Haymakings / Handwashings

'7, Middagh Street' in *Meeting the British* refers to a more recent, and consummated, flight of British writers to North America, though it explores too, the fantasies that accompany such cultural translations. From its opening scenes in which Wystan Auden and Christopher Isherwood take French leave from a Europe at war, to the hasty departure of MacNeice, leaving by the back door of Muldoon's pub or poem at the end, the sequence is fixated on leavings, reverting, in its final line, to that classic *poésie de départs*, Masefield's 'Cargoes', with which it had begun. The key point about the address which provides the sequence's title is that an address is now all that remains of the remarkable household the poem celebrates, the home simultaneously to many writers and artists, including the burlesque artist Gypsy Rose Lee, who is, perhaps, an epitome of them all. Gone to make way for an urban expressway, 7, Middagh Street is the most populated absence in twentieth-century cultural history, now no more than a set of textual traces, recollected in various, diverse memoirs revisited by Muldoon's poem.

The sequence is itself a transportation of cargoes from place to place. The opening poem, 'Wystan', shifts through remnants of biography, running reminiscences of *Spain* into the 'Sonnets from China', and both into recollections of Auden Senior's war service. Wystan Auden may ruminate on the idea that his parents might now be 'tempted to rechristen / their youngest son / who turned his back on Albion / a Quisling'; but he has already been renamed several times, as Parsnip in *Put Out More Flags*, as H. W. Austin the tennis-star in the House of Commons and, conflated in a subliminal pun with the embattled British Prime Minister, as 'Wynstan' by his housemate the novelist Carson McCullers. He himself is prepared to wash his hands of England with the vow that 'I will not go back as *Auden*'. Some leavings are more final than others. In 'Chester', Auden's American lover Chester Kallman stands in for a promiscuity common both to art and life, in that endless circulation of trade-ins inspired by the quest for the new, 'for those time-honoured trophies – / cunts, or fresh, young cocks'. But the whole sequence enacts the same infidelity, as the words which end each separate monologue are traded across, picked up and reused in a new discursive context, in the first line of the subsequent one. Language is constantly on the move, robbing Peter (Pears / Grimes) to pay Paul (Bowles / Bunyan / Muldoon), leaving by the back door as it enters by the front. It is, thus, full of the leavings of other conversations and soliloquies, as Salvador Dali's leaving war-ravaged Barcelona by the back door not only recalls Auden's departure from Spain and from Britain but also prefigures MacNeice's. Dali, Irished by MacNeice as 'O'Daly', epitomises that other sense of leavings, like the lobster / telephone in the painting of which 'Salvador' speaks, which 'droops from a bare branch / above a plate, on which the remains of lunch / include a snapshot of Hitler / and some boiled beans left over / from *Soft Construction: A Premonition / of Civil War.*' These leftovers, one notes, are not from a real meal or last supper, but from a previous painting – in Derrida's neo-platonic terms, the simulacrum of a simulacrum.

A similar preoccupation pervades *The Annals of Chile*[14] (1994), whether in the *At Swim-Two-Birds* poly-narrative exuberance of 'Yarrow' or in that postmodern version of Villon's '*Neiges d'antan*', 'Incantata', with its record of searching 'for some trace of Spinoza or Amelia Earhart, / both of them going down with their

engines on fire', or its recycled sick joke about 'the remnants of Airey Neave...
the remnants of Mountbatten', both victims of IRA bombs, in a world which
is nothing but remnants, and its melancholy catalogues of lost time and
departed glories:

> That's all that's left of the voice of Enrico Caruso
> from all that's left of an opera-house somewhere in Matto Grosso,
> all that's left of the hogweed and horehound and cuckoo-pint,
> of the eighteen soldiers dead at Warrenpoint,
> of the Black Church clique and the Graphic Studio claque,
> of the many moons of glasses on a tray...

Though this ragbag of lists is without hierarchy or precedence, it doesn't
diminish the deaths to which it alludes in the way the joky hocus-pocus of
Madoc does. I'm thinking, for example, of how in that volume the massacre of
Modocs amidst the lava-beds of the American north-west is inexcusably translated at the end of the sequence, by way of a schoolboy pun ('laver-breads'),
into an absurd reprise of the fantasy of Welsh origins: 'May, 1873. The
Modocs, led by Captain Jack, are systematically hunted down on the laver-
breads of Oregon.'[15] The unsifted, disorderly lists of 'Incantata', by contrast,
have a real and urgent rationale, reflecting the confusion of levels and registers in which consciousness is actually constituted.

Hay, Muldoon's playful and inventive but also morally impassioned 1998
volume,[16] combining Derrida's Platonic *spoudē* and *paidia*, has a poem which
hints, in its title, at a Platonic aetiology. 'Symposium' offers what might be the
fruits of a brain-storming session round the conference table: a compendium of
postmodern proverbs which never reach their expected conclusion but run into
each other, in a dizzy circulation of contradictions. This harvest of half-wis-
doms is in one sense an 'aftermath', that word Muldoon uses in several poems,
etymologically a second crop – of alfalfa, hay or whatever – to be garnered late,
in a doubling which is also a diminished repeat of the original thing. Proverbs
in a sense comprise a collective *pharmakon* – a pharmacopia – in that one can
always find one piece of proverbial wisdom that negates another ('He who hes-
itates is lost': 'Look before you leap'; 'Too many cooks spoil the broth': 'Many
hands make light work', etc.). But Muldoon does something more complex
with his miscegenated texts. The poem begins with a slippery evasion of fixity, as the horse led to water migrates through a series of miscegenated
proverbs to have its departure confirmed in the closing couplet: 'There's no
fool like the fool / Who's shot his bolt. There's no smoke after the horse is
gone.'

The lines, in their compacted richness, are an epitome of the contradictory
associations of 'leaving'. To shoot a bolt is both to shut a door and to fire an
arrow (which, while effectual, may also leave one defenceless, the arrow

gone). Bolting an empty stable door won't ensure stability, once the horse has bolted. There's no smoke without fire, but smoke is only the leavings of flame, the trace of something departed. The horse gone, even that trace goes missing. The fusion of the act of leaving with the leavings, the husks of meaning and event left behind, identifies that place of transit which is Muldoon's true homeland. At the heart of this sonnet is an aphoristic complex which relates to the book's title: making hay, hitting a nail on the head, the want of a nail (another horse motif), the sky falling in. 'Hay' itself partakes of the *pharmakon*, as these apophthegms suggest, for while haymaking is a harvesting of plenty, the idiom moves, via 'make hay while the sun shines', to a rather more frivolous implication, as the *OED* makes clear: "To make hay: (a) *lit.*, to mow grass and dry it by spreading it about; (b) *fig.*, to make confusion. *To make hay of*: to turn topsy-turvy."[17]

It is with just such a making hay that the volume begins, with the rumbustious kaleidoscope of narratives and tumbling associations, 'The Mud Room', exploring that edge of things where 'the goats delight to tread upon the brink / of meaning'. This is a poem full of the leavings of existence, the mess and clutter of the mind as of a life, full of the disorderly 'drek / and clutter / of the mud room, the cardboard boxes from K-Mart and Caldor, / the hoover, the ironing-board, the ram's horn / on which Moses called to Aaron, a pair of my da's boots... / Virgil's *Georgics*, Plato's *Dialogues*'. There is, in such a tumbled reality, 'no fine / blue-green line' between one thing and another, or between things and the signifiers in which they come packaged, just as, with regard to his father's boots, it is unclear, as with Flann O'Brien's bicycling policeman, where they ended and the world began. The mind, language, are stuffed like the mud room with 'box after cardboard box / of all manner of schmaltz and schlock from Abba to Ultravox'. But this is a reality full, not empty, of meaning, in which the debris of words, self-referentially, can include the very material presence of 'the stack of twenty copies of *The Annals of Chile* ($21 hardback)'. The self, like its texts, is a remaindered re-minding amidst all this evanescent trash, and if something comes between the she-goat and us it is probably words, words, words.

'They that Wash on Thursday' rings – or wrings – all the changes on the fingers of one hand. It is a poem, indeed, which, recalling Joyce, is all hands, every rhyme in its fifty lines being the one word 'hand', and each usage of the word a variation on its idiomatic, metaphoric and metonymic polyvalency. The signifier gamely runs off, but it is always also pointing back, indexing, one might say, the meanings it has left behind it. Indeed, the accumulation of verbal usages yanks us back to a recognition that, within all the signifying difference, there is an actual physical appendage which, in its wide utility, has generated all these usages, a material, carnal *fons et origo* of all those spilling semes: you need hands. While, then, his mother was 'a dab hand' at child control, and his father 'washed his hands / of the matter', the young Muldoon learned a different lesson, of how to reconcile candour and discretion, indirection and frankness, which his playful way with words holds out as it withholds, holding out on us:

> So I learned first hand
> to deal in the off-, the under-, the sleight-of-hand,
> writing now in that great, open hand
> yet never quite showing my hand.

The poem in its very conclusion performs the same operation, leaving us with the image of an actual person, the real Paul Muldoon, that tangible, real presence allegedly so recently among us, but now departed, as it shifts – sneakily handing on to continuity – to all that's left behind when that person leaves by the back door. What's left is a text, and, punningly, a '"coat of arms"' to be worn on his sleeve: 'on a green field a white hand', that performance known as 'Paul Muldoon, Irish Poet'.

NOTES

1. Paul Muldoon, *New Weather* (London: Faber and Faber, 1973).
2. Paul Muldoon, *Why Brownlee Left* (London: Faber and Faber, 1980).
3. Jacques Derrida, 'Pharmacia', section 1 of 'Plato's Pharmacy', in *Dissemination*, trans. Barbara Johnson (London: The Athlone Press, 1981), pp. 70-5. See also section 4, 'The Pharmakon', especially pp. 97-102. The French original, *La Dissémination*, was published in 1972 by *Editions du Seuil* (Paris).
4. See 'The Makings of a Music', in Seamus Heaney, *Preoccupations: Selected Prose 1968-1978* (London: Faber and Faber, 1980), pp. 65; 68.
5. Jacques Derrida, 'Play: From the Pharmakon to the Letter and from Blindness to the Supplement', section 9 of 'Plato's Pharmacy', pp. 156–7. This might be the point from which to start a discussion of Muldoon's repeated thematics of the double, the copy and the twin, and his verbal and structural doublings and repetitions – what one might coin Muldoon's doubloons, since they so often involve some form of piracy or other, and function like a currency. Compare 'Plato's Pharmacy', section 9, p. 168:
   > To repeat: the disappearance of the good-father-capital-sun is thus the precondition of discourse... The disappearance of truth as presence, the withdrawal of the present origin of presence, is the condition of all (manifestation of) truth. Nonpresence is presence. Différance, the disappearance of any originary presence, is *at once* the condition of possibility *and* the condition of impossibility of truth. At once. 'At once' means the being-present (*on*) in its truth, in the presence of its identity and in the identity of its presence, *is doubled* as soon as it appears, as soon as it presents itself. *It appears, in its essence, as* the possibility of its own most proper nontruth, of its pseudo-truth reflected in the icon, the phantasm, or the simulacrum. What is is not what it is, identical and identical to itself, unique, unless it *adds to itself* the possibility of being repeated as such. And its identity is hollowed out by that addition, withdraws itself in the supplement that presents it (emphases in original).
   >
   Derrida's less enigmatic and succincter formulation a little earlier, that 'Desires, says Plato, should be raised like sons. // Writing is the miserable son', is infinitely suggestive in this context, as are the footnoted observations on the figure of the orphan in Plato ('Plato's Pharmacy', section 8, 'The Heritage of the Pharmakon: The Family Scene', p.145).
6. Cf. Derrida, 'Plato's Pharmacy', section 4, 'The Pharmakon', pp. 104–5:
   > Knowing that he can always leave his thoughts outside or check them with an external agency,

201

with the physical, spatial, superficial marks that one lays flat on a tablet, he who has the *tekhnē* of writing at his disposal will come to rely on it. He will know that he himself can leave without the *tupoi*'s going away, that he can forget all about them without their leaving his service. They will represent him even if he forgets them; they will transmit his word even if he is not there to animate them. Even if he is dead, and only a *pharmakon* can be the wielder of such power, *over* death but also in cahoots with it. The *pharmakon* and writing are thus always involved in questions of life and death.

Suggestively, Derrida later discusses the problematic of work and play by reference to Plato's image of the farmer or husbandman in the *Theaetetus*, contrasting 'the patient, sensible farmer' and 'the Sunday gardener, hasty, dabbling, and frivolous. On the one hand, the serious (*spoudē*); on the other, the game (*paidia*) and the holiday (*heortē*). On the one hand cultivation, agri-culture, knowledge, economy; on the other, art, enjoyment and unreserved spending'; and goes on to observe, in a footnote, 'The opposition farmer / gardener (fruits / flowers; lasting / ephemeral; patience / haste; seriousness / play, etc.) can be juxtaposed to the theme of the double gift in the *Laws*' ('Plato's Pharmacy', 'The Heritage of the Pharmakon', pp. 150–1).

7. Paul Muldoon, *Hay* (London: Faber and Faber, 1998).
8. Jean Baudrillard, 'Simulacra and Simulations', in *Selected Writings*, ed. Mark Poster (Oxford: Polity Press, 1989), pp. 166–184.
9. Paul Muldoon, *Madoc: A Mystery* (London: Faber and Faber, 1990).
10. Cf. Derrida, 'Plato's Pharmacy', p.139: 'A perfect imitation is no longer an imitation. If one eliminates the tiny difference that, in separating the imitator from the imitated, by that very fact refers to it, one would render the imitator absolutely different: the imitator would become another being no longer referring to the imitated.' Derrida offers this as a gloss on Socrates' demonstration that a copy of Cratylus made by some god to be sentient and self-aware would no longer be a copy but would constitute a new, second Cratylus – in anachronistic modern terms, a clone and not a simulacrum.
11. James Wilson, *The Earth Shall Weep: A History of Native America* (London: Picador, 1998), p. 106.
12. Paul Muldoon, *Meeting the British* (London: Faber and Faber, 1987).
13. Wilson, *The Earth Shall Weep*, pp. 122–7.
14. Paul Muldoon, *The Annals of Chile* (London: Faber and Faber, 1994)
15. According to Wilson, this genocidal campaign actually took place in Northern California. Muldoon has altered the location, presumably, to make a tenuous and frivolous connection with the Oregon Trail expedition, on whose participants John Evans's Welsh fantasia had apparently had an influence. On the story of Captain Jack, see Wilson, *The Earth Shall Weep*, pp. 236–7.
16. Muldoon, *Hay*.
17. 'Hay' is also glossed as a hedge, fence, enclosure, park, an extended line of men, a net used for catching wild animals, esp. rabbits, stretched in front of their holes, and a country dance with a serpentine movement.

XII

Cruising to the Podes:
Ciaran Carson's Virtual Realities

'Its map is virtual reality' ('Letters from the Alphabet': 'A')[1]

Ambilocations

Reviewing Richard Murphy's *The Kick* in a piece called, with characteristic wordplay, 'Murphy's Lore',[2] Ciaran Carson was seized by the fact that Murphy's mother was 'ambidextrous',

> and it was all the same to her whether she wrote backwards or forwards. She used to have to ask someone on which side of a blank page she ought to begin. When asked to state her nationality on forms in Ireland during the Second World War, she used to write 'British and Irish'. The family believed that no one spoke English as well as the Anglo-Irish, and that the Anglo-Irish were the best administrators in the Empire.

Murphy's father was the last British mayor of Colombo, so that, as a boy, travelling repeatedly between Ceylon and Ireland, says Carson, 'He was shuttled back and forth for some years between these two extremes of climate, like a kind of hyphen'. Finally, Carson touches on a third aspect of Murphy's identity, remarking that, 'Sexually ambivalent, he managed to marry happily, at least for a while'. These three discrete elements clearly connect in Carson's imagination, making up a kind of conceptual rhyming triplet. Ambidextrous, sexually ambivalent, and, a usage I want to coin here, in the manner of Carson, 'ambilocated'. Ambilocation is a different condition from mere 'bilocation', the mysterious capacity to be in two places at once. Rather it is a matter of being always in neither place, or of being between places, or of being always in one place which may be Belfast, but also at the same time in many other places, dis-located, relocated, mis-placed, displaced, everywhere and nowhere, evincing what 'All the Better to See You With'[3] calls 'just that air / Of neither-here-nor-thereness. Coming in the act of going'.

The theme is ubiquitous in Carson's writings, summed up in the report of the poem 'Alibi' (*OEC*) that everywhere 'murder is done', which prompts the questions, 'Was I there?' and, if not, 'Where was I then?', only to recognise that in the end 'we are accomplices to all assassinations', and have no alibi. It is not always a comfortable place to be, may indeed be a place of intimidation and putative violence. 'Jawbox' (*BC*), for example, speaks of how, travelling on an Ulster bus, 'the border passes through him / Like a knife, invisibly', and of being trapped in the 'Small transgressions', 'caught between "Bel*fast*" and "*Bel*fast", as if in the accordion pleats between two lurching carriages' of the train, with 'terrifying glimpses' of the tracks below.

What links all three of Murphy's doublenesses is indicated by the phrase 'like a kind of hyphen'. This is an original variation on Stephen Gwynn's description of Anglo-Irishness as a form of 'spiritual hyphenation'. For whereas the ambidextrous analogy would suggest a poet both British and Irish, 'a kind of hyphen' rules out both, stranding him in the mere moment of transit between the two, neither both at once nor just one thing or the other, but simply a place where one passes over, is translated, between two worlds. History has many cunning passages, but this moment of passage, this place of transit, is one of the darkest and yet most illuminating places to be, a 'disembodied interim' like that spoken of in 'The Wind that Shakes the Barley'.[4] It is a space that Carson, speaking, as the title of one poem puts it, a 'Second Language', published in the volume *First Language*,[5] has clearly made his own.

This space of hyphenation, not of hyphenated being but of being a hyphen, is given a specifically Northern Irish inflection in that chilling little poem in *Belfast Confetti* called 'Last Orders', its very title loitering between the profane world of the bar and the sacred one of holy orders, with an apocalyptic suggestion of 'last things', personal and collective mortality. Its resonating ambiguities connect, too, with that infamous phrase of morally incompetent self-exculpation, 'just obeying orders'.

The poem is a discourse of double entendres. The buzzer for the fortified bar is like a trigger, the doorman's spyhole is like rifle sights, and the click of the door opening might be that of a killer's finger on the trigger of a gun. The whole experience, 'since you never know for sure who's who, or what / You're walking into', is a kind of semantic Russian roulette, in which you can't guarantee that it won't be the loaded cylinder that the next sentence discharges. Playful similes may suddenly turn deadly literal. If events are this unpredictable, such chance differences could instigate wholly different timelines: a bullet or a bomb now would change the course of many lives. Likewise, the unreliability of language can generate innumerable possible meanings, semantic lines. But this works both ways. Those inside the bar, who take the risk of opening the door to a stranger, might be the victims, not the perpetrators of murder. They too are playing Russian roulette. The sudden lull when the two men enter suggests both anxiety and the sullen lull of hostility. The half-rhyme that picks this up makes the barman's lolling head, inviting an order, suggest the lolling head of a corpse. The innocuous neutrality of the *Harp* lager they order, putatively Danish, yes, and therefore beyond all this fiddle – harping on it – also suggests the musical instrument that might be ordered for a performance in that 'Kingdom Come' to which they could all be blown. Looking daggers in a sectarian Bushmills bar mirror emphasises the identity in difference of these opposed 'orders'. If 'Taig' is written on his face, this is not something the speaker can control, simply a facticity he is fated to. Everything is being read here, but nothing is said beyond the laconic call to last orders. Inhabiting that realm of the hyphen between opposing loyalties, these faces along the bar meet through a mirror, as if, as in Auden's 'September 1, 1939', they are meeting their own complicit reflections. But this encounter also signals a momentary truce in the looking-glass war. What they all share, as human beings, is that they're dying for a drink.

Carson's most remarkable achievement in this poem lies in the deployment of its modest little pronouns, those humble parts of speech round which the whole poem is structured. The second line is skilfully constructed to follow the 'but' which ends a line where, because of the imperative, no prenomial subject is identified: it is only 'someone else' who has you in their metaphoric or possibly literal sights. 'Someone else' is the real subject of this sentence, but it takes second place to the impersonalising 'It's', and is then dispersed into plurality by the colloquial use of 'their'– not because the poem wants to be politically correct about gender, but because this 'someone else' is not a person but a faceless representative of a collective other. The 'you' spoken of in the next line ('you never know for sure who's who, or what / You're walking into') takes on a similar generality, since it is not really 'you', the unique and actual person, but 'one', a collective alterity, that is the subject of this knowledge, or this ignorance, a dispersal into anonymous collectivity underlined by 'who's who, or what'. The poem then comes clean about its dissolution of real subjects into figures, instances in an argument, almost algebraic in their representativeness. The speaker himself could, 'for instance', be 'anybody', the very formulation reducing him to the generic status of an instance. The point is that, to these others, who don't know him from Adam, he *is* anybody, just as each of the others is to *him*. Everybody is, from another point of view, anybody. It is within such alienating distances that the bombers and the gunmen operate, reducing each unique other to a generalised otherness, a mere instance, a disembodied interim, abstract cipher: 'anybody', or 'any body'.

The pronouns operate with some subtlety: 'I'm told' (passive recipient of advice from an unspecific other who is merely the agent of the telling – 'they say'); 'See me', a colloquial invitation to look which is really just a way of identifying the self as speaker; the italicised, apparently determining 'I', insisting on his own uniqueness and particularity, at the very centre of the poem. The juxtaposed 'me / I' quietly emphasises that double dimension in which we exist, in the hyphen / slash between subject and object, self for self and self for others. That buttonholing 'See me' invites the reader in as the speaker's bar companion, to become part of that threatened, but also threatening, 'us / we' who order *Harp*. But if *Harp* is safe because unsectarian – 'everybody' drinks it – that everybody briefly collectivised as a unity is then at once dispersed by the reappearance of a solitary and hostile 'someone' who looks daggers at 'us', the momentary community of thirst falling into sectarian division again.

'Someone', however, has not yet finished its political business. In the opening sentence it was 'someone else' who had 'you' in 'their' sights, and then 'someone' who looks daggers at 'us' – you and I facing a hostile anonymity of faces. The penny drops differently, recognising how easily 'someone / Like ourselves' – a pause on the enjambment holding off the dénouement – could 'walk in and blow the whole place, and ourselves, to Kingdom Come'. There are multiple perspectives here, and that even smaller and even more insignificant word, 'like', is what hits the spot. 'Someone else', yes, but also 'someone / Like ourselves' – in Baudelairean and Eliotic terms, 'hypocrite lecteur, mon semblable, mon frère'. But, for the men already in the bar, 'we' might be just some such other, someone like *their* selves, assassins bringing *their* death.

Carson's masterly deployment of pronouns enacts a whole political history of alienation and mutual hostility, within a gapped culture where all of them, united by the strife which divides them, inhabit the last, secret order of the hyphen. Carson had used the metaphor of hyphenation – not of being hyphenated, but of being a hyphen – in another more overtly political commentary in the bar-room setting of 'Barfly' in the same volume. The buttonholing barfly invites us to figure why The Crown and Shamrock and the Rose and Crown bars are at opposite ends of town, but dismisses the presumed reply, that it is for reasons of politics, with the observation that borders move, odds change, 'Or they're asked to', shifting evasively to the anecdote of an armed raid on a bar earlier that evening. The barfly tells us he 'buzzed off' from this particular scene, his metaphoric vocation turning suddenly literal, a Lord of the Flies looking for trade: 'So now, I am a hyphen, flitting here and there: between The First and Last.'

Carson's a fly guy – like Beelzebub. There are plenty of flies on, or, rather in, his poetry. Another fly may indicate what's going on here – that which in 'Graecum Est: Non Legitur' in *Opera Et Cetera*, in a dive-bombing rendezvous with the page on which the poet is writing, 'made an audible syzygy'. Originally, according to the *OED*, meaning 'conjunction', the word is 'Now extended to include both conjunction and opposition'. Carson's initial sense here would seem to be the next one: 'the conjunction of two organisms without loss of identity', that last word alerting us to a possibly political dimension. But in his poetry, reality regularly enters into a syzygy, 'both conjunction and 'opposition', with fantasy, literal with metaphoric. This is what I mean by ambilocation.

Which brings us to the Podes

Carson's virtual HMS *Belfast*[6] is manned, in apparently unsectarian fashion, by 'Both Catestants and Protholics', the playful transposition suggesting the interchangeability of these opposing creeds but also, perhaps, the fatuousness of their antithesis – in other words, that syzygy which is 'both conjunction and opposition'. But the poem, which sails out on imaginary voyages to some of the places where the real HMS *Belfast* saw service, returns at the end to find its speaker waking up, not bound away but 'bound in iron chains', 'on board the prison ship Belfast', still in dock in a scare-quoted '"old Belfast"'. The real *Belfast* did manage to elude the wreckers' yard, after all its sailings, on the Arctic Convoy to Archangel during the war, and in the Far East after it, acting in 1947 as the relay station for messages to the sloop *Amethyst* beset by Chinese Communist forces a thousand miles up the Yangtse. These elements of the ship's history are obliquely alluded to in the redundancy of taking 'Ice to Archangel, tea to China, coals to Tyne' (the last variant adapting the proverbial cliché, 'coals to Newcastle'), and in the reference to those 'imperceptible horizons, where amethyst / Dims into blue'. HMS *Belfast* survives, however, not as a prison ship in Belfast harbour but as a museum ship in the Pool of London. The conjunction and opposition of museum and prison proposes, as so often in Carson's poetry, that memory can be a prison-house where the subject, fixated on recall as if identity depended on it, is actually thwarted, erased, cancelled by the very proliferation of calls to remember, as 'Schoolboys and Idlers of Pompeii'(*BC*) spells out:

> At times it seems that every inch of Belfast has been written-on, erased, and written-on again: messages, curses, political imperatives, but mostly names, or nicknames… cancelling each other out in their bid to be remembered. *Remember 1690. Remember 1916.* Most of all. *Remember me. I was here.*

The final question here, 'Where does… memory falter, and imagination take hold?', indicates the preoccupation that underlies the syzygy of actual and virtual realities in 'The Ballad of HMS *Belfast*'.

If, on board ship, 'Some sang of Zanzibar and Montalban, and others of the lands unascertained / On maps', the former name probably recalls the ship's ceremonial role in Tanganyikan (subsequently Tanzanian) independence celebrations. 'Montalban', however, though a place in the Philippines, and therefore the Antipodes, may refer instead, as part of that interweaving of fantastic and actual voyages, to the actor Ricardo Montalban, who played the eponymous villain in the *Star Trek* movie *The Wrath of Khan*, who was also the mysterious host on the TV series *Fantasy Island*, an intermediary between the ballad's references to contemporary science fiction, 'boldly go[ing] where none had gone before', Keats's travels in the Homeric 'Realms of Gold' and Jules Verne's Nemo ('No-one', the alias of Odysseus also), captain of the *Nautilus*. Such an interweaving of canonical poetry, sci-fi and historical actuality is signalled near the start of the ballad, which speaks of the ship being 'full-rigged like the *Beagle*, piston-driven like the *Enterprise* / Express; each system was a back-up for the other, auxiliarizing verse with prose', and Charles Darwin with Captain Kirk.

A subsequent couplet extends the wordplay: 'We've been immersed, since then, in cruises to the Podes and Antipodes; / The dolphin and the flying fish would chaperone us like aquatic aunties...' This is an attention-seeking rhyme. If you remove 'pode' from the middle of the first word, it would constitute (in Northern Ireland, anyway), a rime riche: 'Antis / aunties'. The 'pode' we might say, is a hyphen thrusting itself between 'anti' and 'is'. And this reinforces the whimsicality of that neologism, 'Podes'. For of course there is – or was – no such word. And yet it is an eminently sensible word to envisage. For if there is an 'Antipodes', there should, surely, be a 'Podes' for them to be antithetical to.

The *OED* gives as a primary definition of 'antipodes': 'Places on the surface of the earth directly opposite to each other, or the place which is directly opposite to another (*esp.* to our own region)', and, by transference, 'the exact opposite of a person or thing', with a nice quotation from Bacon, 'He will never be one of the Antipodes, to tread opposite to the present world'. The Podes, then, would be the opposite of an opposite. They are an imaginary location, constructed by a process of back formation from the Antipodes. What the 'Ballad' calls 'lands unascertained' are then, like More's Utopia, William Morris's Nowhere, or Samuel Butler's Erewhon, precisely no place at all. And yet, if the 'antipodes' are the geographical opposite of where we are, then where we are should be the Podes. A supposedly 'actual' world, that is, is displaced by an imaginary and 'unascertained' one, that linguistically constructed 'virtual reality' spoken of in the first poem of the sequence 'Letters from the Alphabet' (*OEC*) which stands as epigraph to this chapter, an imagined, imaginary, realm, where fantasy, memory and actuality interpenetrate in kaleidoscopic variations.

Back formation is a recurrent practice in Carson's poetry. Think, for example, of how Horse Boyle gets his name, in 'Dresden' (*BC*): 'Horse Boyle was called Horse Boyle because of his brother Mule; / Though why Mule was called Mule is anybody's guess.' And this imaginary identity is related to the story-telling fantasies which this, as so many of the poems, articulates, though in this case the story-line is called back as soon as uttered: 'I stayed there once, / Or rather, I nearly stayed there once. But that's another story.' 'Nearly' here is that hyphen between actual and imaginary, the slash that splices either / or, that intervenes between this story and another one. In 'Second Language' (*FL*) we're told that, for the young Carson, the Arapaho Indians 'whooped and hollered in their unforked tongue'. But this last phrase, while it obviously alludes to Heaney's use in *North* of the 'forked tongue' as an image of Northern Irish duplicities, is actually a back formation, for it infers that the Arapaho cast the white man as speaking with a forked tongue by contrast with their own 'unforked' tongue. Carson, born into an Irish-speaking family in Belfast, found his own tongue hyphenated from the start by this English / Gaelic duality.

The poem 'Opus 14' (*FL*) asks: 'Did you know that "the set of all objects describable in exactly eleven English words" / Is called an "R-Set"? I didn't. It was dreamed up by the people who put the "surd" in "absurd".' Though the phrase in quotation marks would seem to belong to an R-Set (it comprises exactly eleven words) its apparent autoreferentiality falls apart on examination, since it is not the description of an object but the naming of a category. The real attraction of the 'R-Set' to Carson is that it rhymes with 'Farset', the lost river which gives Belfast its name, and the subject of a prose meditation in *Belfast Confetti*. Though, with admirable restraint, he neither makes the rhyme nor refers to the subject here, it lurks as an underground current in the text, awaiting rediscovery. The conceptual absurdity of all this is opened up in the actual, not quite perfect rhyme of the next line, which has its own sting in the tail. For the usage 'surd', which might appear, like 'podes', to be a word created by back formation from its assumed opposite, 'absurd', actually precedes – just – that of 'absurd'. The earliest instances, according to the *OED*, occur in 1551 and 1557 respectively. Nor, in fact, is it the opposite of 'absurd'. The *OED* records of 'surd', originally meaning 'deaf' and / or 'mute' (French 'sourd'), that 'The mathematical sense "irrational" arises from L. *surdus* being used to render Gr. *alogos* ... *Math*. Of a number or quantity (esp. a root): That cannot be expressed in finite terms of ordinary numbers or quantities: = irrational.' The *OED* glosses 'absurd' as 'Inharmonious. Out of harmony with reason or propriety; in mod. use, plainly opposed to reason'. In other words, 'absurd' and 'surd', far from being antithetical, the one a departure from the other, come punningly down to the same thing. That Greek original, '*alogos*', may be translated as 'irrational'. It could also mean 'without language'.

There is a moral here for Carson's poetry. Whether you stay on the surd and narrow or depart from it, you are wandering in absurdity. But you can never be 'without language'. Antitheses turn out not to work like that at all. Binaries dissolve themselves into multiplicity, incompatible overlapping alternatives. The poem 'Opus Operandi' (*FL*), depicting the antipathetic Paddies and Billies struggling to understand 'the concept "Orange"' and 'the deep grammar of the handshake, the shibboleths of *aitch* and *haitch*' at an empathy class for expectant fathers, observes paradoxically that 'Everything was neither one thing nor the other'. As Carson says of his blue-black Quink in 'Loaf' (*BC*), 'I liked the in-between-ness of it, neither / One thing nor the other', referring simultaneously to the colour of the ink and the made-up portmanteau trade name.

As that 'Catestants and Protholics' in 'HMS *Belfast*' indicates, Carson is not much enamoured of the simple dualities of identity politics. Antitheses and oppositions figure regularly in his writing only to be deconstructed into plurality. The structuralist binary gets short shrift in the opening poem of 'Et Cetera', 'Auditque Vocatus Apollo' (*OEC*), in which the observations by his guide on the ascent of Parnassus are immediately subverted by the poet's silly answers and runaway fancy: '*Our mind*, he said, *is split*. Too true. Like he was Quee and I was Queg – // One of those guys. Orpheus. Apollo. Rilke. Ahab. Dick.' The list overflows itself with subversive non-partners, splitting Melville's Queequeg into a non-existent couple, substituting Orpheus for Dionysus as the usual antithesis to Apollo, and then dislocating the chain of signification altogether by throwing in Rilke, the author of *Sonnets to Orpheus*, before undercutting the whole idea by comically curtailing Moby Dick to a supposed surname (a kind of back formation, this) in a ludicrous coupling as a 'guy' with his pursuer Ahab. The poem lurches further into absurdity with the suggestion that 'climbing Mount / Olympia is like that', where not only has the poem shifted from the mountain of the Muses to that of the Olympian gods (poetry versus power), but in the process has got the name wrong, since Olympia, the site of the Olympic games, is on a level plain, while the gods (allegedly) live on Olymp*us*. But this is nothing beside the absurdity of 'enquiring for the whale' on a mountain.

Both whale hunt and ascent conjoin as apparently unending and fruitless quests, for 'You think you've reached the summit when another distant crest / Appears to challenge you. *Quo vadis?* Something like that'. This I take to be the point of the sequence title, 'Et Cetera' – 'and the rest' – a potentially endless proliferation of associations on which a restless language puns in 'I asked if we could rest'. It performs a similar function, that is, to Muldoon's 'And then some', endlessly deferring closure. If the god appears at the very moment of giving up, announcing, in the last words of the poem '*It's me. Apollo*', this is because, in a slickly autoreferential move, the poem about trying to write a poem has somehow been written in the process of lamenting its own elusiveness. (Carson glosses the Latin tag, from Virgil's *Georgics*, as 'and Apollo hears when invoked'.) But there remains the rest of the sequence, all those other et ceteras to pursue, mountains to climb, whales to hunt, words to pin down, those 'something[s] like that' which are the very embodiment of difference in their parade of approximate similitude.

As the poem over the page in this volume, '*Vox et Praeterea Nihil*' (' a voice and nothing more'), proposes, 'the notes / Are always different, though the tune remains the same; the "quotes" are really "unquotes"'. The Podes, that is, are simultaneously the Antipodes, and yet, as with the campanologists of this poem, they are also '– invariably – ... out of synch on dangling long / Elastic ropes, though all are trying hard to tell their *Ding an sich* from *dong*'. The elastic ropes of language (a better metaphor than the iron chain of signifiers), permit that dodgy pulling of 'dong' into binary coupling with '*Ding*', in a discourse which is always out of synch with the thing itself, which explains, the poem ends, 'why the same refrain is always various', sameness and difference in one *Ding* the very stuff of meaning.

Carson seems as happy amidst the infinite indeterminacies of post-structuralism as a leprechaun in clover, proclaiming in 'Mountain Dew' (*ToN*), that 'everything can be contained in anything', as dragons are implicit in 'dragonfly', so that 'For every line you write are countless thousands not', and that 'For all the prophets claim, the end is never nigh'. Language runs away with meaning. It is always, in Carson's recurrent image, 'out of synch' with the real. There can be, in reality, no 'Narrative in Black and White', despite the claim made by the poem of that title in *Belfast Confetti*. It is easy to 'misconstrue' blurred reconstructions, the poem argues, and all one usually encounters in any narrative is 'a faded diagram from which / You'd try to piece together what the action was' (another instance of a kind of back formation). In tale-telling as in telling tales, it continues, 'people don't go shooting off their mouths like that'. At times, however, language can dive-bomb shockingly into the thing itself, as metaphor turns murderously actual, carrying us across that frontier to a place where words are taken literally, and mouths are shot off for real. Earlier in the same volume, 'The Mouth' had already opened up the idiomatic cliché which concludes 'Narrative in Black and White': 'There was this head had this mouth he kept shooting off. / Unfortunately', biting off 'more than he could chew'. The poem concludes, chillingly, with the literal application of the metaphor, the indiscreet gossiper's face blown off by (wordplay insinuates) Provisional gunmen. Carson here makes a literal application, too, of his usually playful rhetorical trick. The face of the murdered man is reconstructed by back formation, from the tooth marks in the last apple he ever ate, by – the malapropism a final insult to 'what he used to be' – the 'Forscenic Lab'.

The Groves of Blarney

The question, '*Was it a vision or a waking dream?*', that opens the title poem of *The Irish for No* (originally published 1987)[7] calls up Keats as a drugged or drunken companion in hyphenland, and the joky intertexts that pervade the poem place everything within 'the dangling / Quotation marks of a yin-yang mobile'. But though the poem 'slips away to perilous seas as things remain unsolved', confronting the death – murder or suicide? – of the UDR corporal on the headland, or the Belfast businessman with thirteen Black and Decker drill-holes in his head, the one phrase from its Keatsian repertoire that it does not open charmed casements on to is 'fairy lands forlorn'.

It is precisely this domain that Carson addressed in *The Twelfth of Never*, in 1999. The volume explores a fantasy island which, like the island of Dr Moreau, is what 'Sod of Death' calls 'the realm of the Metamorphoses, / Whose shapes are as innumerable as Chaos / Ever burgeoning with versions of our species'. The labyrinthine intertextuality of this volume finds its guiding thread in calling up Keats, Coleridge, de Quincey and other Romantics as the connoisseurs of a chaos where the dreams and visions of Romance metamorphose into the Nightmare Life-in-Death and Belle Dame sans Merci of addictive political traditions. Those twee eighteenth-century personifications, 'Hibernia' and 'Erin', the sentimental repertoire of Irish popular and patriotic song, and the kitsch folkloric Pooka, cluricaine and leprechaun, lead astray tourists and terrorists alike in pursuit of fairy gold at the end of the rainbow. The Irish theme pub called 'The Elfin Grot', where 'Karaoke singers mouth their lip-synch rhymes' in the Keats-baiting poem 'Hippocrene', is less likely to be located in Ireland than in that Japan which is one of the sequence's ambilocations. This simulacrum of Ireland and Irishness can be displaced to an oriental antipodes because it only ever really existed in discourse, fantasy, delusion, rounds of drinking or of drunken song. One can cruise to these Irish Podes anywhere. 'Hibernia' can beckon from across the sea if one drinks too much green tea below the snows of Fujiyama ('Green Tea'); one can enter an Irish Paradise by going with the flow, getting high on Japanese poteen and joss sticks in a Tokyo shebeen ('Sod of Death').

What the sequence explores is a karaoke politics lip-synched by nationalist and unionist alike, addicted to a 'Tape-loop music' for which Kafka's absurdist 'K is the leader of the empty orchestra of karaoke'. Of the many names the sequence offers for this fantasy realm, the most comprehensive is 'The Groves of Blarney', for it suggests the extent to which the Ireland of both major traditions is a rhetorical and self-deluding construct, a set of interpenetrating, interactive tall tales and fairy stories on or off the native soil, where the fetishised icons of allegiance come with authorising narratives attached, whether the Stickies' 1916 lily or the Loyalists' 1914–18 poppy. The archetype of martyred heroism is actually an otherworldly phantasm, 'The Man-from-god-knows-where'. Humble praties can be retrospectively mythologised, through the rear-view mirror of the 1840s, into glamorously addictive poppies in the poem '1798', where Keats's fairy beldam, encountered in 'the garden where the poppies grow', 'suck[s] the broken English from my Gaelic tongue'. 'Fear' sums up all these mythical beasts and succubi, 'the gremlins that have colonised my brain', in terms of Lewis Carroll's comic creation: 'I fear the Jabberwock, whatever it might be'. As in 'Sunderland and Spencer', the coy periphrases and sentimental personifications of an eighteenth-century discourse recruit acolytes 'smitten by the lovely Erin, who'd / Seduced them by her words of faery glamour'. The reality remains that of the hanged man in 'Spraying the Potatoes', with 'popping eyes of apoplectic liberty'.

But the sequence's central concern is with what the title of one sonnet calls 'Legions of the Dead', whether their icons of allegiance are the Red Hand of Ulster or the harp that once through Tara's halls, etcetera. Both alike belong to 'The indecipherable babble of days of yore', the schmaltzy archaism of that phrase suggesting just how banal were the causes for which these armies of 'hieroglyphic men / Like us' marched through history. But if, as the poem concludes, 'Opposing soldiers are at one within our regimen', it does not forget that these wasted generations are, as that innocent-seeming little connective reminds us, 'Like us', ambiguously leaving open whether the likeness resides in a common humanity or in conscription to a partisan fantasy. As 'Banners' puts it, 'dear old Ireland: / Fields of corpses plentiful as dug potatoes'.

'1798' allows Carson to make a brilliant and daring leap, via 'The Year of the French' (the title of another sonnet), to the 'Galactic battalions of those fallen in war', all the way from that Pharaonic Egypt rediscovered by Napoleon's archaeologists, through his invasion of Russia, to the battlefields of Flanders and beyond the present to Star Wars of the future. All have died, or will die, the volume's closing poem, 'Envoy', suggests, for nothing, for 'high cockelorum', the imaginary land of Cockaigne where everything is slightly out of synch. The punning allusion to 'cocaine' echoes back to the American hobos' song of the Big Rock Candy Mountain of the opening sonnet, 'Tib's Eve', and implicates all the other drugs that have created delusory allegiances, life-threatening addictions and intoxications throughout the sequence (to name a few, poppy, 'the emblem of Peace and the Opium Wars', tobacco, 'Catmint Tea', 'Green Tea', belladonna, 'Drops of Brandy', 'Wallop', 'Mountain Dew', 'Saké', 'Digitalis', 'Milk of Paradise', 'Crack', 'Doctor Ecstasy'). 'Tib's Eve' speaks of this fantasy Ireland as a realm 'Where everything is metaphor and simile', where the adjective 'green' valorises all impossibilities, like the linguistic philosopher's hypothetical 'green rose', and Zeno's paradox creates an intercalated space and time that's a paradise for stumbling somnambulists. 'Envoy' depicts the legions of the lost propping their ladders against the gates of an imaginary Heaven where all their grand endeavours will be rewarded with 'campaign haloes' on the Twelfth of Never. But as 'Twelfth Day' makes clear, this volume is not a sectarian tract. The Shakespearian fairies with which the sonnet opens mutate rapidly into the 'tiny Arcadians' of a Lilliputian world such as the ambilocated Swift imagined, 'troops of little fellows marching up and down... as if transistorised', 'the whole field pulsing like an Orange drum'. The 'Glorious Twelfth', another fantasy time replete with its baggage of myths, is also a variant on the Twelfth of Never, since it never really existed except in discourse. The Battle of the Boyne actually took place on the First of July 1690, but an adjustment was made when eleven days were lost with the change from Julian to Gregorian calendar in 1752. The absurdity of this iconic false chronology compounds the definition offered in the book's epigraph from *Brewer's Dictionary of Phrase and Fable*, a non-time to match the back-formed, utopian no-place of the Podes: 'St Tib's Eve. Never. A corruption of St Ubes. There is no such saint in the calendar as St Ubes, and therefore her eve falls on the "Greek Calends", neither before Christmas Day nor after it.'

This is not as straightforward as it sounds. The 'original' of St Tib is the St Ubes of which it is a corruption. But if St Ubes doesn't exist either, it is in a sense a back formation from St Tib, as the Eve – the night before – of St Tib is in turn a back formation from the non-existent saint's day, and the 'Greek Calends' are a non-existent back formation from the actual Roman Calends. Similarly, Brewer's apparently paradoxical last sentence is skewed into a kind of commonsense by verbal slackness. For if St Tib's Eve is neither before nor after Christmas day, the unintended implication is that it could be Christmas Day itself, that Saturnalian time of intercalated merriment when the world is turned upside down and another mythic saint, Santa Claus, briefly (mis)rules. The Twelfth of Never also, of course, suggests Twelfth Night, another eve of transition and reversal that connects, in the sonnet 'Twelfth Day', with the syzygial 'Glorious Twelfth' of Unionist celebration.

The Twelfth of Never opens with a recollection of that Victorian pseudo-archaism which bedevilled generations of schoolchildren required to sing it: 'There is a green hill far away, without a city wall'. Why on earth would anyone expect a green hill to *have* a city wall in the first place? The double meaning of 'without' – outside, as well as lacking – confirms Carson's vision of the world as a nexus of hermeneutic cruces, clouded by the linguistic residues of defunct idioms and ideologies. But it is interesting that this schoolboy puzzle finds an echo of sorts in another problematic inversion in the sequence's final sonnet. Following on from 'The Ambassadors', the title of 'Envoy' at first sight suggests that it is some kind of diplomatic envoy, carrying news or instructions from the spiritual capital, where true authority and significance reside. It turns out, however, to be a parting *Envoi*, which also sends its readers packing. What it dismisses is, in part, the meaningfulness of any message an envoy might bear from that assumed, anterior authority. It does this by garbling its own verbal authority: 'These words the ink is written in is not indelible'. The word order of the line is itself 'slightly out of synch', as the lack of agreement in the verb confirms, and this leads to a confusion of ends and means (words / ink). In scholarly fashion one should perhaps note: '*scilicet*: The ink these words are written in is not indelible'. Is this a misprint, or a breaking theme? If, as the next line tells us, every fairy story has its variorum, every sentence can be re-phrased, even though some rephrasings are just plain wrong. What Carson is doing here is underlining the textuality of the whole bundle of ideological narratives he's been negotiating, by reminding us of the textuality of the sequence itself, as prone to misprints and misprisions as are the conflicting 'histories' it deconstructs. For, as the octet concludes, 'the printed news is always unreliable'.

The Twilight Zone

A bundle of aphorisms:

(1) 'The world', said Wittgenstein, 'is everything that is the case.'
(2) 'The limits of my language mean the limits of my world.'
(3) 'Philosophy is a battle against the bewitchment of our intelligence by means of language.'
(4) 'What is your aim in philosophy? – To show the fly the way out of the fly-bottle.'
(5) 'What can be said at all can be said clearly; and whereof one cannot speak thereof one must be silent.'

This isn't particularly erudite. These five magical and familiar one-liners are the philosopher's total oeuvre, as collected in *The Concise Oxford Dictionary of Quotations* (1993). Carson's poetry enters into complex negotiations with all of them, seeking to show all those Irish flies that buzz around his poetry the way out of their fly bottle. And he does this by speaking clearly about the host of confused sayings that constitute the dark passages of a culture, and by refusing to remain silent about that of which, one might be warned, it would be better not to shoot off one's mouth. Carson's natural element, that is, is that Pynchonesque 'interface' he writes of in 'Intelligence' (*BC*), where

> We track shadows, echoes, scents, prints; and in the interface the information is decoded, coded back again and stored in bits and bytes and indirect addressing; but the glitches and gremlins and bugs keep fouling-up, seething out from the hardware, the dense entangled circuitry of back streets, backplanes, while the tape is spooling and drooling over alphanumeric strings and random-riot situations...

'The world is everything that is the case'. 'Everything' is a favourite word of Carson's. Paradoxically, its very inclusiveness may reduce all specific things to one thing, their mere totality. Yet regularly, his deployment of the word is in contexts which emphasise evanescence, indeterminacy, volatility, displacement, the deconstruction of the totality 'everything' would appear to posit: 'Like a fishnet stocking, everything is full of holes' ('Snowball', *IFN*); 'everything as full of holes as a Swiss cheese' ('Whatever Sleep It Is', *IFN*); 'Everything dissolves' ('All the Better to See You With', *BC*); 'everything's chalked up, and every now and then, wiped clean' ('Barfly', *BC*); 'Difficult to keep track: / Everything's a bit askew' ('Gate', *BC*); 'Everything was neither one thing nor the other' ('Opus Operandi', *FL*); 'everything can be contained in anything' ('Mountain Dew', *ToN*); 'Everything reverses south' ('Yes', *BC*); 'For the moment, everything is *X*, a blank not yet filled in'('Punctuation', *BC*); and so on.

This is repeatedly the condition of the city, which, as the title of one of those remarkable prose sequences in *Belfast Confetti* puts it, is perpetually a 'Revised Version': 'For everything is contingent and provisional; and the subjunctive mood of these images is tensed to the ifs and buts, the yeas and nays of Belfast's history.' Or again, in 'Question Time' (*BC*), a place of shifting sands and shifting meanings,

> The junk is sinking back into the sleech and muck. Pizza parlours, massage parlours, night-clubs, drinking-clubs, antique shops, designer studios momentarily populate the wilderness and the blitz sites; they too will vanish in the morning. Everything will be revised... sliding back into the rubble and erasure.

This is where Carson renegotiates Wittgenstein, for 'everything that is the case' also includes everything which is not, those mere possibilities of the actual as possible contemplated by Stephen Dedalus, which pervade his poems, the subjunctives of Belfast's history, the 'plan of might-have-beens, legislating for all the possibilities' he speaks of in 'Revised Version', which we each carry in our heads,

> For maps cannot describe everything, or they describe states of mind, like Dubourdieu's 'very incorrect' plan of 1811, which shows *streets and blocks of buildings which have never existed... a bridge ... proposed but not carried out...* the intoxicating draught of futures swallowed at one gulp, as someone sets another up.

'Everything' is, quite literally, indescribable. If the limits of our language are the limits of our world, that world, as *The Twelfth of Never* demonstrates, includes all those negatives and subjunctives that not only crowd around the actual but pervade it, shape it, force revisions upon it, in an endless interaction of the imaginary and virtual with the actual and factual. In 'Dresden' the young Flynn, gaoled for seven years, learns in prison 'to speak / The best of Irish', which includes the not exactly useful 'thirteen words for a cow in heat; / A word for the third thwart in a boat' and 'the extinct names of insects'. But he also learns to redefine himself within the quotation marks of a nationalist fantasy. 'F', in the sequence 'Letters from the Alphabet', registers the unreality of a world constructed by discourse, in which it seems 'everything was dubbed: / The *mise en scene*, the plot, the lines'. 'H' affirms that 'Everything is in the way / You say them', for whether the *H* in H-Block is pronounced as 'aitch' or 'haitch' sorts out which tribe you belong to, and can mean the difference between life and death. On this fantasy island language is so important that its speakers may have to be subjected to a form of institutionalised karaoke, so that when prisoners complain of ill-treatment through a spokesman, 'We cannot reproduce his actual words here, since their spokesman is alleged / To be a sub-commander of a movement deemed to be illegal.'

The 'shibboleth' is an important motif in Carson's poetry, but it needs to be read in tandem with the idea of the karaoke. Nuances of pronunciation can assume such ideological importance for his characters that when 'H' says, of the dubbed Republican spokesman, 'An actor spoke for him in almost-perfect lip-synch', purists complained that the Belfast accent 'wasn't West enough', while apparently accepting the whole absurdity of this Thatcher-years embargo on the voice of the man himself. 'Opus 14' repeats the topos: 'Spokesman for censored political party spoke in someone else's lip-synch / So perfectly, you'd think it was the man himself, though much of this is double-think'. 'You'd think' is picked up by 'double-think', in a way which destabilises the whole communicative process by not clarifying what 'this' refers to. The implication remains that the phrase 'the man himself' may well be the deepest double-think, presupposing a free, self-articulating subject, when the speaker is merely repeating the mantras of a discourse that has become depersonalised, self-sufficient, so emptied of authentic meaning that an actor can mouth them, karaoke style, with as much conviction and authenticity as a supposed true believer. Wittgenstein's 'bewitchment of our intelligence by language' is Carson's central theme, but living in the hyphen, in the slash of the either / or, he responds to all the ambiguity and ambilocatedness (another back formation there) of that 'bewitchment'. What is almost but not quite a malapropism sums this up when the prose meditation 'Brick' (*BC*) observes that 'Belfast has again swallowed up the miniature versions of itself in its intestine war'. An educated reader night think '*scilicet*: "internecine"'; an even more educated one might observe the play on the Latin *bella intestina*: civil wars.

The prose reflection 'Farset' (*BC*) starts in the realm of language, attempting to understand Belfast by pursuing the multiple possible etymologies of its name – a kind of back formation in which the imagining of origins is slowly transformed into an elaborate fantasy spun out of their interactions, after the fashion of Borges' story 'The Garden of Forked Paths'. The idea that that 'which gives Belfast its name' can somehow explain its present reality soon succumbs to a sense, like that attributed to George Benn in the 1820s, of 'The utmost obscurity and perplexity [which] attend the derivation of the name... of *Bealafarsad*', 'a matter of complete hypothesis', with 'further room for further speculation' – what Carson dubs 'all this watery confusion'. This quest for origins, however, turns into a different kind of project in 'The Exiles' Club'

(*IFN*) and 'Schoolboys and Idlers of Pompeii', both of which report the regular meetings of the Falls Road Club in Adelaide's Woolongong Bar, its members, according to the latter poem, products of the emigrations of the 1950s and 1960s, 'immersed in history, reconstructing a city on the other side of the world, detailing streets and shops and houses which for the most part only exist now in the memory'. Carson's interpenetrating, plural histories, the stories, memories, mental maps of many generations sliding in and out of each other in discourse, as in the multiple parallel universes of science fiction, *Star Trek* and *Sliders*, then take on a more tangible form, as 'Schoolboys and Idlers' imagines a city which is a physical palimpsest of centuries of real estate, of all the building and streets that ever existed on the site, recreated simultaneously in the one packed, multidimensional space:

> Running back the film of the mind's eye, the alphabet soup of demolition sorts itself into phrases, names, buildings, as if, on the last day, not only bodies are resurrected whole and perfect, but each brick, each stone, finds its proper place again.... bridges within bridges... who will sort out the chaos?

It is a remarkable postmodern parable of the way in which language can accommodate, in its very insubstantiality, the dense competing clutter of the real which appears to crowd it out, but which is itself as evanescent as smoke, as 'the very city recycled itself and disassembled buildings – churches, air-raid shelters, haberdashers, pawnshops' ('Brick', *BC*). Such a perception relates to that astonishing poem, 'Queen's Gambit' (*HMSB*), in which diverse narratives intersect and disrupt each other, not only in the levels and layers of their telling, but in the actual, on-the-ground unfolding of events, as a series of narratival interference patterns that leak into and disrupt each other, 'Like the names on a school desk, carved into one another till they're indecipherable', or 'the sketch that's taking shape on the Army HQ blackboard, chalky ghosts / Behind the present, showing what was contemplated, Plan A / Becoming X or Y; interlocked, curved arrows of the mortgaged future'; or, most evocatively, like the tea spilt on a discarded *Irish News*, so that 'A minor item bleeds through from another page, blurring the main story. / It's difficult to pick up without the whole thing coming apart in your hands...'.

But I want to end back in the Twilight Zone of the Podes, by focusing on the poem 'The Words', which opens the sequence 'Alibi: after Stefan Augustin Doinas' in *Opera Et Cetera*, precisely because this sequence is crucially ambilocated, neither one thing nor the other – neither translations nor original poems but creations 'after' (but for us standing *before*, in front of, blocking out) a completely different text. In other words these poems inhabit the space of the hyphen between Ciaran Carson and Stefan Doinas. They are literally an elsewhere from which both Carson and Doinas are absent, yet in which they are also presences. 'The Words' declares as much in *its* opening words, conceding

'Yes – someone lived here once'. The poem could be speaking about itself, but it is also talking about the words that constitute it, and about the nature of all language. It is 'like the hieroglyph / Of where we are'. Where we are, however, is not here. Being 'like' is not the same as being identical with. 'Like', similitude rather than identity, is the hyphenic space where all language operates, and 'where we are' becomes simply the sign or written trace of a departed presence, a hieroglyph. The very crudity of Carson's similitudes reinforce the idea of the discrepancy between 'real presence' and presence in language, between 'the pungent dragon-whiff' and the ghostly music of the sea blown from conches, between 'The dog-rough breath that slabbered here' and the 'mere miasma' it is 'now'. The limestone sea of the geological metaphor is now imaginable only in back formation from the limestone deposits of its once-living denizens. In this liminal place, 'the guardian angels of its threshold are connected to us by an ampersand / When we talk in our sleep'. All discourse is in a sense sleep-talking, since it stumbles on things we do not know, do not intend, which come as 'revenants' from elsewhere, from that 'reservoir of silence, or a Twilight Zone'. The capitalised phrase poises equivocally between the 1960s TV sci-fi series (or its 1980s remakes) and the high-brow apocalyptics of some *Untergang des Abendlandes*, in, that is, an ambilocated space, the place of the hyphen, the true location of all Carson's poetry – and, in retrospect, of the whole literary lineage charted in this study.

NOTES

1. Ciaran Carson, *Opera Et Cetera* (Newcastle upon Tyne: Bloodaxe Books, 1996); hereafter *OEC* in the text.
2. Ciaran Carson, 'Murphy's Lore', *The Guardian* (London), 3 August 2002. Richard Murphy, *The Kick: A Memoir* (Cambridge: Granta, 2003).
3. Ciaran Carson, *Belfast Confetti* (Newcastle upon Tyne: Bloodaxe Books, 1990); hereafter *BC* in the text.
4. Ciaran Carson, *The Twelfth of Never* (London: Picador, 1999); hereafter *ToN* in the text.
5. Ciaran Carson, *First Language* (Belfast: The Gallery Press, 1993); hereafter *FL* in the text.
6. Ciaran Carson, *The Ballad of HMS Belfast* (London: Picador, 1999); hereafter *HMSB* in the text.
7. Ciaran Carson, *The Irish for No* (Newcastle upon Tyne: Bloodaxe Books, 1988); hereafter *IFN* in the text.

Select Bibliography

This Bibliography is not intended to be comprehensive, but confines itself largely to works discussed or cited in the present study, or directly relevant to it.

Allen, Michael (ed.) (1997) *Seamus Heaney: Contemporary Critical Essays*. London: Macmillan

Althusser, Louis (1971) *Lenin and Philosophy and Other Essays*, trans. Ben Brewster. London: New Left Books

Auden, W. H. (1930) *Poems*. London: Faber and Faber

Auden, W. H. (1936) *Look, Stranger!* London: Faber and Faber

Auden, W. H. (1966) *About the House*. London: Faber and Faber

Auden, W. H. (1968) *Secondary Worlds*. London: Faber and Faber

Banville, John (1997) *The Untouchable*. London: Picador

Baudrillard, Jean (1989) *Selected Writings*, ed. Mark Poster. Oxford: Polity Press

Beckett, Samuel (1934) 'Humanistic Quietism'. *The Dublin Magazine*; repr. as 'Foreword' in Thomas Dillon Redshaw (ed.) *Collected Poems* of Thomas MacGreevy (Dublin: New Writer's Press 1971)

Beckett, Samuel (1954) *Waiting for Godot*. New York: Grove Press

Beckett, Samuel (1954) *Molloy*. Paris: Olympia Press

Beckett, Samuel (1979) *The Beckett Trilogy*. London: Picador

Beckett, Samuel (1990) *The Complete Dramatic Works*. London: Faber and Faber

Benjamin, Walter (1973) *Illuminations*. ed. Hannah Arendt. London: Fontana

Birkett, Jennifer and Kate Ince (eds) (2000) *Samuel Beckett*. London: Longman

Brown, Terence (1975) *Louis MacNeice: Sceptical Vision*. Dublin: Gill and Macmillan

Brown, Terence (1985) *Ireland: A Social and Cultural History 1922–1985*. London: Fontana

Brown, Terence (2001) *The Life of W. B. Yeats.* Oxford: Blackwell

Carson, Ciaran (1976) *The New Estate.* Belfast: Blackstaff Press

Carson, Ciaran (1988) *The Irish for No.* Newcastle upon Tyne: Bloodaxe Books

Carson, Ciaran (1990) *Belfast Confetti.* Newcastle upon Tyne: Bloodaxe Books

Carson, Ciaran (1993) *First Language.* Belfast: The Gallery Press

Carson, Ciaran (1996) *Opera Et Cetera.* Newcastle upon Tyne: Bloodaxe Books

Carson, Ciaran (1999) *The Ballad of HMS Belfast.* London: Picador

Carson, Ciaran (1999) *The Twelfth of Never.* London: Picador

Carson, Ciaran (2002) 'Murphy's Lore', *The Guardian* (London), 3 August 2002

Clarke, Austin (1974) *Collected Poems* (three vols) ed. Liam Miller. Dublin: The Dolmen Press

Coffey, Brian (1971) *Selected Poems.* Dublin: New Writers' Press, Zozimus Books

Coffey, Brian (1975) *Advent, Versions, Leo,* in *Irish University Review: Brian Coffey Special Issue* 5. 1

Coffey, Brian (1976) *Advent VI: Denis Devlin Special Issue.* Southampton: Advent Books

Connolly, Peter (ed.) (1982) *Literature and the Changing Ireland.* Gerrards Cross: Colin Smythe

Corcoran, Neil (1986) *Seamus Heaney.* London: Faber and Faber

Corcoran, Neil (ed.) (1992) *The Chosen Ground: Essays on the Contemporary Poetry of Northern Ireland.* Bridgend: Seren Books

Corcoran, Neil (1997) *After Yeats and Joyce: Reading Modern Irish Literature.* Oxford: Oxford University Press

Coughlan, Patricia and Alex Davis (eds) (1995) *Modernism and Ireland: The Poetry of the 1930s.* Cork: Cork University Press

Dante Alighieri (1981) *Literature in the Vernacular,* trans. Sally Purcell. Manchester: Carcanet

Davie, Donald (1952) *Purity of Diction in English Verse.* London: Chatto

Davis, Alex and Lee M. Jenkins (eds) (2000) *Locations of Literary Modernism.* Cambridge: Cambridge University Press

Dawe, Gerald (1978) *Sheltering Places.* Belfast: Blackstaff Press

Dawe, Gerald (1985) *The Lundys Letter.* Dublin: The Gallery Press

Dawe, Gerald (1991) *How's the Poetry Going? Literary Politics & Ireland Today.* Belfast: Lagan Press

Dawe, Gerald (1991) *Sunday School.* Oldcastle: Gallery Press

Dawe, Gerald (1993) *Sheltering Places & Company.* Biddulph Moor: The Rudyard Press

Dawe, Gerald (1993) *False Faces: Poetry, Politics & Place.* Belfast: Lagan Press

Dawe, Gerald (1993) *A Real Life Elsewhere.* Belfast: Lagan Press

Dawe, Gerald (1995) *Against Piety: Essays in Irish Poetry.* Belfast: Blackstaff Press

Dawe, Gerald (1995) *Heart of Hearts.* Oldcastle: Gallery Press

Dawe, Gerald (1998) *The Rest is History: A Critical Memoir.* Newry: Abbey Press

Dawe, Gerald (1999) *The Morning Train.* Oldcastle: Gallery Press

Dawe, Gerald (2000) *Stray Dogs and Dark Horses.* Newry: Abbey Press

Dawe, Gerald (2003) *Lake Geneva.* Oldcastle: Gallery Press

Derrida, Jacques (1976) *Of Grammatology*, trans. Gayatri Chakravorty Spivak. Baltimore: Johns Hopkins University Press

Derrida, Jacques (1978) *Writing and Difference*, trans. Alan Bass. London: Routledge & Kegan Paul

Derrida, Jacques (1981) *Dissemination*, trans. Barbara Johnson. London: The Athlone Press

Derrida, Jacques (1982) *Margins of Philosophy*, trans. Alan Bass. Brighton: Harvester Press

Devlin, Denis (1937) *Intercessions.* Paris: Europa Press

Devlin, Denis (1953) St-John Perse, *Exile and Other Poems.* New York: Pantheon Books

Devlin, Denis (1964) *Collected Poems*, ed. Brian Coffey. Dublin: Dolmen Press

Devlin, Denis (1967) *The Heavenly Foreigner*, ed. Brian Coffey. Dublin: Dolmen Press

Devlin, Denis (1989) *Collected Poems of Denis Devlin*, ed. J. C. C. Mays. Dublin: The Dedalus Press

Dunn, Douglas (ed.) (1975) *Two Decades of Irish Writing.* Cheadle Hulme: Carcanet Press

Durcan, Paul (1982) *The Selected Paul Durcan.* Belfast: Blackstaff Press

Durcan, Paul (1984) *Jumping the Train Tracks with Angela.* Manchester: Carcanet

Durcan, Paul (1985) *The Berlin Wall Café.* Belfast: Blackstaff Press

Durcan, Paul (1987) *Going Home to Russia.* Belfast: Blackstaff Press

Durcan, Paul (1988) *Jesus and Angela: Poems.* Belfast: Blackstaff Press

Durcan, Paul (1990) *Daddy, Daddy.* Belfast: Blackstaff Press

Durcan, Paul (1993) *A Snail in My Prime: New and Selected Poems.* London: Harvill Press

Durcan, Paul (1996) *Christmas Day*, with 'A Goose in the Frost'. London: Harvill Press

Durcan, Paul (1999) *Greetings to Our Friends in Brazil.* London: Harvill Press

Durcan, Paul (2001) *Cries of an Irish Caveman: New Poems.* London: Harvill Press

Ellmann, Richard (1967) *Eminent Domain.* New York: Oxford University Press

Eliot, T. S. (1951) *Selected Essays.* London: Faber and Faber

Fallon, Padraic (1974) *Poems*. Dublin: The Dolmen Press
Fallon, Padraic (1983) *Poems & Versions*, ed. Brian Fallon. Dublin: Raven
    Arts Press
Foster, R. F. (1989) *Modern Ireland 1600–1972*. London: Penguin Books
Foster, R. F. (1997) *W. B. Yeats. A Life: The Apprentice Mage, 1865–1914*. Oxford:
    Oxford University Press
Goldmann, Lucien (1964) *The Hidden God*, trans. Philip Thody. London:
    Routledge & Kegan Paul
Goodby, John (ed.) (2003) *Irish Studies: The Essential Glossary*. London: Arnold
Graves, Robert (1953) *Poems 1953*. London: Cassell
Gwynn, Stephen (1926) *Experiences of a Literary Man*. London: Butterworth
Haffenden, John (ed.) (1981) *Viewpoints: Poets in Conversation*.
    London: Faber and Faber
Heaney, Seamus (1966) *Death of a Naturalist*. London: Faber and
    Faber
Heaney, Seamus (1969) *Door into the Dark*. London: Faber and Faber
Heaney, Seamus (1972) *Wintering Out*. London: Faber and Faber
Heaney, Seamus (1975) *North*. London: Faber and Faber
Heaney, Seamus (1979) *Field Work*. London: Faber and Faber
Heaney, Seamus (1980) *Preoccupations: Selected Prose 1968–1978*.
    London: Faber and Faber
Heaney, Seamus (1980) 'A Tale of Two Islands: Reflections on the Irish
    Literary Revival', in P. J. Drudy (ed.) *Irish Studies I*. Cambridge:
    Cambridge University Press
Heaney, Seamus (1983) *Among Schoolchildren*. Belfast: John Malone Memorial
    Committee
Heaney, Seamus (1983) *Sweeney Astray*. London: Faber and Faber
Heaney, Seamus (1984) *Station Island*. London: Faber and Faber
Heaney, Seamus (1984) *Place and Displacement*. Grasmere: Trustees of
    Dove Cottage
Heaney, Seamus (1985) 'Envies and Identifications: Dante and the
    Modern Poet', in *Irish University Review* (Spring 1985)
Heaney, Seamus (1987) *The Haw Lantern*. London: Faber and Faber
Heaney, Seamus (1988) *The Government of the Tongue*. London: Faber
    and Faber
Heaney, Seamus (1988) 'Interview with Rand Brandes', *Salmagundi* (Fall,
    1988)
Heaney, Seamus (1991) *Seeing Things*. London: Faber and Faber
Heaney, Seamus (1995) *The Redress of Poetry*. London: Faber and Faber
Heaney, Seamus (1996) *The Spirit Level*. London: Faber and Faber
Heaney, Seamus (1998) *Opened Ground: Poems 1966–1996*. London:
    Faber and Faber
Heaney, Seamus (2001) *Electric Light*. London: Faber and Faber

Howes, Marjorie (1996) *Yeats's Nations: Gender, Class, and Irishness.* Cambridge: Cambridge University Press

Jordan, Carmel (1987) *A Terrible Beauty: The Easter Rebellion and Yeats's 'Great Tapestry'.* Lewisburg, PA: Bucknell University Press

Joyce, James (1916) *A Portrait of the Artist as a Young Man.* New York: W. B. Huebsch; (1945) Stockholm: Zephyr Books

Joyce, James [1922] (1937) *Ulysses.* London: The Bodley Head

Kavanagh, Patrick (1972) *Collected Poems.* London: Martin Brian & O'Keeffe

Kenneally, Michael (ed.) (1995) *Poetry in Contemporary Irish Literature.* Gerrards Cross: Colin Smythe

Kearney, Richard (1997) *Postnationalist Ireland.* London: Routledge

Kennedy-Andrews, Elmer, as Elmer Andrews (ed.) (1998) *The Poetry of Seamus Heaney.* Duxford: Icon Books

Kennedy-Andrews, Elmer (ed.) (2002) *The Poetry of Derek Mahon.* Gerrards Cross: Colin Smythe

Kiberd, Declan (1995) *Inventing Ireland.* London: Jonathan Cape

Kirkland, Richard (1996) *Literature and Culture in Northern Ireland Since 1965: Moments of Danger.* London: Longman Studies in Twentieth-Century Literature

Lacan, Jacques [1949] (1968) 'The Mirror-phase as formative of the Function of the I', trans. Jean Roussel, *New Left Review* 51 (Sept.–Oct.)

Lacan, Jacques (1977) *The Four Fundamental Concepts of Psychoanalysis*, ed. Jacques-Alain Miller. London: The Hogarth Press

Larrissy, Edward (1994) *Yeats the Poet: The Measures of Difference.* Hemel Hempstead: Harvester Wheatsheaf

Lodge, David (1985) *Small World.* London: Penguin Books

McCormack, W. J. (ed.) (2001) *The Blackwell Companion to Modern Irish Culture.* Oxford: Blackwell

McDonald, Peter (1997) *Mistaken Identities: Poetry and Northern Ireland.* Oxford: The Clarendon Press

MacGreevy, Thomas (1934) *Poems.* London: Heinemann

MacGreevy, Thomas (1971) *Collected Poems*, ed. Thomas Dillon Redshaw. Dublin: New Writers' Press

MacGreevy, Thomas (1991) *The Collected Poems of Thomas MacGreevy: An Annotated Edition*, ed. Susan Schreibman. Dublin: Anna Livia Press; Washington, D.C.: Catholic University of America Press.

McGuckian, Medbh (1982) *The Flower Master.* Oxford: Oxford University Press.

McGuckian, Medbh (1984) *Venus and the Rain.* Oxford: Oxford University Press

McGuckian, Medbh (1988) *On Ballycastle Beach.* Oxford: Oxford University Press

McGuckian, Medbh (1992) *Marconi's Cottage.* Newcastle upon Tyne:

Bloodaxe Books

McGuckian, Medbh (1994) *Captain Lavender.* Oldcastle: Gallery Press

McGuckian, Medbh 1997) *Selected Poems.* Oldcastle: Gallery Press

McGuckian, Medbh (2001) *Drawing Ballerinas.* Oldcastle: Gallery Press

McGuckian, Medbh (2002) *The Face of the Earth.* Oldcastle: Gallery Press

McGuckian, Medbh (2003) *Had I a Thousand Lives.* Oldcastle: Gallery Press

McGuckian, Medbh (2004) *The Book of the Angel.* Oldcastle: Gallery Press

MacNeice, Louis (1929) 'Our God Bogus', in *Sir Galahad*, 2, (14 May 1929)

MacNeice, Louis (1935) 'Poetry To-day', in *The Arts To-day.* Geoffrey
    Grigson (ed.), London: The Bodley Head

MacNeice, Louis (1938) *Autumn Journal.* London: Faber and Faber

MacNeice, Louis (1938) *Modern Poetry: A Personal Essay.* London: Oxford
    University Press

MacNeice, Louis (1941) *The Poetry of W.B. Yeats.* London: Faber and Faber

MacNeice, Louis (1965) *The Strings Are False.* London: Faber and Faber

MacNeice, Louis (1965) *Varieties of Parable.* Cambridge: Cambridge
    University Press

MacNeice, Louis (1966) *The Collected Poems.* London: Faber and Faber

MacNeice, Louis (1987) *Selected Literary Criticism of Louis MacNeice*, ed. Alan
    Heuser. Oxford: Clarendon Press

Mahon, Derek (1968) *Night-Crossing.* London: Oxford University Press

Mahon, Derek (1970) *Beyond Howth Head.* Dublin: Dolmen Press

Mahon, Derek (1972) *Lives.* London: Oxford University Press

Mahon, Derek (1975) *The Snow Party.* London: Oxford University Press

Mahon, Derek (1979) *Poems 1962–1978.* London: Oxford University Press

Mahon, Derek (1979) *The Sea in Winter.* Dublin: Gallery Press

Mahon, Derek (1981) *Courtyards in Delft.* Dublin: Gallery Press

Mahon, Derek (1982) *The Hunt by Night.* Oxford: Oxford University Press

Mahon, Derek (1984) *A Kensington Notebook.* London: Anvil Press

Mahon, Derek (1985) *Antarctica.* Dublin: Gallery Press

Mahon, Derek (1991) *Selected Poems.* Oldcastle: Gallery Press

Mahon, Derek (1992) *The Yaddo Letter.* Oldcastle: Gallery Press

Mahon, Derek (1995) *The Hudson Letter.* Oldcastle: Gallery Press

Mahon, Derek (1996) *Selected Prose,* ed. Terence Brown. Oldcastle: Gallery
    Press

Mahon, Derek (1997) *The Yellow Book.* Oldcastle: Gallery Press

Mahon, Derek (1999) *Collected Poems.* Oldcastle: Gallery Press

Mahon, Derek and Peter Fallon (eds) (1990). *The Penguin Book of
    Contemporary Irish Poetry.* London: Penguin

Montague, John (1958) *Forms of Exile.* Dublin: Dolmen Press.

Montague, John (1971) *Tides.* Dublin: Dolmen Press

Montague, John (1972) *The Rough Field.* Dublin: Dolmen Press

Montague, John (1975) *A Slow Dance.* Dublin: Dolmen Press

Montague, John (1977; rev. edn) *Poisoned Lands* Dublin: Dolmen Press
Montague, John (1984) *The Dead Kingdom*. Portlaoise: Dolmen Press
Montague, John (1986) interview with Shirley Anders, *Verse* 6
Montague, John (1988) *Mount Eagle*. Dublin: The Gallery Press
Montague, John (1995) *Collected Poems*. Oldcastle: The Gallery Press
Muldoon, Paul (1973) *New Weather*. London: Faber and Faber
Muldoon, Paul (1980) *Why Brownlee Left*. London: Faber and Faber
Muldoon, Paul (1983) *Quoof*. London: Faber and Faber
Muldoon, Paul (ed.) (1986) *The Faber Book of Contemporary Irish Poetry*.
    London: Faber and Faber
Muldoon, Paul (1987) *Meeting the British*. London: Faber and Faber
Muldoon, Paul (1990) *Madoc: A Mystery*. London: Faber and Faber
Muldoon, Paul (1994) *The Annals of Chile*. London: Faber and Faber
Muldoon, Paul (1998) *Hay*. London: Faber and Faber
Muldoon, Paul (2000) *To Ireland, I*. Oxford: Oxford University Press
Muldoon, Paul *Poems 1968–1998*. London: Faber and Faber, 2001
Muldoon, Paul (2002) *Moy Sand and Gravel*. London: Faber and Faber
Murphy, Richard (2003) *The Kick: A Memoir*. Cambridge: Granta
Norman, Edward (1971) *A History of Modern Ireland*. London: Penguin Books
O'Kelly, Michael J. (1993) *Early Ireland: An Introduction to Irish Prehistory*.
    Cambridge: Cambridge University Press
Ormsby, Frank (ed.) (1992) *A Rage for Order: Poetry of the Northern Ireland
    Troubles*. Belfast: Blackstaff Press
Parker, Michael (1994) *Seamus Heaney: The Making of the Poet*. London:
    Macmillan
Paulin, Tom (1984) *Ireland and the English Crisis*. London: Faber and Faber
Paulin, Tom (1992) *Minotaur: Poetry and the Nation State*. London: Faber and
    Faber
Paulin, Tom (1996) *Writing to the Moment: Selected Critical Essays 1980-1996*.
    London: Faber and Faber
Plath, Sylvia (1963) *Ariel*. London: Faber and Faber
Regan, John M. (1999) *The Irish Counter-Revolution 1921–1936*.
    Dublin: Gill and Macmillan
Shklovsky, Victor [1925] 'Art as Technique', in *Russian Formalist Criticism: Four
    Essays* trans. Lee T. Lemon and Marion T. Reis. Lincoln, NE: University
    of Nebraska Press (1965)
Skelton, Robin (ed.) (1962) *Six Irish Poets*. London: Oxford
    University Press
Smith, Stan (1976) 'Frightened Antinomies: Love and Death in the Poetry of
    Denis Devlin', in Brian Coffey (ed.), *Advent VI: Denis Devlin Special Issue*.
    Southampton: Advent Books
Smith, Stan (1978) 'Precarious Guest: The Poetry of Denis Devlin'. *Irish
    University Review* 8.1

Smith, Stan (1982) *Inviolable Voice: History and Twentieth-Century Poetry.* Dublin: Gill and Macmillan

Smith, Stan (1983) 'Against the Grain: Women and War in Brian Coffey's *Death of Hektor'. Etudes Irlandaises* 8

Smith, Stan (1985) *W. H. Auden.* Oxford: Basil Blackwell

Smith, Stan (1990) *W. B. Yeats: A Critical Introduction.* London: Macmillan

Smith, Stan (1994) *The Origins of Modernism: Eliot, Pound, Yeats and the Rhetorics of Renewal.* Hemel Hempstead: Harvester Wheatsheaf

Smith, Stan (1998) 'Mystical Estates and Legal Fictions: Modernism's Apostolic Successions', in Lieve Spaas (ed.) *Paternity and Fatherhood: Myths and Realities.* London: Macmillan

Stallworthy, Jon (1995) *Louis MacNeice.* London: Faber and Faber

Stevens,Wallace (1959) *The Collected Poems.* London: Faber and Faber

Stevens,Wallace (1967) *Letters*, ed. Holly Stevens. London: Faber and Faber

Sweeney, Matthew (1981) *A Dream of Maps.* Dublin: Raven Arts Press

Sweeney, Matthew (1983) *A Round House.* London: Alison & Busby

Sweeney, Matthew (1985) *The Lame Waltzer.* London: Alison & Busby

Sweeney, Matthew (1989) *Blue Shoes.* London: Secker and Warburg

Sweeney, Matthew (1992) *Cacti.* London: Secker and Warburg

Sweeney, Matthew (1997) *The Bridal Suite.* London: Jonathan Cape

Sweeney, Matthew (2000) *A Smell of Fish.* London: Jonathan Cape

Sweeney, Matthew (2002) *Selected Poems.* London: Jonathan Cape

Swift, Jonathan [1704] (1909) *A Tale of a Tub and Other Satires*, ed. Lewis Melville. London: J. M. Dent

Todorov, Tzvetan (1975) *The Fantastic: A Structural Approach to a Literary Genre*, trans. Richard Howard. Ithaca, NY: Cornell Unversity Press

Walker, W. M. (1972) 'Irish Immigrants in Scotland: Their Priests, Politics and Parochial Life', *The Historical Journal*, xv

Wilson, James (1998) *The Earth Shall Weep: A History of Native America.* London: Picador

Yeats, W. B. (1914) *Responsibilities: Poems and a Play.* Dundrum: Cuala Press

Yeats, W. B. (1919) *The Wild Swans at Coole.* London: Macmillan

Yeats, W. B. (1921) *Michael Robartes and the Dancer.* Dundrum: Cuala Press

Yeats, W. B. (1928) *The Tower.* London: Macmillan

Yeats, W. B. (1929) *The Winding Stair.* New York: Macmillan

Yeats, W. B. (1932) *Words for Music Perhaps and Other Poems.* Dublin: Cuala Press

Yeats, W. B. (1934) *Letters to the New Island*, ed. Horace Reynolds. London: Oxford University Press

Yeats, W. B. (1935) *A Full Moon in March.* London: Macmillan

Yeats, W. B. (1937; rev. edn 1962; 1981) *A Vision.* London: Macmillan

Yeats, W. B. (1938) *New Poems.* Dublin: Cuala Press

Yeats, W. B. (1939) *Last Poems and Two Plays.* Dublin: Cuala Press

Yeats, W. B. (1961) *Essays and Introductions.* London: Macmillan

Yeats, W. B. (1962) *Explorations.* New York: Macmillan

Yeats, W. B. (1965) *The Autobiography of William Butler Yeats.* New York: Macmillan

Yeats, W. B. (1972) *Memoirs*, transcribed and ed. Denis Donoghue. London: Macmillan

Yeats, W. B. (1975) *Uncollected Prose*, two vols, ed. John P. Frayne and Colton Johnson. London: Macmillan

Yeats, W. B. (1977) *The Variorum Edition of the Poems of W. B. Yeats*, ed. Peter Allt and Russell K. Alspach. New York: Macmillan

Yeats, W. B. (1978) *A Critical Edition of Yeats's A Vision (1925)*, ed. George Mills Harper and Walter Kelly Wood. London: Macmillan

Index